LONDON

How to use this book

The main text provides a survey of the city's cultural history from its foundations under the Romans to the present time. It is illustrated with paintings, sculpture, architecture and general views and includes a chapter on **London Treasures** which describes in detail the scope and contents of the larger museums and galleries.

The map (pp. 238-39) shows the principal monuments, museums and historic buildings, using symbols and colours for quick reference.

To find a museum or gallery turn to Appendix I, which lists them alphabetically, with their address and opening times, followed by a brief descriptive note. Page numbers indicate where these are mentioned or illustrated in the text.

To find a historic building or church turn to Appendix II, which gives a similar alphabetical list of important buildings, monuments, squares, streets, etc. Grid-references enable the most important places to be easily located on the map (e.g. St Paul's Cathedral, XY, means horizontal reference X, vertical reference Y).

For information on artists—painters, sculptors and architects—turn to Appendix III. Here are listed those who contributed to the cultural greatness of London and whose works are now to be seen there. Each entry consists of a biographical note, details of where the artist's main works are located, and references to the main text where they are mentioned or illustrated.

World Cultural Guides

LONDON

David Piper

163 illustrations
in colour and black and white

special photography
by Edwin Smith

Holt, Rinehart and Winston
New York • Chicago • San Francisco

'Among the noble cities of the world that are
celebrated by Fame, the CITY OF LONDON, seat of the
Monarchy of England is one that spreads its
fame wider, sends its wealth and wares further, and lifts
its head higher than all others.

William Fitzstephen, 1174
A Description of the Most Noble City of London

The World Cultural Guides
have been devised and produced by
Park and Roche Establishment, Schaan.

Copyright © 1971 by Park and Roche Establishment, Schaan.
All rights reserved, including the right to reproduce
this book or portions thereof in any form.
Published simultaneously in Canada by Holt, Rinehart
and Winston of Canada, Limited.
Library of Congress Catalog Card Number: 77-155540
First Edition

SBN: 03-08659-8

Printed and bound in Italy by Amilcare Pizzi S.p.A.

Contents

Aerial photographs pp. 50, 54, 100,
158, 182 by Aerofilms Ltd.

Jacket illustration: Trafalgar Square
with St Martin-in-the-Fields, at night.

End-paper illustration: engraving by
T. Bowles, 1751. The Mansion House,
right, and spire of St Michael
Cornhill in the distance.

Significant dates
in the history of London

55-54 BC	Julius Caesar invades Britain.
AD 43	Britain occupied by Romans. Roman London begun.
61	Boadicea's hordes sack London
410-42	Rome withdraws her legions from Britain.
604	Ethelbert, King of Kent, builds first St Paul's.
787	First recorded raid by Danes in England.
886	King Alfred occupies London.
1065	Consecration of first Westminster Abbey.
1066	William the Conqueror crowned at Westminster.
1087	Fire destroys greater part of the city and St Paul's. Norman Cathedral begun.
1097	The White Tower is completed. William Rufus begins to build the great hall at Westminster.
1176-1209	London Bridge, first stone bridge, built.
1189-1199	Richard I. Rule by mayor established.
1245	Rebuilding of Westminster Abbey begun.
1272-1307	Edward I. Institutions of English state begin to take shape.
1340-1400	Geoffrey Chaucer, son of London burgher, attached to John of Gaunt's circle.
1348-49	Black Death in London.
1381	Wat Tyler's Peasant Revolt.
1419-20	Richard Whittington, third time Mayor of London.
1450	Jack Cade's rebellion.
1476	Caxton's printing press set up at Westminster.
1485	Accession of Henry Tudor.
1509-47	Henry VIII. St James's Palace built.
1558-1603	Elizabeth I.
1566	Royal Exchange set up.
c. 1584	Shakespeare arrives in London.
1603-25	James I (James VI of Scotland). First large migration of Scots to London.
1619-25	Inigo Jones builds Banqueting House.
1631	Covent Garden laid out.
1642	Quarrels between Charles I and Parliament lead to Civil War. King forced to leave London: defeated and executed 1649.
1660	Restoration of Charles II.
1665	The Great Plague.
1666	The Great Fire.

1666-1723	Christopher Wren designs and builds St Paul's and 51 churches in London.
1688	'Glorious Revolution'. Accession of William and Mary.
1694	Bank of England founded.
1698	Palace of Whitehall destroyed by fire.
1714-27	George I.
1739-1750	Westminster Bridge built.
1753	Sir Hans Sloane's collection forms basis for the British Museum (built 1828).
1760-1820	George III.
1764	Dr Johnson's Literary Club founded.
1768	Royal Academy of Arts founded.
1768-72	Robert and John Adam build the Adelphi.
1815	John Nash lays out Regent's Park, Portland Place, Regent Street and the Mall.
1824	National Gallery founded.
1829	First London bus.
1836	London University receives royal charter.
1837	Buckingham Palace becomes permanent residence of the Sovereign.
1837-1901	Victoria.
1820-40	Trafalgar Square laid out.
1835-60	Houses of Parliament built.
1851	The Great Exhibition.
1852	Victoria and Albert Museum founded.
1863	Metropolitan railway, first part completed.
1867-71	Royal Albert Hall built.
1890	First electric tube railway.
1894	Tower Bridge built.
1914-18	World War I. Damage from Zeppelin air raids.
1939-45	World War II. The Blitz. Second Great Fire of London. Thousands of buildings destroyed.
1944	County of London plan for redevelopment of City area.
1951	Festival of Britain. South bank of Thames reclaimed and designed as cultural centre. Royal Festival Hall built.
1971	The Barbican. Completion of new twin development scheme.

The first thousand years

The first thousand years of London may not be buried quite so deep as the ruins of ancient Troy, but they are still, perhaps, more difficult to get at; as 20th-century London is vital and busy above them, a controlled strategy of archaeological excavation is generally impracticable. The cultural remains of that millennium are therefore fragmentary: some surviving patches of the lower part of the Roman wall; the groundwork of the Mithraic temple; and a somewhat haphazard collection mainly of bits and pieces, tessellated pavements, sculpture, as well as the debris of domestic life, now concentrated mainly in the London and the Guildhall Museums, plus some important pieces in the British Museum.

The civilization to which these battered and crumpled objects bear witness was nevertheless, in its beginnings, a rich and sophisticated one, and the first London, the Roman *Londinium*, grew and flourished through four centuries, almost as long as the post-medieval period of history till now. The Romans were the true founders; before them, when south-east England was dominated by an Iron-Age people originally from north-eastern Europe (the Belgae), there were settlements along the Thames banks, but nothing concentrated. Their implements can be found in the museums, and a very few objects of high artistic quality (notably the famous bronze 'Battersea' shield in the British Museum) are evidence of a lost culture of some calibre. Their capital, however, was miles to the north-east of London, at Colchester. The first Roman penetrations were those of Julius Caesar in 55 and 54 BC, but the first colonizing invasion was only in AD 43 under the Emperor Claudius, and this being successful, the Romans took over the existing capital of Colchester. In the first seventeen years of Roman rule, however, London was implanted, took root, and grew rapidly. To the historian looking back, the choice of site for the ultimate capital seems inevitable. The spot the Romans pitched on owned a conjunction of virtues. It was the first raised ground hard by the banks of the river for those coming in from the sea up miles of marshy estuary. It was also the first point at which the Thames was decently fordable, and the furthest point down-river at which a bridge was practicable. The Romans promptly bridged it, and the present London Bridge still crosses the river very near its original site; a bridge at that point was

◁
The Roman Wall, Cooper's Row. Begun in the 2nd century AD, the wall contained London for over a thousand years.

the only bridge in all London for some 1,700 years, until Westminster Bridge was begun in 1738. The Thames is the great divide of southern England from west to east, and so its main crossing at London Bridge became the focus of the web of roads that the Romans characteristically spanned across the country. Thus, though not a *colonia* like Colchester, London thrived, as port and centre of trade and commerce, and, as was noted by Tacitus, it was famed for its prosperity and 'packed with traders'.

The first London lasted only those first seventeen flourishing years, for in AD 61, following atrocities by the Roman Procurator, the native Iceni revolted. Led by their Queen Boadicea, they sacked London, and after an appalling massacre, razed it to the ground by fire. A mourning stratum of black ash, struck during excavations below the church of All Hallows Barking on Tower Hill, is almost the sole certain physical witness of the first London. The revolt did not remain successful, for all the inspiration of its romantic queen; though she has remained a national heroine, and can still be seen, resurrected into a surely sweetened version of Amazon in a late Victorian statue by Thomas Thornycroft at the approach to Westminster Bridge, she was a tough and probably uncherishable character — according to one early writer,

Temple of Mithras used by the Zoroastrian cult of Mithras, 1st-4th centuries AD, rediscovered during excavations in Queen Victoria Street, 1954.

'huge of frame, terrifying in aspect, and with a harsh voice'. Her forces were routed by the Romans, and a new Procurator, Classicianus, set about settling the country with a magnanimous and constructive policy far removed from that of his predecessor. His tombstone can be seen in the British Museum.

For the first but not the last time, London arose from its ashes. The site was the same: essentially the twin hills north of the river and, round the bridgehead south of the river, the 'suburb' that was later to become Southwark. The hills were gravelly and well-drained, good to build on; they were divided by a stream (Walbrook) running down to the Thames, while to the west there ran a small tributary of the Thames, the Fleet river. The horizon to the south was contained by the ridge of the Surrey hills, and to the north by the high ground where Hampstead and Highgate are now. The famous wall that defined London was not begun for some time, and before its construction there grew a large military fort, at the end of the 1st century AD, built northwest of the town (Cripplegate) and covering some 11 acres; this was not properly excavated until after the Second World War. The wall itself was only started perhaps a century later, and for reasons that are not yet entirely clear. It was, however, an assertion of considerable

confidence and ambition, running north from the Thames where the Tower of London is now, then turning west, and finally south again west of St Paul's Hill to rejoin the river bank — over two miles in all, and enclosing over 330 acres. Thus defined, London was by far the largest city in Britain and indeed the fifth largest city in the western Empire. What is perhaps more remarkable is that this definition contained London for almost a thousand years; only after the Norman Conquest did significant expansion begin. The wall was punctuated by gateways, to which modern street names still bear witness (Aldersgate, Aldgate, Bishopsgate, etc.) and whence the great Roman roads drove imperiously out to straddle Britain.

The original height of the wall is unknown; almost all of it, of course, has vanished. Where fragments still stand, only the lower courses are Roman, dug out below ground level, for the fabric of the wall was, through the centuries, ripped and ravaged, patched and made good up to medieval times. The surviving pieces can best be seen on Tower Hill at Trinity Place, or better Cooper's Row, where the upper parts reach 33 feet high, though these are medieval. In the gardens at Trinity Place there is an evocative cast of a Roman soldier and also one of the tombstone of the benevolent Classicianus. Further north (off London Wall) in St Alphage churchyard there is also a spectacular section of the wall in rugged contrast to the sleek postwar office blocks that tower above it; the medieval (15th-century) superstructure here is battlemented. At the roots of these sections, the Roman work can be clearly recognized, of grey ragstone bonded at intervals with red brick. The stone is not native to London, but was brought, in all probability by barge (the remnants of one, still part laden with this stone, was found in the mud of Thames bank in 1963) from quarries in Kent.

The fabric of the city, domestic, commercial and industrial, that grew within the wall has foundered, but the archaeologists have demonstrated that it was of a grand scale and some splendour. The major civic building, a Basilica (its foundations lost partly under the present Leadenhall Market) was well over 975 feet long, longer than the Basilica Julia in Rome, and with an attendant forum over 487 feet wide. This has vanished, with all the attendant buildings of stature that the city must have owned, except for one: the Temple of Mithras. This can now be seen raised up and, as it were, lying in the lap of an enormous modern development, Bucklersbury House on Queen Victoria Street. It was discovered in excavating the site for the latter in 1954. Enough remains (the floor and the lower courses of the wall, as though a ground-plan in relief) to show that here was a temple of basilica pattern, approximately 65 feet by 23, with nave and columned aisles and an apse. An important cache of sculptural fragments, apparently originally deliberately buried on the site, proved the association with the cult of Mithras, introduced to the Roman Empire from the East early in the 1st century BC and surviving till the 4th century AD. It was a virile and martial cult, with much emphasis on grades, initiations and tests of courage, but was also developed by the commercial classes, as lawgivers as well as conquerors. The unusual size and the richness of the objects discovered with the temple suggest this was not a purely military Mithraeum. The hoard is now in the Guildhall Museum, including a good marble head of Mithras himself with Phrygian cap, and a later group of Dionysus with Silenus on a donkey. There is also a charming little round silver box, chased with hunting scenes. A relief of Mithras slaying the bull, now in the London Museum, is probably associated too with this temple, though it was found separate, in Walbrook, and much earlier (1889).

Other haphazard survivals will be found in the museums, ranging from luxurious tessellated pavements to the now precious junk thrown away by London's citizens in Roman times, fragments of glass, pottery (much imported from Gaul, but also London-made), tools, jewelry, even clothes. Leather is most durable, especially shoes — but the strangest survivor, in its startlingly contemporary brevity, is the equivalent of a modern bikini. These witnesses to a life long dead are most broken, and mute — but not all, for not only have some traces of writing materials survived, but also written messages, some still of poignant urgency. Thus (on a wax writing-tablet from the bed of the Walbrook): 'Take good care you turn that slave-girl into cash'; or, much less solicitously, scratched on a famous piece of lead known as the London Curse' (and repeated twice): 'Titus Egnatius Tyrannus is hereby solemnly cursed, likewise Publius Cicerius Felix'. But most hauntingly pathetic, perhaps the very imprint of mortality, the impression of a child's foot as he (she?) stepped on a clay tile when it was still wet, and which was, centuries later, found in the flue channel of a Roman bath in Cheapside.

For Rome indeed came to decline and fall. By the 3rd century AD the protection of Roman military power was proving vulnerable, at first in Europe whose troubles hit hard on Britain's export trade; then the direct raids on the island by the Saxons began, and London started

Saxon Cross. One of the rare survivors of the northern art before the introduction of the Romanesque. All Hallows Barking.

to decay (probably already the third London, as enormous damage had been done by a fire of about AD 125); edicts at the end of the 4th century grant permission for the use of building materials taken from abandoned temples. Then, in 410, as the Goths struck into the heart of the Empire, into Italy itself, Rome withdrew from Britain, and London withdrew almost, it seems, from history for some two hundred years. These are the true Dark Ages; from Britain the appeal went to Rome — 'The barbarians force us to the sea, and the sea forces us back to the barbarians' — but no answer came. The central authority of London dissolved, and Britain split into warring factions, of which the raiding Saxons took full advantage. If the documentary evidence of this time is sparse and above all confusing, the physical remains in London are almost nil — a small scatter of coins of Londinia or Londinium registering some form of survival. Society was far from urban-minded, and that London decayed there is no doubt. But it was never entirely abandoned.

In 597 Augustine's missionary monks landed in Kent, and a sense of enduring institution and continuity was reborn. In 604, at the request of Bishop Mellitus, a church was built at the high point of London, and thus the Cathedral of St Paul's was founded. A slow revival of London's metropolitan ascendancy as capital of the East Saxons seems to have begun, till Bede could proclaim it as *'multorum emporium populorum terra marique venientium'* ('the market-place of many peoples coming by sea and land'). But upon the now indigenous Anglo-Saxons there then fell the raiding assaults of the Danes, and London's fortunes fluctuated wildly. It was sacked by the Danes in 851, rebuilt and refortified by the great King Alfred in 886, yet again sacked by the Danes in 982.

To expect a rich witness of Anglo-Saxon culture in London is therefore obviously vain. There are fragments of jewelry, a barbarous eroded collection of brutal swords, but the only major hoard of Anglo-Saxon art has come very recently to London, the wonderful assembly of grave goods (probably of King Ethelhere of East Anglia, and dug up near Ipswich in 1939), known as the Sutton Hoo Treasure and now in the British Museum. There is a fine Danish gravestone, exhumed from St Paul's churchyard, and now in the Guildhall Museum, but perhaps the most eloquent commentary on this broken phase of London's history is to be found in the crypt of the church of All Hallows Barking on Tower Hill, a palimpsest of history first revealed in full by a much later sack of London. The church was founded about 675, but in the crypt you can see a tessellated pavement, still *in situ*, from Roman times (and below that, invisible, as already mentioned, the black line of ashes of London's first burning). When the church was bombed and gutted in 1940, a Saxon arch with Roman tiles incorporated was laid bare, of somewhere about 650 — the earliest arch in London. At the same time, amidst the shattered masonry, there fell fragments of two Saxon crosses.

In the early 11th century, a Danish king, Canute, consolidated England into a relatively peaceful unity. On his death, the crown reverted to the old royal line, and to a king, Edward the Confessor, who, although his name lives still as founder of Westminster Abbey, was not the strong man needed in more mundane affairs. On his death, England fell apart, and after the battle of Hastings in 1066, the invader William, Duke of Normandy, took over. On Christmas Day, 1066, he was crowned in Westminster Abbey, and the tangible history of modern London begins.

Edward III, reigned 1327-77; effigy by John Orchard, 1378. Westminster Abbey (see p. 39).

The Middle Ages

No one would claim that London or England from the 12th century through the 16th — that is, through the Middle Ages — was a halcyon period of peaceful consolidation and growth. Still, certain characteristics were established then, and the society that formed them also — in its institutional buildings at any rate — produced a number of buildings of such monumental scale and durability that they have lasted till today. There was also, though the core of the City remained within the area defined by the Roman walls, a fairly continuous expansion, notably to the west along the north bank of the Thames, between the City of London and Westminster. The period sees in fact the establishment of a second centre for London, two miles west of the City, at Westminster, and these two concentrations of power and business, each of very different kinds, still remain in the 20th century. The City first. Already by the time of the arrival of the victorious Normans, London was of considerable wealth and power, and conscious of its independence as the most important city in England. As such, it was treated by William the Conqueror with every respect. He granted it a royal charter which gave some assurance that he would observe its privileges, but also, fairly promptly, he set up warning that the king was the supreme power, not open to abuse, in the form of three substantial castles on London's perimeter. Of these, two have long vanished almost without trace, but the third, easternmost, one remains as one of the most famous sights of the city, the so-called 'White Tower', the heart and kernel of the great concentric accretion of walls and towers that gradually accumulated about it during this period, the Tower of London.

The White Tower — actually pale grey, of Caen stone though it was originally whitewashed — was completed by 1097. It was sited almost straddling the eastern extremity of the Roman wall, traces of which can still be seen in the Tower's grounds (notably at the Byward Tower, just south-east of the White Tower), and although later superficial modifications have somewhat lightened its aspect, the impression is still of formidable military strength. In form, it is of the rare, very English (rather than French) type of castle known as a 'hall-keep', and larger (107 x 118 feet in plan) than any in England except Colchester: roughly square, its floors are each divided into three compartments, and each of the four angle turrets has an ogee cap (later, and much less severe in mood; it is these, plus the enlargement of the windows on all except the south front, that modify the aggressiveness of the tower's original expression). It is, though, unmistakably a fortress, literally a 'keep', and Londoners must have felt it always uneasily, over their shoulders, as a presence of external authority. It has since served many functions, notably, like much of the later buildings that surround it, as a prison (a role it began to play almost at once, as its part builder, Ranulph, Bishop of Durham, ironically was imprisoned there in 1101). Now it houses much of the national collection of armour. The architectural jewel that it contains is, however, original: the Chapel of St John on the first floor, the most impressive, pure and moving piece of Early Norman space in London, in a naked and massive austerity. Its impact is monumental and breathtaking, for all its small extent: a tunnel-vaulted nave with apse, groin-vaulted aisles, pillars of squat yet most exact proportion, almost without ornament. It seems the essence of endurance, and the strange ceremonies that it has seen through the centuries irrelevant to it. But here the murdered Henry VI lay in state, and Elizabeth of York also, in a galaxy of 800 candles. Mary Tudor here married Philip of Spain, by proxy, and the Chapel is where for many years aspirant Knights of the Order of the Bath, one of England's oldest orders of chivalry, after a ritual washing, kept vigil through a long night with their armour spread in dedication before the altar.

The subsequent development of the Tower area is essentially connected with changing practice in military architecture, and so the Norman central keep of the White Tower was modulated (mainly by Henry III) into a Gothic-type fortress with curtain walls — the latter encircling the White Tower with two defensive screens, inner and outer, each strengthened at its angles with bastion towers, and the outer one girt with a moat (some 130 feet wide, drained only in 1843). The whole area (some 18 acres) is an extraordinary agglomeration of building of all periods, remarkable not so much for architectural felicities, as for its impressive picturesque — grey mass of fortress bulk on the slope of Tower Hill, with Thames beyond — as ensemble, and for its historical associations, many of them macabre and murderous; the predominant aura is of claustrophobic prison and violent death. The Tower was the major state prison through much of its history (and could still so serve, I think, in cases of high treason, as it certainly did between 1939 and 1945). In it were murdered probably two kings of England (Henry VI, and Edward V, one of the 'little princes' believed to have been smothered to death in the Bloody Tower in 1485); was drowned, in a butt of Malmsey wine, a prince of the blood royal, the Duke of Clarence; were executed three queens of England (two wives of Henry VIII, Anne Boleyn and Katherine Howard, and the 'ten-days queen', the seventeen-year-old Lady Jane Grey), as also — here,

The White Tower, finished by 1097, the heart of the Tower of London; from the south, showing the original windows.

on a scaffold the site of which is marked with granite, or upon Tower Hill outside the Tower — some of the greatest names in English history: Bishop Fisher, Thomas More, Robert Earl of Essex, and countless more. Sir Walter Raleigh, that epitome of the various Elizabethan genius, was incarcerated here for thirteen years; so also, much more briefly though unexpectedly, was Samuel Pepys, and so even, most recently, Rudolf Hess. Eloquent and pathetic witness can be found in the countless graffiti, names and exclamations scratched into the stone throughout the buildings of the Tower.

But the Tower was other things too: one of the royal palaces until the mid-17th century; a wardrobe; a garrison (till the 1960s); more unexpectedly, the Royal Menagerie (at the Lion Tower, where the modern visitor enters) till 1834, when it transferred to the present Zoo in Regent's Park. It houses also, besides the collections of armour, the Crown Jewels, recently resited in a secure but visitable cavern beneath the old barracks-building; these almost all date from after the

Tower of London: the complex of curtain walls, subsidiary towers, and moat enveloping the White Tower, developed through the Middle Ages.

Restoration of Charles II in 1660, for the early regalia was melted down in the Civil Wars. There are even odd, charming, domestic accents relieving the fortress air, such as the black-and-white Tudor timber work over Traitors' Gate. The custodians of the Tower are known as Beefeaters, in Tudorish dark blue uniforms, and the ravens are domiciled for centuries past, officially on the muster, with a weekly allowance for meat. Distinct from the Norman chapel in the White Tower, is the Chapel of St Peter and Vincula on the hill above, now much as it was when rebuilt by Henry VIII after 1532, with some interesting monuments and a Father Schmidt organ, but depressive with the scaffold site just outside, and the chopped bodies of the three queens (among others) named above under its floor.

The medieval city that lay to the west of the Tower expanded in numbers, but kept largely within the confines of the old wall. Pressure for space grew more and more intense. The plan of the City was originally determined by relatively large manorial holdings, giving way gradually to a very condensed medieval urbanism of overhanging houses in continuous lines along mainly very narrow streets and alleys. Part

of one of these later grand merchants' manors has survived, the great hall of Sir John Crosby's mansion (1466) built near Bishopsgate. This was taken down in 1908, but rebuilt on Chelsea Embankment, where it can still be visited. It gives a vivid impression of the scale of life of London's richer merchants. This is of stone, with a magnificent timber roof, but most of the domestic structures, large and small alike, were wooden-framed, and so ephemeral. Certain enduring institutions one might expect to leave more enduring memorials — the municipal organization, including the Guilds; the military orders; the Church — and this would indeed have been so had it not been for the Great Fire of 1666 which razed most of the square mile of the City.

The Guilds were of great power and importance; from being social and religious fraternities designed to protect practitioners in a craft

PP. 20/21

Tower of London: the Chapel of St John in the White Tower, one of the purest survivors of Early Norman church architecture.

Ampulla and spoon (Tower of London); basically 12th and 14th centuries respectively. For the anointing at coronations, the oldest surviving regalia.

or trade (usually concentrated in one area, a habit still recalled by names such as Milk Street or Bread Street), they grew to have great influence on the government and administration of the City as a whole, and indeed acquired the power (which in their more modern name of Livery Companies they still have) to elect the Sheriffs and the Lord Mayor of London. But setting aside the destructions of the Great Fire of 1666, they did not build ambitiously as some of their counterparts in Europe did. The main central building, the Guildhall, was of scale and grandeur, and this still survives. The skeleton of the Gothic hall (built by John Craxton, early 15th century) is, however, much overlaid: the stone shell of the hall itself (very large, 163 feet long) is original, as also the porch, and the vaulting of the crypt is magnificent, but the façade is a very idiosyncratic mixture of Gothic and classical idiom (rather agreeable once you've got used to the idea) supplied by George Dance in 1788. The building must have been impressive in its justifiable pride, but in all its history has never been the climax of a great forum or ceremonial place. In this it is entirely typical of an enduring characteristic of the City, of its habit of concealing its treasures, its almost wilful rejection of large-scale urban compositions in terms of

St Edward's Crown (Tower of London) made for Charles II, and still used for coronations. Weight: five pounds.

spectacle. This is because, though so few medieval buildings remain, the City has, in its perpetual refashioning of its buildings through the centuries, retained almost literally the old, cramped street pattern of the Middle Ages. What is lost in composed spectacle is offset by a curious gain in nervous tensions — even now the City retains an endless capacity to surprise, and it can only be satisfactorily investigated on foot, up nooks and crannies, through canyons of buildings opening a sudden oasis of abandoned churchyards, the walker always in suspense as to what the rounding of the next corner may reveal.

In the case of the Guildhall, the Lord Mayor's Rolls-Royce, as he alights for a ceremonial function, may seem to fill the entire forecourt. The Guildhall still serves a number of administrative and ceremonial purposes of the City, and houses also notably a great library, with a rich collection of books relating to London's history. Its Museum, however, at the time of writing, awaits a permanent home, and is temporarily housed nearby on London Wall (see p. 226). In the main hall of the Guildhall are some ambitious homages in sculpture to national heroes of the 18th and 19th centuries — the two Pitts, Nelson and Wellington, the most vigorous being the monument to the elder

Pitt by John Bacon the elder, 1782. The Guildhall also houses earlier statues salvaged from now demolished buildings, including three probably from the first Royal Exchange and probably by Nicholas Stone (Edward VI, Elizabeth I, Charles I), and two good if battered baroque statues, by Quellin, from the old College of Physicians.

The medieval churches of the City were almost wiped out by the Great Fire. Their number is an index not only of parochial and guild piety, but of the flourishing wealth of London. Through the Middle Ages there were never less than 100 in the square mile of the City. Besides the parish churches there were the religious houses. Most of these needed more space than could be found inside the City walls and so built outside: at Westminster, as we shall see, the Benedictines, the Cluniacs at Bermondsey and so on. The friars, however, always tried to build within towns, and accordingly in the 13th century, Dominicans (Blackfriars), Franciscans (Greyfriars), Crutched Friars and Augustinian Friars all built churches in the City (all dispossessed and destroyed after the Reformation). About the same time charitable foundations were established, some of which still survive. Rather earlier was the Augustinian Priory of (Great) St Bartholomew, founded by one Rahere, together with attached hospital. Church and hospital still exist, the hospital entirely rebuilt, the church a fragment — but a monumental fragment. What remains is essentially the crossing, and transepts, with the chancel of the old priory: the nave has vanished, but the whole was some 293 feet long. The fragment has been somewhat restored, but still impresses as Norman architecture of massive quality and huge dignity. The Lady Chapel at the East End, though restored (once used as a printing works, where the young Benjamin Franklin was employed) is of 1330, and a charming oriel window high in the side of the chancel was a prior's private oratory inserted in the early 16th century. There are a number of monuments, notably that of the founder Rahere (retrospective, of about 1500). Hogarth was baptised in this church. As you go in, do not miss the pretty half-timbering over the gateway, it is Elizabethan and a very rare survivor.

The chapel in the White Tower and Great St Bartholomew are the major witnesses to the Norman style in London. In the crossing of the latter, you can see, however, pointed arches, heralding the Gothic, which in the Temple Church (consecrated 1185) has arrived, if inset in unusual circular form. This was the church of the Knights Templar, a military order originally founded in Jerusalem in 1118 after the First Crusade, and the round nave is a tribute to the Sepulchre of Christ in Jerusalem. The chancel is later (consecrated 1240), and is one of the finest surviving representatives of English 13th-century Gothic — spare but airy, the vault beautifully sprung from elegant piers of Purbeck marble. Though nave and chancel were both scoured by 19th-century restoration and much rebuilt after aerial bombardment, they constitute one of the most satisfying churches in London. In the nave, blitz-ravaged husks on the floor are what remain of the 13th-century effigies of the crusaders.

The Temple Church is now the oldest element in that strange legal precinct, comprised of courts and gardens, that rambles from the Thames northward for nearly a mile, and to which we shall return later (p. 91). It is also clear to the west of the old London wall, and clear of the

◁
St Ethelburga, Bishopsgate: one of the few surviving medieval (basically 14th/15th centuries) churches in the City.

reach of the Great Fire of 1666. Other medieval churches which survived the Fire are, away to the east, All Hallows Barking (see p. 14; its medieval shell was gutted in the Blitz, and restored); Southwark Cathedral, the very much rebuilt church of a 13th-century priory, St Mary Overy (most interesting for a series of wooden 15th-century bosses), south of the river by London Bridge; and to the north, both off Bishopsgate, St Ethelburga and Great St Helen's. St Ethelburga is architecturally unimportant, but enchanting as a picturesque grace-note, *piccolo* in a 20th-century roar of traffic and mammoth office building — it looks almost squeezed to death by its giant neighbours. It is mainly 15th century, a rag-faced modesty with a prim little 18th-century square bell-turret; it is small but its parish was small — only three acres.

Great St Helen's, a few hundred yards south down the road, is very different, although, now with a lofty Manhattan-style skyscraper bursting almost from its churchyard, it has a similar precious quality of a haphazardly surviving relic. It is, however, much bigger, and much odder, for it is a double purpose church, with two naves (originally

St Bartholomew the Great, Smithfield. Norman, originally a vast Augustinian Priory Church (founded 1123), of which the chancel survives.

separated), one of which served the parish and the other a Benedictine nunnery. For the purist, the architecture is not compulsive. The church is very much an agglomerate of elements from the 13th to the 17th century, most notably of a fascinating range of tombs and monuments — a fragmentary illustration of the wealth and pomp of the great men of the City, as Westminster Abbey, on a vastly more extensive scale, is of the great men of the nation. The best early effigies are late 14th century, to John of Oteswich and his wife; here also the already mentioned merchant Sir John Crosby (1476) and his wife. The Crosby fortunes rested probably mainly on wool; St Helen's also has copious representation of the 16th- and early 17th-century material pride continuing beyond the grave in elaborate, often gaudy, tombs, coarse in quality, glaring with colour, the funereal art, it seems, of the *nouveaux-riches*. There is, however, an admirable conceit, worthy of John Donne, in the case of Sir Julius Caesar Adelmare (1636, by Nicholas Stone), and further, most significantly, a simple but grand, austere but superb, sarcophagus, very classical in treatment. This is the most apt memorial to, and tomb of, the City's presiding economic

Temple Church, 12th and 13th centuries, with round nave and Purbeck marble effigies of the Templar Knights, whose church this was.

and financial genius in the 16th century, Sir Thomas Gresham (d. 1579). Gresham was personally responsible for much of the transformation of London, of the City, from an outlying, if important, cog in European commerce and finance, into a central market for trade that, from the 16th century on, rapidly became global. Taking advantage of political and religious upheaval on the Continent, Gresham helped to switch the focus of the manufacture and trade in woven cloth from Antwerp to London: to build great reserves of capital in the City; and finally to establish the dominance of London traders at sea, to the New World and beyond, a dominance sealed by the great naval victory over the Spanish Armada in 1588. The architectural symbol of Gresham's achievement was the first Royal Exchange, on the model of the Antwerp Exchange, built in 1566 (burnt in 1666, and again in 1838, all that remains in the present early Victorian version of the building is the stone pavement); Gresham's symbol, a giant grasshopper, still acting as weather vane, has been claimed to be the original. His tomb, in Great St Helen's, makes the other memorials there look gauche and provincial, and he was indeed a great European prince of the Renaissance.

But the enchantment of St Helen's is its atmosphere as ensemble, sunk, dark and mysterious, in the giant booming welter of commercial London that almost engulfs it. For the architectural specialist, however, it contains one illuminating illustration in the shape of two doorcases,

The first Royal Exchange, built by Sir Thomas Gresham as centre and symbol of English commercial eminence. Opened by Elizabeth I in 1566. Destroyed by fire in 1666, and since twice rebuilt.

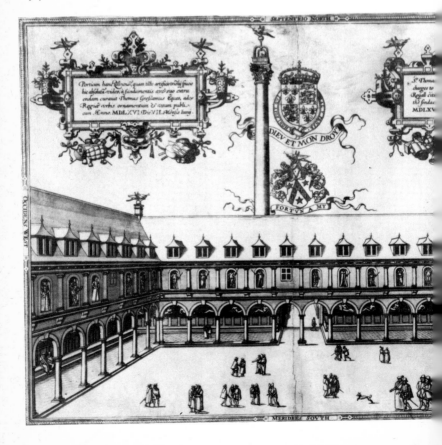

rare witness of a style that the Great Fire obliterated from the City — this time not a medieval style, but the classical one that followed on Inigo Jones. Both doorcases are of the 1630s, but the west one is the 'City-merchants'' version of it, coarse and uncertain of the principles behind it, whereas the south one is chaste, correct and elegant — the 'Court' version, showing a sophisticated comprehension. The contrast is like that between the presumptuous tombs of the more local magnates and that of Gresham.

The ecclesiastical medley of the City had its focus, soaring from the westward of the two London hills — Old St Paul's Cathedral, longer than the present cathedral and with a spire some 520 feet high. This had developed from the church founded by Mellitus in 604 into one of the great Gothic cathedrals of Europe, mainly 13th-century in fabric but before it burned in 1666 provided with a strange classical portico by Inigo Jones. We know something of its aspect now, the soaring nave and aisles, mainly from Hollar's engravings, though one remarkable pre-Fire monument, among other battered fragments, survives essentially intact in modern St Paul's — the shrouded, erect figure of the metaphysical poet John Donne, carved to his order by Nicholas Stone in 1631 — as vividly macabre an image as any you will find in his poetry.

One of the most spectacular signs of London's growing importance in the early Middle Ages was the building of a new London bridge,

Old St Paul's Cathedral. One of the major medieval cathedrals of Europe, mainly 13th century in its final form. Etched by Hollar, 1645, before its destruction in the Great Fire of 1666.

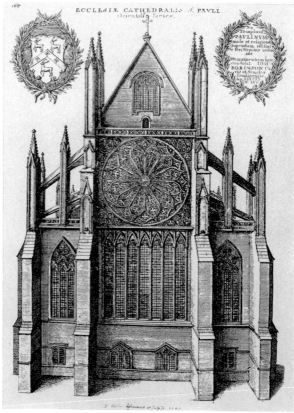

between 1176 and 1209, for the first time in stone. This was a major and famous monument with its nineteen arches and a picturesque furniture of shops and houses that gradually grew up on it, including a chapel, a drawbridge and a gatehouse (on which, by way of macabre welcome to those entering the city from the south, were impaled the heads of executed traitors). The bridge was of unique importance in the network of internal English trade, and stood for some six centuries, being replaced only in 1831. It crossed the river at what was then the end of the tide, and so was the terminus on the one hand for seaborne trade and the port of London, and on the other for the pullulating domestic river traffic of the town. For centuries the Thames was London's main thoroughfare, a fact difficult to remember now: since the multiplication of bridges (following on the second one, at Westminster, first built in 1738) and the improvement of road surfaces, London seems almost to have turned its back on the Thames.

At the south end of the bridge, the suburb of Southwark naturally flourished, among other things, as a kind of transit camp for travellers, replete with inns. But a much more important development was taking place along the north of Thames bank, to the west, for there a twin growth that would eventually balance, or at times rival, the importance of the City itself, was growing, two miles away, at Westminster. By 1066, London was already probably England's capital city in the sphere of trade and commerce, but it was not the capital in terms of national government. The seed from which the latter function was to grow was provided by a religious institution, a Benedictine foundation on a gravel island called Thorney. This was in existence by 750 (its origins are clouded by glamorous demonstrably false myth), but was fairly modest until Edward the Confessor adopted it. The big Norman church that Edward built there was consecrated late in 1065 (an impression of it is recorded in the Bayeux Tapestry); the king died eight days later. In the following year, as we have seen, the coronation of William I, the Conqueror, was celebrated in Westminster Abbey on Christmas Day. The church lasted some 200 years, until rebuilt in Henry III's reign, from 1220 on, in the Gothic form in which we know it. But of more lasting consequence for the mundane affairs of both London and England than the establishment of this great church, was Edward the Confessor's building of some sort of palace between the Abbey and the river. This was not, to begin with, either the main personal residence of the king or the seat of government: the English court was to remain peripatetic for many years, but as the organization of government, ever increasing in complexity, began to make some kind of settled headquarters essential, it began to settle in effect at Westminster — the Exchequer in the 13th century — and has been thereabouts (now a few hundred yards to the north, in Whitehall) ever since.

The building that now hides the site of the Palace of Westminster still has the same title, though the only time the monarch goes there is at the annual state-opening of Parliament to read a speech written not by herself but by the Prime Minister. In the long processes of democracy the royal palace has become the Houses of Parliament, and though the fabric at first glance may look venerably Gothic, it is Gothic of the rebuilding after the great fire of 1834. Little survived that fire. The undercroft of St Stephen's Chapel remains, but it is mostly restoration; this Chapel — a two-storey counterpart of the Sainte-Chapelle in Paris — was in its time of seminal importance, built between 1292 and 1360 and announcing certain trends of the Decorated style

Westminster Hall, from about 1090, but re-modelled by Henry Yevele with hammerbeam roof by Hugh Herland, finished 1402.

and also in aspect heralding much later royal chapels like Henry VII's in Westminster Abbey. Apart from this, the agreeable Jewel Tower of 1365/6 remains with its moat, but the truly monumental survivor of the palace is Westminster Hall, built originally by William Rufus (the Conqueror's son) around 1090: much of the stonework is original, but the great glory of this huge, chill and memory-haunted arena (221 x 75 feet) was provided three hundred years later (under Richard II), the grandest (and largest: 67 foot span) timber hammerbeam roof in the world, installed by Hugh Herland, carpenter. The Hall has filled many roles, from banqueting to the most solemn processes of justice; many of the judicial courts were established here until the Law Courts were built in the Strand in the 19th century. It was here that Charles I was tried and sentenced to death; it was here that Sir Winston Churchill lay in state.

It ceased, mainly or entirely, to be a royal residence in the 1520s, when Henry VIII, in the gradual process of dispossessing his greatest but fading statesman, Cardinal Wolsey, took over the London mansions of the see of York, just north of the Palace of Westminster on the river bank, and re-christened it Whitehall. The Palace of Whitehall, much added to and altered, was one of the main residences of the monarchy until it too was obliterated by fire in 1697. It seems always to have been an incoherent agglomeration of buildings, but that it had accents of grandeur can be seen from Holbein's cartoon of Henry VIII and Henry VII (National Portrait Gallery), part of the design for a grandiose celebration of the Tudor dynasty frescoed by Holbein on the walls of the Whitehall Privy Chamber. Other survivors — more purely eloquent of the arrival of the Italian Renaissance idiom in England in Henry VIII's reign — are roundel terracotta reliefs, by Giovanni da Maiano, of Emperors which came from one of the palace gateways (demolished only in the mid-18th century) and were transplanted to a gateway at Hampton Court; from the same source is a vivid poly-chrome bust of Henry VII, ascribed to Torrigiani, now in the Victoria and Albert Museum. The only building of consequence which remains is Inigo Jones's Banqueting House (see p. 69), but by the time Whitehall burned the whole area was irrevocably associated with the processes of government, and remained so, with the House of Commons sitting in old St Stephen's Chapel, the judiciary in Westminster Hall, and the offices of government gradually establishing a stranglehold on the street now known as Whitehall, which name has long since been synonymous, for Englishmen, with bureaucracy.

For the ordinary visitor, however, the remaining medieval fabric of major interest in Westminster is the Abbey itself, the great church of St Peter. No longer dominant on the skyline as it once was, it is nevertheless of impressive bulk (some 553 feet long), though never

PLAN OF WESTMINSTER ABBEY

KEY: 1 West Door; 2 St. George's Chapel; 3 Grave of Unknown Warrior; 4 North Aisle; 5 Nave; 6 South Aisle; 7 Organ loft; 8 North Choir Aisle; 9 Choir; 10 South Choir Aisle; 11 North Entrance; 12 North Transept; 13 Sanctuary; 14 High Altar; 15 Chapel of St. Benedict; 16 Chapel of St. Edmund; 17 Chapel of St. Nicholas; 18 St. Edward's Chapel and Coronation Chair; 19 Henry V's Chantry Chapel; 20 Henry VII's Chapel; 21 Tomb of Mary Queen of Scots; 22 Tomb of Henry VII; 23 RAF Chapel; Battle of Britain Memorial Window; 24 Tombs of Mary I and Elizabeth I; 25 Chapel of St. Paul; 26 Chapel of St. John the Baptist; 27 Islip Chapel; 28 Poets' Corner; 29 South Transept; 30 Chapel of St. Faith; 31 Chapter House; 32 Chapel of the Pyx; 33 Undercroft Museum; 34 Cloisters.

(right) Westminster Abbey nave, continued by Henry Yevele from 1375 in the style of the earlier building.

The Wilton Diptych, c. 1400 (?) National Gallery. Richard II kneeling, with three patron saints, Edmund, Edward the Confessor and John the Baptist.

completed — its external expression was indeed fundamentally modified as late as 1735-40, when the twin towers over the west front were added by Nicholas Hawksmoor, a fascinating 18th-century baroque exercise in the Gothic idiom, if not quite massive enough for the context. Of the Confessor's Norman work, fragments can be found (off the cloisters: the Chapel of the Pyx, and the Undercroft, now the Abbey Museum), but the body of the church is English 13th-century Gothic in style, though planned by one well aware of contemporary developments in cathedral architecture in France. Henry of 'Reyns' was in fact Henry III's master mason, and the plan of the east end of Westminster (polygonal apse with ambulatory and radiating chapels)

is very close to Rheims, as are certain details — the bar tracery, the naturalistic foliage carving. There are also echoes of Amiens, and of the Sainte-Chapelle. Yet the polygonal, and most beautiful, Chapter House is pure English.

The overriding impression on entering the church (preferably from the west door) is of singular lofty architectural coherence. It is an impression that is immediately knocked askew (if the visitor is set single-minded on architectural appreciation) by the jumbled accretion, at eye level, of tombs, monuments, and the paraphernalia of the illustrious English dead from the 13th century till today. For the Abbey has for centuries been, not only the chosen site for national religious

(above) Detail, Henry VII's tomb,
by Pietro Torrigiani, 1512-18.

(right) The Sanctuary,
Westminster Abbey.

ceremonials — especially, of course, coronations — but also the cemetery of England's élite — a sort of *Who Was Who* composed in terms
of monumental statuary, tombs, slabs, lapidary inscriptions — all, for
pressure of space, wedged in upon one another with total disregard
for conflicting styles and materials. The Abbey is indeed, among other
things, a museum of the history of English funereal and figure sculpture; this can have a fascination, both sentimental and formal, of its
own, but initially the architectural enthusiast is well advised to turn
his eyes to heaven rather than to the grave.

The coherence of the march of the soaring bays of the nave towards
crossing and chancel is in fact deceptive, for the west end of the nave
is the newest part of the main fabric of the church. Chancel and transepts, the beginning of the nave, and also the Chapter House, were
complete by 1269 when the Confessor's body was solemnly translated
to the new building. (The Confessor, by now canonized, was Henry
III's patron saint, and the new building was perhaps essentially conceived as a carapace to encapsulate Edward's shrine, behind the high
altar.) Thereafter, however, work ceased for over a hundred years,
and the nave was completed only between 1375 and about 1500; the
architect then mainly concerned was the great builder Henry Yevele,
and what is extraordinary — and to posterity most praiseworthy — is
his respect for, and loyal continuation of, a style entirely outdated by
his day, so that the church stands essentially as of the 13th rather than
of the late 14th or 15th centuries.

The heart of the church is still the Confessor's shrine, raised up in the

*Tomb of Queen Elizabeth I (died 1603), Westminster Abbey.
Finished 1606, by Maximilian Colt, for £765.*

feretory behind the high altar. Its focus was originally a raised-up coffer of 'purest gold and precious stones', lost probably in the Reformation, and replaced by the present one in Mary I's time. The base on which it rests, as well as the paving of this area, is original, including elaborate patterning in porphyry and glass mosaic. It is Roman, Cosmati work, signed by Odericus and Petrus Romanus (father and son), 1268-70; they worked also on the similar pavement by the high altar (both these tend to be covered; their effect can be gauged, perhaps more brilliantly than from the originals now, from Holbein's painting of the 1530s, *The Ambassadors* (National Gallery) wherein part of the floor is copied). About this shrine of the Confessor are ringed tombs, almost as if battlements, of the early Plantagenet kings — Edward I; Henry III (also Cosmati work about 1280) with a slender, sensitive gilt bronze effigy by William Torel, 1291; Eleanor (Queen of Edward I), effigy also by Torel; Queen Philippa of Hainault (d. 1369), by a Parisian sculptor Hennequin De Liège, in blue marble, bruised by time but with a new, less stylized, liveliness; Edward III (d. 1377), a most dignified patriarchal effigy, probably by John Orchard, with admirable toy-like weepers; and Richard II and Anne of Bohemia, 1394-95, the gilt bronze effigies exquisitely stylized (by Nicholas Broker and Godfrey Prest) yet convincingly individual. (Richard II's likeness can be checked against that in a monumental panel painting *c*. 1400, of him in majesty, that hangs on a pillar by the west door, and by his profile in the exquisite Wilton Diptych in the National Gallery — both these paintings, in the 'International Gothic Style', much disputed

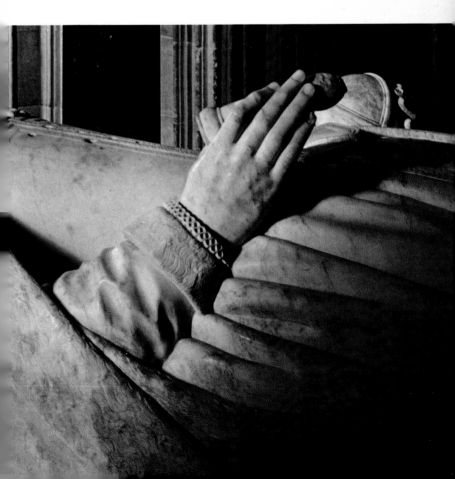

as to authorship, French or English.) Also in the feretory area is the Coronation Chair, joined rather roughly by Master Walter in 1300-01 with a place under the seat to hold the charismatic Stone of Scone that Edward I had brought from Scotland — this is still used for coronations. At the end of the feretory is the chantry chapel for Henry V, about 1448-50, rich in lively Perpendicular detail; the effigy of the king has lost its head (which was of silver). Other important medieval monuments will be found in the Abbey, mainly in the chapels of the apse, mingled with much later ones — Edmund Crouchback, Earl of Lancaster (d. 1296), cross-legged, with strange weepers; and his wife Aveline; Aymer de Valence (d. 1324); John of Eltham (d. 1337) — an early example of the use of alabaster, and with very courtly, affected, weepers. Abbot Islip (d. 1532) has an important Perpendicular-style chantry built into one of the apse chapels, its detail reiterating his rebus (eye and a man slipping). The sculptural detail high in the Abbey vaults needs binoculars for study, but is rewarding — especially many of the bosses, but most of all perhaps the angels in the transepts, smiling for ever mysteriously, magic almost as those at Chartres.

In the early 16th century came a spectacular alteration to the east end of the church — a gesture of piety by Henry VII, founder of the new dynasty, the Tudors, and probably not uninfluenced by more worldly considerations. Having achieved the crown at the battle of Bosworth by force of arms, Henry was much concerned to support the Tudor claim by other propaganda. Thus he intended to instal Henry VI's body in his new chapel, as evidence of continuity and piety to the past, but also to establish a monument to himself. His building (1503 to about 1512) replaced the former lady-chapel, and, following on the grave dignity of the 13th-century chancel, strikes almost as an explosion of pageant movement, light and colour.

Its plan is of a nave, with aisles at each side, terminated by a polygonal chancel with radiating chapels, but the aisles are invisible to the visitor entering, and what fills the eye is the high, light space of the nave, laced with a richness of decoration of dazzling virtuosity. The nave is flanked by dark tall stalls with fretted canopies, of about 1520 and perhaps by Flemish craftsmen; above them in the middle air float the many-coloured banners of the Knights of the Order of the Bath (this is their ceremonial chapel, and little enamelled mosaic splashes of colour are added by their heraldic plates on the stalls). The middle heights of the side walls are serried with the stone figures of almost 100 saints, probably by imported Netherlandish carvers, and by far the richest and finest concentration of late Gothic figure sculpture to survive in England; that they survived the iconoclasm under the Tudors is comprehensible, as they are part of the Tudor family shrine, but how they remained unbroken through the later Puritan massacre of images is a mystery for which posterity can be grateful. But to the eye rising heavenward, they are only the prelude to the triumphant tracery of the roof. The roof appears to be a singularly elaborate version of that uniquely late Gothic development of the fan vault (as at King's Chapel, Cambridge, and St George's, Windsor); in fact it is almost as if the architect (William Vertue) had realized the fan vault could be developed no further, and had decided by a brilliantly perverse *tour-de-force*

◁
Coronation Chair, Westminster Abbey, in which the monarchs of England have been crowned since the 14th century.

Henry VII's Chapel, the banners of the Knights of the Bath.

to produce a fan vault that was not a fan vault, for this vault is structurally a groin vault, and the 'fans' (a foam of cusped tracery, though
of most solid heavy stone) are floated from the ribs of the groin vault
(you can see these vanishing up through the tracery). It is a virtuoso
conception, but, unlike many such, entirely successful, convincing and
exhilarating. Elsewhere the detail matches it (note the almost zigzag-
ging articulation of windows in the apse, or, alternatively, the lively
plebeian anecdotes carved in the misericords under the seats of the
stalls). The chapels at the apse are somewhat overstuffed with monuments, and the altar (with painting by Vivarini) is a modern substitute
for the lost original by Torrigiani. But all is not lost — behind the
altar, set in the defences of a tall ribbed and pierced bronze screen,
is one of the finest monuments in England, and by Torrigiani (the
wild youth who broke Michelangelo's nose) made between 1512 and
1518: twin effigies, of Henry VII and Elizabeth of York, recumbent.
This is the heart of a triumph of art, none the less so because in it
there meet, in improbable harmony, two almost contradictory modes

◁
*Henry VII's Chapel, built as a new Lady Chapel 1503-12, uncommonly
richly variegated in texture.*

(right) The Chapter House,
Westminster Abbey. c. 1250.

(above) Details from the floor
tiles, mid-13th century.

of style and vision — the late English Gothic and the Italian Renaissance. Such sweetly portly cherubs, such a Latin madonna, such a sumptuous sarcophagus, can never have been seen in England before — especially in a tomb, a serene and suave insistence, not on the corruption by death of the flesh, but on the enduring pleasures of the senses for anyone still alive to possess them. Yet all this — so remote from the doom-charged, worm-raddled cadavers of many English 15th-century tombs — consorts entirely agreeably with the magnificent screen that surrounds it, which is English Gothic in spirit, even if elegant in its angularity; and the whole forms a consistent focus for the quintessentially Gothic exuberance of the rest of the chapel's architecture. As it should, for the placid figures of man and wife represent peace, a union stronger than death of the two great warring factions of the civil Wars of the Roses, the Houses of Lancaster and of York, by the marriage of Henry Tudor and Elizabeth of York. Another beautiful effigy by Torrigiani, of Lady Margaret Beaufort, is in the south aisle (and is easier to see than the other), as also a bronze medallion by him of Sir Thomas Lovell, with the tomb erected for Mary Queen of Scots by her son James I. In the north aisle is the tomb and effigy, with gaunt fierce face, of the greatest of the Tudors, Elizabeth I.

The monastic buildings that once extended to the south of the Abbey have mostly gone, but the cloister remains (built at various periods between 1245 and 1366), with more monuments. Off the cloisters is the magnificent austere octagonal shell of the Chapter House, finished by about 1350, its vault flowing from the jet of its single central pillar. The floor tiles are original, and among them the confident inscription *Ut rosa flos florum sic domus ista domorum* (As the rose is the flower of flowers, so this is the house of houses) seems justified. (The Abbey Museum nearby, in the Norman undercroft to the vanished dormitory, should not be missed; it includes the startling wax effigies used for state funerals, ranging from Edward III to Nelson.) This area is associated not only with monastic administration, but with the beginnings of a centralized national government, for early parliaments had met in the Chapter House, while in the Chapel of the Pyx the coinage was annually assayed for weight and metal. Although the old buildings further to the south have vanished, something of the warren-like atmosphere is perhaps preserved, and a visitor finding his way out through Little Dean's Yard and Dean's Yard may detect a whiff of monastery. But it is a different kind of monastery, a range of buildings housing Westminster School, one of the great public schools (meaning that it is fee-paying, private, and confined to the male sex) of England, founded about 1560 on the stock of an earlier monastic school. Adjacent to the west front of the Abbey is the Jerusalem Chamber (where Henry IV died), and round the next flank a small church sits on the Abbey lawns like a rather prim detached chapel — but it is quite separate, St Margaret's Westminster (the parish church of the Houses of Parliament). This is mostly late Gothic (early 16th century), though restored in the 18th century, but is chiefly remarkable for a rare Flemish window made for Katherine of Aragon, Henry VIII's first queen, about 1501 — perhaps intended for Henry VII's Chapel and, like it, in style a telling witness of transition from Gothic to Renaissance.

▷

(above) The vault of the choir and stiff-leaf bosses c. 1250.

(right) Part of the Cloisters (east). Westminster Abbey.

The survival of this great medieval and Tudor complex is due to its close association with the Crown. When all the other monastic foundations of London were all but swept away in the Reformation, the Abbey, though switched to the Reformed Religion in the 1530s, reverted to the Old Faith under Mary I only to be reclaimed for Protestantism under Elizabeth I. The Abbey, nevertheless, stood. It is still, technically, a 'royal peculiar': its Dean is responsible to the Crown rather than to Canterbury.

London has other things to thank the Crown for, that date in essence mostly from the early Tudors: the royal palaces, some surviving in more or less rebuilt or altered form as enduring monuments in the changing texture of London, and most of them with accompanying open grounds, now virtually public property. Hence these miraculous expanses of grass, trees and water in which London, from the centre to the periphery, is so happily rich — the Parks. The first of the remaining palaces (apart from the Tower) is rather earlier — away to the south and east at Eltham; this was a favourite royal resting-place in the 14th and 15th centuries, but decayed thereafter. Little remains now other than its splendid focal point, the Great Hall with a magnificent hammerbeam roof erected by Edward IV, which survived through later centuries because it was serviceable as a common barn, and is now restored. But the great sequence of royal palaces really flourished in the 16th century under the Tudors, a march of noble buildings linked by the Thames. To the east was Greenwich, then known lyrically as *Placentia*, which gave way entirely to rebuilding under the Stuarts (see p. 64); but the palace grounds, rising steeply to the heights of Blackheath over the river, remain as open, and now public, ground. Then, as we have glimpsed, there was Westminster, with Whitehall bordering on it, the one now translated into the seat of Parliament, the other razed to the ground.

A little to the west of Whitehall, somewhat clear of the river, the Palace of St James's still stands. This was essentially, like Whitehall, another of Henry VIII's appropriations. He dispossessed a lepers' hospital maintained by a religious foundation there about 1532, and built a fairly modest palace (perhaps originally as annex to Whitehall); of this the typical red brick Tudor gatehouse tower survives, and also the chapel with a most rich, intricate coffered ceiling (traditionally but probably wrongly ascribed to Holbein, but of quality worthy of his name). St James's attained major importance only after Whitehall burned, but then became the central *pied-à-terre* of the monarch when in town and the focus of the court, until Victoria moved a few hundred yards down the road to Buckingham Palace (see p. 146); it is still to 'the court of St James' that foreign ambassadors are accredited. The palace is not open to the public but its complex of courtyards (mostly much later, but retaining an atmosphere of picturesque Tudorish flavour) can be perambulated. With St James's has survived St James's Park, one of the world's most agreeable parks, at the heart of capital. In its present form, with its irregular lake, its sparkle of rare and brilliant birds, its great trees and subtle undulation of ground, St James's Park reflects the early 19th-century taste for the natural-seeming but in fact most carefully contrived picturesque, as laid out in the time of John Nash. But it was once part of the great royal hunting reserve,

▷

St James's Palace, built for Henry VIII in the 1530s; later altered and enlarged by Wren and Kent.

Buckingham Palace Gardens from the air — the only part of the former royal hunting chase in London still kept private by the Crown.

open land that swept up for miles from Westminster to the west and north. Gradually this area, even though much of it was lost to the houses of the expanding city, was defined, and made over to the public (St James's Park first in the early 17th century); and though all are still Crown property, they are maintained by the Ministry of Public Buildings and Works, and Londoners for centuries have regarded them as their own.

The exception is Buckingham Palace Garden, park-like in size, and adjacent to the west extremity of St James's Park; this is private, as gardens of the London residence of the monarch, and to visit them you must qualify for invitation to the garden parties that the Queen holds there in the summer. But Green Park, extending north-west from St James's Park, is public, and so too, across Hyde Park Corner

to the west, is the largest of the inner London parks, Hyde Park. Hyde Park gives imperceptibly on to Kensington Palace Gardens, and it is possible to walk, from Westminster to Kensington Palace, nearly three miles over grass and through trees, though still in the centre of one of the greatest cities of the world. At the east end of Hyde Park is Rotten Row, a ride where horses are still to be seen though it is no longer, as it was once, the parade ground for high London fashion, like the Bois de Boulogne in Paris. The Park has water (the Serpentine, with boats and bathers), a restaurant, and further west, some famous statuary, including a controversial early work by Epstein, *Rima,* and (in Kensington Palace Gardens) the famous bronze of *Peter Pan,* the children's favourite. (Also, in the north-west corner, a curious inhumation of eccentric English culture, a dogs' cemetery with inscribed

St George's Chapel, Windsor. The
interior, with its fan vault at
the crossing (finished 1528, probably
to William Vertue's designs),
is, with King's College Chapel,
Cambridge and Henry VII's Chapel,
Westminster, the finest flower
of English late Gothic (see p. 41).

tombstones.) Its westward progress is halted by Kensington Palace, a later addition to the royal dwellings, built by William III after Whitehall burned (see p. 116). But to the north, though separated now by almost a mile of dense urban building, a further substantial segment of Henry VIII's old hunting *chase*, Regent's Park, is still grass and trees and water, though (like St James's Park) most delicately and civilly modulated for pleasure under John Nash, and closed at its northern extremity by the Zoo.

These are the big inner London Royal Parks. The three outer ones are far up-river to the west. At Richmond, the turreted Tudor palace built by Henry VII has vanished almost without trace, but its Great Park remains, some 2,358 acres of it, 2½ miles across; and still further west, among its superb gardens, Hampton Court Palace stands in considerable and magnificent substance. Hampton Court, like Whitehall, was originally the creation of that potentate of the first part of Henry

Windsor Castle — the prime out-of-town residence of the monarch; the Round Tower goes back to the time of Henry II.

VIII's reign, Cardinal Wolsey. It was built and furnished to answer the sumptuous pride of a great prince of the Catholic Church, and to rival any other palace in Europe. Henry VIII watched Wolsey make it, and then, in 1526, made it clear that the time was ripe for Wolsey to hand it over for the greater glory of the English Crown. It remained very much a royal abode, even if for Charles I it was both a site for honeymoon bliss and, later, a prison. With Kensington, it enjoyed the special favour of William III after Whitehall was destroyed, and the rebuilding that Wren did at Hampton Court for William we shall discuss later (p. 114). Wolsey's building was planned round five great courtyards, of which most notably the Green Court and Clock Court (with the original intricately enormous astronomical clock still in working order) and the Gate-Tower remain. Modern though Wolsey was, the architecture is still Gothic Perpendicular expressed in beautifully laid red brick, rather than Renaissance, and almost monastic in

conception. The fully Renaissance terracotta roundels of Emperors, set in the walls (though some of them came later from Whitehall), by Giovanni da Maiano, show that Wolsey was at least superficially aware of changing fashion, and a good idea of the original decor of the interior can be gained from the recently restored Wolsey's Parlour, richly, almost too lavishly, decorated. Wolsey's entertainments, at Hampton Court as at Whitehall, became legendary for their lavish ostentation, and the enormous kitchens at Hampton Court provide a sense of scale of the nourishment offered. Henry VIII's most spectacular improvement was the Great Hall, perhaps the finest such surviving in the country, with a celebrated timber roof. Since 1839, the Palace has been open to the public, and now serves as one of the main displays of the treasures of the Royal Collection to the public — particularly Italian and Dutch paintings, and portraits (including the celebrated series of Lely's *Beauties* — the admirably upholstered ladies of Charles II's court) — but best of all, a major treasure surviving from Charles I's collection, Mantegna's cartoons for the *Triumph of Julius Caesar*.

Perhaps the most regal, and most enduring, of the palaces is some way out of London, completing the riverside thread of royal residences, away to the west at Windsor. The origins of Windsor Castle go back before the Norman Conquest, and the dominant accent on its long skyline is still the great Round Tower, refashioned by Edward III about 1344, on an earlier one built by Henry II, as a centre for the senior order of chivalry in England, the Knights of the Garter. Into the wandering system of curtain-walls, the Castle's most beautiful component was built by the early Tudors (though started by Edward IV in 1473), St George's Chapel, which, with King's College Chapel, Cambridge, and Henry VII's Chapel at Westminster, is the finest flower of late English ecclesiastical Gothic. The Knights of the Garter still meet there, and their banners adorn the Chapel. Many kings are buried at Windsor, including Henry VIII, Charles I and Queen Victoria. The castle (much rehandled by the architect Wyattville for George IV) is still the main royal residence out of London, and houses the Royal Library, with its formidable Old Master drawings, including the great Holbein series of portrait drawings and incomparable wealth of Leonardo da Vinci; also the brilliant collection of portrait miniatures, and, hung through the state rooms, some of the finest paintings in the Royal Collection, including the famous Van Dycks of Charles I and his family. Windsor Castle broods both in and over the picturesque little town of Windsor, with the most famous of English schools, Eton College, in the valley below; its silhouette against the sky has a true romantic grandeur.

The sequence of palaces built mainly by the early Tudors had a slightly less grand counterpart in the development by the great courtiers and nobles of large London estates. Many of these lay conveniently between London and Westminster, with easy access to either along the three linking routes, Holborn, the Strand and the Thames itself. These estates, and the rich mansions in them, have long since almost entirely vanished, but remain of significance because, through the 17th and 18th centuries, the ground-plan of the subsequent urban development was to reflect in a broader pattern their parcelling of territory. Now they are no more than street-names that echo the great names of the

Clock Court, Hampton Court. Built for Cardinal Wolsey in the 1520s; finest Tudor brickwork with imperial terracotta roundel (by G. da Maiano) inset, and Astronomical Clock by Nicholas Oursian, 1540.

past, though in some cases (more to the west and north) the original families, until very recently, still owned the land and drew rich incomes from it.

The profound and violent religious and political turmoil of the 16th century had wide-reaching effect on the actual fabric of London, particularly as an immediate consequence of the reformation of religion in the 1530s, and the dissolution of the monasteries. The Crown drew rich dividends from this; it is heralded by the royal take-over, in the 1520s, of Cardinal Wolsey's readymade palaces at Whitehall and Hampton Court. Then St James's, for example, replaced a religious foundation. Elsewhere, through all London, monastic territory was made over to the great officers of the Crown: Grey Friars, Black Friars, White Friars all vanished, and many others. There are, however, survivors in part. The Charterhouse, made over to Sir Edward North, came, after various tribulations (it was one of the few institutions to resist dispossessions, and has its roll of martyrs), to a rich coal

St George's Chapel, Windsor Castle, one of the finest late Gothic buildings in England. It is the royal chapel of Windsor Castle, and of the Order of the Knights of the Garter.

merchant, Thomas Sutton, who in 1611 founded there 'The Hospital of King James in Charterhouse' — a charitable foundation which has endured (though its famous school moved out to Surrey in 1872) with much of a monastic atmosphere and lay-out. The Gatehouse, built in 1504, of the Priory of St John of Jerusalem also survives (much later, Samuel Johnson worked in it when it was the offices of the *Gentleman's Magazine*); the priory was of the military order of the Knights Hospitaller, originating like the Templars in Jerusalem. Like them, too, it was identified with a round church — the site of this is marked by a circular pattern of stones in the roadway: the later church was blitzed in 1941 and rebuilt, but the Norman and early English crypt survives.

Of the old aristocratic palace-houses, virtually the sole survivor is Lambeth Palace, south of the river on the waterfront just west of Westminster, and now, as originally, the London seat of the Archbishops of Canterbury. Though much altered and enlarged in the 19th century (and also bomb-damaged in the 20th) this remains a highly picturesque amalgam of domestic buildings on the grand scale through the ages. The typical gatehouse, red brick with black diapering, is of about 1495 and heralds a complex of varying date all subordinate to a most picturesque sky-line. The old central feature, the Hall, with its buttresses, lancets and noble high hammerbeam roof, might seem original, but is in fact an interestingly archaic exercise in the Gothic style (with classical and Italianate detail when you look close) of the mid-17th century, built to replace the old hall destroyed during the Commonwealth. The Chapel had to be entirely restored after the Blitz, but its undercroft goes back to the early 13th century. (The Palace has interesting portraits, including a fine Van Dyck of Archbishop Laud, and the Library is celebrated for its manuscripts; entrance to the Palace is normally by previous arrangement only.)

The 16th-century landscaping of the ground north and south of the river, and beyond, must have been dominated by buildings such as Lambeth, with their sky-fretting towers and gables, and clustered about by minor service buildings. The more urban texture of the City itself

St Bartholomew the Great, Smithfield. A rare survivor of Tudor black-and-white timbering (1595), revealed by Zeppelin bombing in 1915.

was still essentially medieval, and by now extremely dense — a close-packed town, mainly timber-built, angular with gables, with the upper storey of the houses projecting full-bellied over narrow streets, the skyline thronged with Gothic church spires, dominant among them, high on its hill, Old St Paul's — as indeed one can glimpse London in the first maps and bird's-eye views produced of it. Of this rich and swarming texture, so vulnerable to decay and to fire, survivors of domestic buildings are very rare. They include most notably the black-and-white gateway to Great St Bartholomew's (already mentioned); another gateway, to Inner Temple, in Fleet Street, built in 1610 with, in its upper room (open to the public), a well-preserved plaster ceiling bearing the Prince of Wales's feathers and P.H., the initials of James I's eldest son, Prince Henry. In the same area, Middle Temple Hall offers another example of the grandiose central feature of medieval and Tudor communal life, the Great Hall — opened by Elizabeth I in 1576 — with an excellent example of the elaborate Elizabethan screens at the end. Here Shakespeare's *Twelfth Night* received its first performance.

Lambeth Palace, residence of the Archbishop of Canterbury. Entrance gateway (Martin's Tower, 1490), with St Mary's, Lambeth, alongside.

Staple Inn, once part of the Inns of Court. Elizabethan black-and-white still fronting a modern High Holborn.

The most celebrated and spectacular survivor of Elizabethan black-and-white timber architecture belongs to the former Staple Inn, confronting most improbably the modern traffic on Holborn: here are most of the characteristics, oriels and overhanging upper storeys, built between 1545 and 1589. Though inevitably somewhat restored, its façade is much as it always was. Another example is the 'Queen's House', built by Henry VIII in the Tower of London. As an evocation of the interiors of the time, the period rooms at the Victoria and Albert Museum (p. 214) are probably best, but to glimpse in substance the colour and brash and intricate pride of the great citizens of Elizabethan London, the best way is to contemplate their enormous tombs, blazing with heraldic hues, in Great St Helen's and Westminster Abbey.

Their more essential vitality and passion is of course captured for all time in the incredible flowering of drama, above all in the plays of Shakespeare. If under court protection, these might be staged, as we have seen, in such places as the Halls of the Inns of law, but their true London homes were the theatres on the South Bank, in Southwark, where they were not subject to the censoring restrictions of the City — most famously, at the Globe Theatre, the site of which now lies buried under a brewery.

By 1600, London, with the Court centring ever more closely on Westminster (and Parliament moved out of the Chapter House at the Abbey into St Stephen's Chapel where, approximately, it still sits) and the City flourishing on the economic and commercial impetus given it by great merchants such as Thomas Gresham, was truly a capital city.

Its population seems to have more than doubled in the preceding century, swollen, most significantly, by the influx from the Continent of Protestant refugees, including many skilled craftsmen and artists. The immigrant weavers tended to congregate outside the City walls, mainly to the east, but elsewhere expansion was inevitable. Although alarmed authority was promulgating, already in Elizabeth's reign, fierce laws forbidding building outside the City walls, these could not be sustained. The City was consolidating physically with Westminster, and, politically, in the time of the Tudors, there was also on the whole a considerable harmony between them and a mutual respect, a growing awareness of national interest. Yet the City always maintained its independence very jealously, and that the forthright Lord Mayor Fitzthomas's uncompromising qualification of loyalty to the Crown was a very real and enduring one, the Stuarts had to learn by bitter experience in the next century — 'My Lord', said Fitzthomas to the King, 'so long as unto us you will be a good lord and king, we will be faithful and duteous unto you.'

London from the Tudors to the Great Fire

Through the 16th century the English attitude to the artistic principles behind the Italian Renaissance was somewhat coy and superficial, almost flirtatious. A very few artists of high calibre, fully involved with the Renaissance, worked in London — Holbein, whose art seems to marry the monumentality of Raphael with the spiritual tensions of the north, in the 1530s; Torrigiani, fellow student in his youth of Michelangelo (and underrated perhaps in the shadow of that great name and because he was tactless enough to break Michelangelo's nose in a brawl), and a number of lesser Italian artists attracted by Henry VIII; and, in the 1570s, very briefly, Federico Zuccaro. They left a number of masterpieces — Holbein's portraits and his wall-painting in Whitehall, Torrigiani's tombs in Westminster Abbey — but these remained isolated and essentially at variance with the main stream of English practice. In architecture especially the prevalent practice showed an increasing interest in Renaissance motifs from about 1520 on, but these were applied, as it were, at first as novelties and then as superficial if established fashion — or as cosmetic on an underlying structure that tended to remain resolutely Gothic. Such is the use of da Maiano's imperial roundels inset on the Gate-Tower at Hampton Court. Much of this came via France rather than direct from Italy — thus in Chelsea Old Church there are two capitals, one dated 1528, which are almost twins of one at Chambord of 1532; and when Henry VIII, from 1538 on, built his last and most up-to-date palace, the long-since entirely destroyed Nonsuch in Surrey, it was probably in direct rivalry with Francis I's project at Chambord. Nonsuch, too, was copiously adorned with plaster reliefs of classical scenes, reminiscent of Fontainebleau; some painted 'grotesque' panels (deriving from Raphael's work at the Vatican Loggias) said to be from Nonsuch can still be seen at Loseley Park near Guildford, some 30 miles south-east of London.

In the mid-century this decoration thickened up, became much more elaborate and rich, as the impact of Flemish Italianate style became predominant. From Antwerp came the contorted mode of decoration known as 'strapwork', stone or plaster imitating interlacings of cut paper or leather, a fashion that ran riotously across Elizabethan architecture and monumental sculpture, as can be seen in the great dynastic tombs in the side chapels off Westminster Abbey apse. Evidence of a more fundamental concern with Renaissance principles is rare but not non-existent, and between 1547 and 1552 there was built, on the Strand, for the greatest noble in the land, the Duke of Somerset, Protector or Regent of the boy-king Edward VI, the first house in England to attempt sustained composition within the classical discipline of architecture. This was Somerset House, on the site of which Sir William Chamber's 18th-century building now stands: built in ashlar, with a flat, balustrated roofline and a loggia, it reflected French practice of the period. A little later, Flemish Italianate in very advanced form was introduced in a major mercantile building in the City — Sir Thomas Gresham's Royal Exchange, built by Flemish workmen in imported stone. The courtyard of the Exchange was arcaded with round arches on Doric columns, niches with statues of the English kings, and Ionic pilasters articulating the upper storey. These isolated elements stood, however, almost alone in the hotch-potch of London's urban texture; the buildings whose example was to change the face of London came only in the beginning of the 17th century, and the name for ever held in reverent association with them is that of Inigo Jones.

Inigo Jones was of the great generation of Shakespeare (son of a Smithfield clothworker, he was born in 1573, nine years after the poet). His early history is obscure, but he certainly visited Italy, and later, in 1613, made a protracted tour ranging from Venice to Rome, in the entourage of the first great English aristocratic virtuoso and collector of the arts, the Earl of Arundel. With Jones went his copy of Palladio and this, lavishly annotated, still survives (at Worcester College, Oxford). Till then, most of his contemporary fame rested on his revolutionary theatrical designs for Court masques, but in 1615 he was appointed Surveyor of the King's Works, and remained so until 1642, and in that long period was especially concerned with the royal palaces in London. The first project was the 'Queen's House' at Greenwich, begun in 1617 for Queen Anne of Denmark, left incomplete at her death in 1619, but continued from 1629. It was the first strictly classical building in England, and still survives (part of the National Maritime Museum, see p. 115) at the heart of the great architectural fanfare of Greenwich Hospital that the later Stuarts created about it (p. 115). It was originally a double house, with the main London-Dover road dividing it into two (the two parts were linked with bridges, and were consolidated into one building only in 1661); in spite of this, its general inspiration and atmosphere, and a great deal of its detail, come straight from Palladio. It is a very chaste, at first sight even austere, building: smooth rustication below, plain cement rendering above, the roof invisible behind the horizontal of the balustrade: on the garden side, at first floor level, a loggia with slender columns. The great room of the interior is the hall, a perfect cube the full height of the house: the simple pattern of the ceiling (wherein once were Gentileschi paintings, that can now be seen in Marlborough House, Pall Mall) echoes that of the black and white marble floor. But the most enchanting part of the house is the staircase: a cantilevered stair, a circular well with beautifully elegant iron balustrade and a tulip motif.

▷

Queen's House, Greenwich, by Inigo Jones. The 'tulip' staircase, though perhaps rather 'fleur-de-lis' for Charles I's French queen, Henrietta Maria.

The quality of the impact that this simple box must have made on Jones's contemporaries can be gauged by comparison with the only well-preserved survivor of the great Jacobean 'prodigy houses' in the London area. This is conveniently near Charlton House, and can be seen comfortably on the same day as Greenwich. Charlton, though symmetrically composed (its plan is the shape of an E), derives from the Gothic Perpendicular domestic style: red brick, with stone groins; batteries of tall leaded windows, turrets with cupolas, twisted chimneys; and, in its 'frontispiece', the central projecting entrance, an

Charlton House near Greenwich. About 1607, typical of the grandiose mansions built by James I's courtiers. (right) The 'frontispiece'.

explosion of ornament of contorted fantasy (derived in fact from the designs of the German mannerist architect, Wendel Dietterlin). The serenity of Jones's building contrasts with the tension and busyness of Charlton, yet the latter was built only a few years earlier (1607-12) than the Queen's House. Its owner was even from the same circle as Jones: Sir Adam Newton, who was tutor to Henry, Prince of Wales, for whom Jones also worked (and in the grounds of Charlton there is even a very plain little summer house, with Tuscan pilasters, which has been ascribed not unreasonably to Jones, about 1630).

In 1619, Inigo Jones began his most celebrated contribution to London's architecture, this time at Whitehall Palace: the Banqueting House. This was to replace an earlier structure that had burned down; it was intended, as the name indicates, for state banquets, but also for other pageant ceremonies and masques. Though direct quotations are not obvious, this is again an essay in the manner of Palladio: it consists of a great hall, this time not a single but a double cube, divided into seven bays with tall windows, and demicolumns and pilasters, Corinthian over Ionic. A cantilevered balcony runs round the wall, and this noble room is crowned with the greatest ceiling painting in England: the *Apotheosis of James I*, commissioned in 1629/30 by Charles I, for the greater glory of the arts and of the Stuart dynasty, from Rubens, when the painter/diplomat was in London on a diplomatic mission. The movement of this exuberant design bursts from the rich deep coffering of the ceiling; in the middle panel is King James, enthroned but also levitating heavenwards through swirling allegorical figures; elsewhere he points to Peace and Plenty embracing, while Minerva thrusts Rebellion down into hell (a prophecy not to be fulfilled for Charles I, who indeed walked to his own execution at the hands of rebellion on a scaffold outside a window in an annex to this very building). Through the panels, Virtue in various personification overcomes Wrong while the north panel demonstrates the Union of England and Scotland. The paintings seem to fall into perpective best from the far (south) end of the hall, but recently learned argument has arisen as to whether they are in fact disposed in the order Rubens originally intended.

The exterior of the Banqueting House is the precise expression of the interior, the attached columns, again Corinthian over Ionic, dividing the windows; the elevations relate to Palladian designs for town houses, but omitting the central door, and the subtlety of modulation, the very slight swell of emphasis in the centre bays, produce an ensemble that is new. The building is crowned with a balustrade, and the lower storey, almost undercroft, has low massive vaults inside to support the hall. It may have been intended originally to build entirely in Portland stone, but in fact this was only achieved many years later when the House had to be refaced. But from now on, Portland stone increasingly adds its strange quality to the fabric of London, its virtue being that, on surfaces exposed to weather, it washes itself into a crystalline pallor against which the black of London dirt, accumulating in the shelter of protected areas of the stone, tells with a velvet dark.

The Banqueting House has not always been tactfully treated, although it was here that Charles II was acclaimed by Parliament after his restoration to the throne in 1660, as in 1689 it was here that William of Orange and Mary II were offered and accepted the crown. But after the destruction of Whitehall Palace in 1698, when it was the only major element of the palace that survived intact, it was turned into a chapel, and in 1890 into a museum. In 1963 the Queen made it over to the nation, and now restored, it can be seen in its true magnificence.

Most of Jones's work for the Crown elsewhere has vanished, though some of it was of extreme magnificence, notably the chapel and its fittings at Somerset House, which had become a residence of Charles I's French (and Catholic) Queen, Henrietta Maria. An earlier chapel, finished in 1627, also a setting for the Mass for the Queen at St James's

◁

Banqueting House, Whitehall, by Inigo Jones, 1619-22. The only major survivor of the old Palace of Whitehall.

Palace, has however survived (though now separated from the Palace by the road through into St James's Park, and almost part of Marlborough House). This has suffered much remodelling because, although always the chapel of queens, it has had to answer the liturgical needs of their very varying creeds (from Catholic to Dutch Reformed, German Lutheran, and even Danish for Edward VII's consort, Alexandra); a restoration of 1950 brought it back as close as possible to its original appearance, so that the design, the proportion and calm are clearly recognizable, especially the curved recess of the reredos.

Jones was also responsible for a very strange ecclesiastical re-arrangement at Old St Paul's Cathedral which, in its west front particularly, was much decayed; to the most Gothic body of that great church, Jones married a huge monumental Corinthian portico, very scholarly and almost purely Roman — destroyed in the fire of 1666. There was, however, a further side of Jones's activities, unconcerned with court developments, but of major interest for the future development of London: this related to a commission of buildings first set up in 1618 to attempt some control over both design and fabric of building in London. This commission was concerned first with Lincoln's Inn Fields, but rather with the nature of 'its fair and goodly walks' than with its surrounding houses: later, from 1630, it was very much connected with the development of an estate, lying between the City and Westminster, which belonged to the Earl of Bedford — Covent Garden.

This was already somewhat cluttered with a motley of old building, and its creation involved initially a clearing operation, followed by new building to a co-ordinated plan. This was the first instance of the semi-geometrical development by private estate-owners which was to condition the urban character of west London for two centuries and more — the birth of the London square. Though the urge for order was perhaps initiated by the fastidious taste of King Charles I himself — the Earl of Bedford's son later spoke of 'new buildings erected by special direction of the then King and his Council with much ornament and beauty and to a vast charge' — the vast charge was incurred by Bedford, and to Bedford went the income. Covent Garden was London's first formal space: a rectangle, with a uniform, classical, terrace of private houses on two sides; on the third, a church, while the fourth, to the south towards the river, was left open. The houses (probably by a French immigrant colleague of Jones's, Isaac de Caus) were arcaded, and reflected both French and Italian established practice — the term 'piazza', which applies properly to the whole 'square', was perverted by some freak of popular London usage to designate the arcades. The originals are long vanished, but a recent reconstruction of the 1880s (north-west corner) gives some idea of their appearance.

The church has also gone, another victim of fire in 1795, but a perhaps rather over-precise replica was built immediately, and its design is almost certainly very close to Inigo Jones's. According to a famous story, the Earl of Bedford (doubtless concerned about the 'vast charges' arising from the Covent Garden development, and seeking economy) asked for something 'not much better than a barn' — whereupon Jones promised him 'the handsomest barn in Europe', and duly built it, at considerable expense. The present reconstruction is very bare, indeed barn-like inside (though with many memorials associated with the theatrical profession which later constellated about Covent Garden). The external porch, however, is probably close to Jones's original, extraordinarily massive, an exercise in pure Tuscan with huge eaves, and also most ambivalent because, the church being correctly orientated, its east end, which fronts on Covent Garden, could not have an entrance opening straight on to the altar. The 'porch' has no door, and never has had one, though it is a famous trysting place and also the spot where Bernard Shaw, in *Pygmalion*, sites the momentous meeting of Professor Higgins and Eliza Doolittle.

Covent Garden was certainly intended as habitation and show-place to answer the quality and decorum of the aristocracy of high fashion, but its subsequent history is famous for other reasons. The Bedford family discovered it was profitable to let it out as what became the great fruit and vegetable market of London, its central garden filled with an arcaded building of iron and glass, stacked with wooden crates, and at its peak of business between 6 and 8 in the morning. As such, with the adjoining Royal Opera House and Drury Lane theatre adding their nocturnal glamour on its periphery, it has been one of the most picturesque and vital arenas of London life in action. This will cease in the early 1970s, when the market will move south of the river to Nine Elms, and Covent Garden may become again a possible piazza, wide open to the most exciting possibilities of imaginatively planned development. How modern London will rise to this challenge remains to be seen.

St Paul's, Covent Garden. Near-facsimile of 1795 of Inigo Jones's original (destroyed by fire) of 1633.

Covent Garden had early influence on another development north and east of itself, also outside the City walls — Lincoln's Inn Fields and Great Dean Street. These were developed by a private entrepreneur, William Newton, between 1629 and 1643 — terrace houses conforming to a regular classical design. Whether Jones was involved in this is uncertain, but his influence is beyond question, and the only original surviving house — Lindsey House (1640) in Lincoln's Inn Fields — has long been ascribed, quite reasonably, to him and is indeed historically the most important house of the period surviving in London. It is in three storeys, five bays wide. The ground floor is unemphatically rusticated, then the upper two storeys are handsomely united by pilasters, and there is a balustrade at roof level. The house is built of brick, and the brickwork in the upper storeys between the pilasters was originally exposed, giving slightly more variety than the present stucco (there was originally a single central door, but the house was later divided internally into two). It is very Palladian, very politely urbane, if grand entirely discreet; if it should seem even 'ordinary' to 20th-century eyes, this is simply because its idiom has been absorbed entirely into the enduring vocabulary of one part of English urban architecture. It is an idiom of proportion, symmetry and balance, and of restraint; instead of the cumulative nature of medieval urban building, a composition that can be demonstrated geometrically, that is resolved in mathematical terms and cannot be added to without wrecking the whole. What Inigo Jones achieved for London was to lay the basis, almost to establish the module for the development, in the squares and terraces of London, of a new architectural mode. So it became inevitable for Inigo Jones to become almost the patron saint of subsequent architects, who referred back to him again and again; of this there is most eloquent witness precisely next door (Nos. 57-58) to Lindsey House, in the shape of a nearly exact repetition of it, but almost a hundred years later, built in 1730 by Henry Joynes in homage to the great master's style. That Inigo's impact was immediate and overwhelming is, however, far from true. He was a court artist, and his style a court style, and although there were brick houses of classical order erected elsewhere in London, and echoes of his manner even in the City (as we have seen in the case of a doorway at Great St Helen's), the general evolution towards an ordered urbanity was slow. As representative of the court, Inigo Jones was no doubt suspect. (In 1642, at the outbreak of the Civil Wars between Crown and Parliament, he withdrew — there is a curious glimpse of him at the sack of Basing House in 1645, the old man being 'carried away in a blanket, having lost his clothes' — but in London he built no more till his death in 1652.) That tolerance, if often strained, of mutual respect between Crown and City that had prevailed in Elizabeth I's time, was wrecked by the drive towards absolutism of the first two Stuart kings, James I and Charles I, in their insistence on divine right. Charles I we have glimpsed in characteristic princely concern, not only for the visual manifestation of his court, but for the capital city of London at large, in the case of the Covent Garden development. But the Caroline spendour, the brilliant explosion of all the arts, was primarily a court concern, and the City was not greatly impressed; it was much more nearly touched by the arbitrary imposition of taxes.

The 1630s were a decade of rising tension in which the City composed its stand firmly against the Crown; but also, as far as the court was concerned, it was a flowering time of magnificence. There were the court masques — their great writer, Ben Jonson, their arch impresario

Vintners' Hall. Sumptuous interior (c. 1671) typical of the Livery Companies' rebuildings after the Great Fire (see pp. 93-94).

of décor, Inigo Jones (though the two quarrelled irreconcilably in 1631); there was the establishment of a new and learned refinement in the arts, led by Charles's personal flair in the creation of one of the finest collections of painting of all time (p. 188) and the presence, from 1631 till his death in 1641, of Van Dyck, who recorded so glamorously the sophisticated yet somehow, in his work, already visibly doomed generation of the Cavaliers. But between 1642 and 1649, rebellion raised its head, and this time Minerva proved not to be on the Stuarts' side, and the City, with its enormous wealth, was almost solidly against him, in support of Oliver Cromwell and the Parliamentarians.

Banqueting House ceiling. The rich coffering to Inigo Jones's design, the paintings, which constitute an apotheosis of the Stuart dynasty, by Rubens. Painted in Antwerp and delivered to London in 1635 for £3,000 (and a knighthood, in anticipation, for Rubens) (see p. 69).

Court Room, Goldsmiths' Hall, Foster Lane. The Goldsmiths stand fifth in precedence in the great Livery Companies. Their present building (by P. Hardwick, 1835) is a magnificent re-expression of the City's confidence and opulence in the 19th century (the Company was incorporated in 1327).

PP. 78/79

The Temple, Essex Court. Originally the home of the military crusading order of the Knights Templars (1119), then of the Knights Hospitallers of St John, the Temple has been associated with the law since the 15th century.

77

Lincoln's Inn, the Old Hall. Built 1490-92, with fine carved screen, early 17th century, and Hogarth's St Paul before Felix, 1748 (see p. 92).

The tragedy drew to its inexorable close when, on a bleak, snow-laden January morning, Londoners came in thousands to see the King of England step to the scaffold and execution in Whitehall outside Inigo Jones's Banqueting House.

The hostilities barely affected London's main texture, and in the ensuing Interregnum — when England made her precocious but premature essay at Republicanism — there emerged no 'Commonwealth' style. A fascinating aspect of the Interregnum is indeed its search, ultimately vain, for a viable form with which to replace the monarchical structure. Cromwell avoided the crown, but in the end, by a kind of popular necessity, when he made his final appearance — after his death, by proxy in the shape of his funeral effigy standing in state at Somerset House — he did so crowned, robed, with sceptre and orb. There had been some real destruction meanwhile, not only in the ripping-out, for example, of the lavish Catholic setting devised by Inigo Jones for Henrietta Maria at Somerset House, but more importantly in the implementation by the extreme Puritan wing of the revolution of the second phase of iconoclasm, a fury of image-breaking that destroyed most of such medieval figure sculpture in the churches as the first wave, in the 1540s and 1550s, had left. They offered by way of reparation no departure in church architecture — they built none, and in fact during the whole century — 1550-1650 — almost no churches were built in London. An interesting exception is St Katherine Cree on Leadenhall Street in the City, consecrated by Charles I's Archbishop Laud in 1631. The 'Laudian revival' stressed once again the importance of the material setting of the liturgy, and the church is not without magnificence — in style a strange transition out of the then still-fashionable (for churches) Gothic Perpendicular tradition — round arches on Corinthian columns, but the vault still a Gothic rib vault though in plaster.

In 1660 a relieved England welcomed back Charles II from exile to the throne of England, and the City too was, at least outwardly, enthusiastic in its greeting. The Royal Office of Works moved into action again; royal building started again; the restoration of the much dilapidated Old St Paul's was considered anew, and at a meeting concerned with this, in August 1666, a young mathematician and architect, Christopher Wren, made the astonishing suggestion that the Gothic tower of St Paul's be replaced by a dome. But the week after, the greatest calamity in the history of modern London kindled. The City burned, and Old St Paul's with it.

London after the Great Fire

The Great Fire of London started late on a Saturday night, 1 September 1666, in a baker's shop in Pudding Lane. Samuel Pepys lived through it, at close quarters, and left a vivid running commentary in his diary. Driven by a fierce east wind, the flames spread, uncheckable, through the densely packed inflammable City. On the Sunday night, Pepys was on Bankside, south of the river, and 'there staid till it was dark almost, and saw the fire grow; and, as it grew darker, appeared more and more, and in corners and upon steeples, and between churches and houses, as far as we could see up the hill of the City, in a most horrid malicious bloody flame, not like the fine flame of an ordinary fire . . . ' until, later, 'we saw the fire as only one entire arch of fire from this to the other side the bridge, and in a bow up the hill for an arch of above a mile long . . . ' London burned for four days, and when the flames sank on a blackened desolation, four-fifths of the City within the wall had been destroyed, and with it most of the City's medieval heritage.

Yet, even before the fire ended, some foresighted Londoners perceived that one outcome must be the opportunity to build a planned city on a vast site, the terrible razing of which might come to seem a divine blessing. The ground had been scoured, not only of its old-fashioned, mainly timber, buildings, but also of the lurking threat of the plague — for the fire must have appeared to Londoners as the second wave of catastrophe. The first, the plague that had raged through London all through the hot summer of the previous year, 1665, had indeed been far more terrible in terms of loss of life; astonishingly few people died in the fire, but the plague's toll was of the order of 100,000 deaths —

perhaps one out of every four citizens died. The opportunity was to build not only an up-to-date, ordered and magnificent capital, but a healthy one.

Before the ashes were cold, within a week from the end of the fire, two plans had been submitted to the King, and a royal proclamation had announced a new city, with broader streets, and built in brick. The mood of *resurgam* is incorporated in the memorial Monument (finished 1677) to the fire, designed by Wren or perhaps by Robert Hooke (or both together) and erected hard by Pudding Lane where the fire had started. It is a Roman Doric column, 202 feet high and its base 202 feet from the fatal baker's shop. It has a spiral staircase inside, and the view from the top has been a point of pilgrimage for the more energetic Londoners and visitors ever since. On its plinth, a large relief, sculptured by C.G.Cibber, depicts Charles II in Roman dress allegorically supervising the resurrection, 'providing with his Power and prudent Directions for the Comfort of his Citizens, and the Ornament of his City'. Inscriptions record the catastrophe (including the loss of 89 churches, 13,200 dwelling houses, 400 streets over 436 acres); one inscription, however, which attributed the destruction of 'this Protestant City' to the 'Treachery and Malice of the Popish Faction', was erased upon the accession of Catholic James II, recut ('very deep') under William and Mary, and finally obliterated in 1831.

The two best-known plans for redevelopment were those by the virtuoso and diarist, John Evelyn, and by Christopher Wren. Both paid tribute to the urban genius of the Paris of Louis XIV (whither Wren had been on a visit the year before), featuring *rond-points* as focuses for a systematic and regular pattern of streets; Evelyn's plan was more of a rigid geometrical grid than Wren's. Almost everything in these, and other, plans proved vain. Even the proposed survey turned out to be impracticable as an all-embracing exercise; a fully planned redevelopment would have involved the pooling of all private property and the exercise of powers that the Crown did not in practice possess. The Englishman's home was his castle, even when it consisted of a burned-

(left) The Monument. Once dominant in the City skyline, rising from clustered streets by Billingsgate Market; built (1671-77) by Wren to commemorate the Great Fire of 1666.

(right) Detail of the relief by C. G. Cibber — Charles II directs the building of the new City.

The Hoop and Grapes, a public house in the City, one of the very few timber-frame houses built since the Great Fire, 1666.

out blackened patch of ground, and the old hotch-potch of property divisions proved unamenable to rationalization. There was also enormous pressure from the homeless to rebuild forthwith without any delaying measures.

The only new streets cut through were two (Queen Street and King Street, between Guildhall and the river), and the ground-plan of the re-built City within its walls remained essentially that of the old medieval confusion. On one point, however, government was able to legislate in 1667: the standardization of house-building into four classes, from the grand on the principal streets, a uniform four storeys in height, to two storeys in 'by-lanes'. Brick or stone was to be a *sine qua non,* and other fire precautionary measures were incorporated. None of the brick houses in the City of this first rebuilding survive; but the evidence is that the scale successfully imposed a degree of regularity without monotony, while the houses, that do survive bear unexpected witness that enforcement of laws was not water-tight, for these houses are of timber-frame construction (*e.g.,* the pub, the Hoop and Grapes, at No. 72 Leadenhall Street, or Nos. 41-42 Cloth Fair, adjacent to Great St Bartholomew's). Glimpses of the late 17th-century texture, however, are still visible outside the square mile of the City; and to the west and north especially, great areas are still laid out according to the new trend and rational attitude to town development that in the City, had been thwarted by the existing ground-plan.

The Water Gate, Victoria Embankment, attributed to Balthasar Gerbier, 1626. Originally for river-access to the Duke of Buckingham's York House.

The Fire provided a dramatically urgent impetus to the already existing tendency for private citizens to move westward, and the demand for accommodation towards Westminster proved not an ephemeral one. Population during the 17th century increased rapidly to about half-a-million at the time of the Fire; disease and flame had revealed the perils of City dwelling, and even in normal times the intense consumption of fuel, the 'Hellish and dismall Cloud of SEACOAL', made the City's air noisome and dirty for domestic living. Close into the City precincts, the demand for new housing was met in considerable part by an ingenious, ruthless and energetic speculator called Dr Nicholas Barbon, operating between 1670 and his death in 1698. He was busy on former large estates south of the Strand, where the great houses came down and were replaced with roads running down to the river. Buckingham Street is one, having something of its original appearance, and also, near its river end, a rare survivor, a fragment of the Duke of Buckingham's former house, the Watergate (built in 1626, perhaps by Balthasar Gerbier, a picturesque and grand porch on to what was the river, but now high and dry as the river has been pushed back about 100 yards from it by the Victoria Embankment). To Buckingham Street (No. 12) Samuel Pepys came to live between 1679 and 1688, like so many other Londoners moving out of his house in the City towards the west. Barbon houses can also be seen further north (Bedford Row, Nos. 36-43), though allowance has to be made for later alterations, especially the replacement of the casement windows by the ubiquitous sash-windows, a Dutch innovation that swept through London from about 1710, modifying her entire superficial expression. Expansion by Barbon and others in the Strand and Holborn area was fast and dense, but more important was that further west, and specifically the development by the Earl of St Alban's of the St James's Square area, planned even before the Fire, and that by the Earl of Southampton in Bloomsbury, to the north. These established various patterns for aristocratic landowners anxious to extract maximum income from their land (and often unable to sell it outright as it was entailed in the family). By letting plots leasehold, they drew steady ground rents, while the land remained theirs to revert to them at the expiration of the lease (which gradually became standardized in London at 99 years); at the same time, as owners of the land, they were able to maintain some control (varying greatly in degree) over the lay-out, design and structure of the houses, and even their maintenance and services. Lord Southampton had built himself a grand house in Bloomsbury in the 1650s, and granted the first leases for plots round a proposed square in front of it as early as 1661: Bloomsbury is the first London square actually to be called a Square. But it was not created in a void, but rather from the start considered as part of a living unit, with market provided, and ancillary streets of more modest dwellings.

Similarly, Lord St Alban in St James's, who planned not only a square, an attendant market, but also a site for a church (which Wren later dignified by what seemed to him the most successful of all the parish churches that he built). St James's Square, neighbour to St James's Palace, was naturally much sought after, as the site for their town houses, by the great aristocratic servants of the court. Pall Mall was possibly the grandest of St James's streets, ending more or less within the precincts of St James's Palace, and with a view to the south across the Park. The most famous of Charles II's mistresses, Nell Gwynn, lived there. (In 1671 the somewhat prim John Evelyn was shocked to see her, one early spring morning, engaged over her garden wall 'in very familiar discourse' with the King.) The Duke of Schomberg built (rather later, in 1698) an unusually grand town house of brown brick with red trim, interesting not only because it—or at least its façade—has survived, giving a rare glimpse of the period, but also because later Thomas Gainsborough lived there after his move from Bath to London.

Further down, a little back from the road and neighbouring St James's Palace, the celebrated Duchess of Marlborough had Wren design her a house, which also survives, though much altered since; its interior has good fireplaces, the Gentileschi painted ceilings removed from the Queen's House at Greenwich, and triumphant frescoes of Marlborough's victories by Louis Laguerre.

The subsequent development of what is now inner London, through the 18th century and well into the 19th, follows in large part the pattern set by St James and Bloomsbury. It produced an entrancing, truly urban character; a reasonably but not tediously regular street plan; a module of urban domestic housing on a terrace principle, with a fairly, but again not boringly, uniform roof line, conforming to

▷

St James's Square. Laid out from 1662, one of the earliest and most fashionable of London squares. No. 4 (facing) is of c. 1726, by Shepherd.

Gray's Inn Gardens. Loved by Londoners since the time of Pepys who promenaded his wife here. The oldest catalpa is legendarily said to have been planted by Francis Bacon (who had chambers here) from cuttings brought from America by Sir Walter Raleigh.

comfortably broad streets and lining them with an agreeable discreet warmth of brick; and, ever and again, the opening out, the lift of the spirit in the squares, with their central gardens, their invitation to perambulation. Though the original houses in the older squares have almost all been replaced through the centuries, the *allure* of the street-order, the rhythm of life that it suggested, remained inviolate almost until the motorcar arrived to tear it asunder.

The example of St James's was quickly followed, though there were immediately no followers of quite such ambition. It was in the late 17th century that London's West End established its heart—Piccadilly, for many visitors now synonymous with London, the beginning of the main road out of London to the west, became first a focus for great houses, as the Strand had been earlier. One of the most famous, and architecturally influential, mansions was that of Lord Clarendon, the great historian and Lord Chancellor of England, but it lasted barely twenty years before its demolition in 1683 to make way for street developments; and there indeed ran Bond Street (the north/south axis of modern Mayfair), rapidly built up and soon reported as 'inhabited by persons of Quality'. Bond Street records the name of Sir Thomas Bond, who was but one speculator among many: the names of others live on in Clarges Street, Panton Street, Storey's Gate and, until its name was changed to Soho Square, in King Square.

By 1700 London was fairly densely built up along the north bank of the Thames from east of the Tower to Horseferry opposite Lambeth, some 5 miles—a long, relatively thin city, its basis clearly the river. London Bridge was still the only bridge, and thence Southwark had spread somewhat to the east along the river, but there was relatively little development south of the river. The population had about doubled in the century, to about 750,000 people, and Londoners already claimed their city as the largest in the world; the most compact one it certainly was not, and for citizens travelling the river was still a main highway, with some 4,000 wherries. But the wheelborne traffic was increasing steadily — '700 hackney-coaches (besides 4 times the Number, who probably keep their own)' — on the roads running between the mercantile City to the east and the luxurious Court-life of Westminster to the west. The City had difficulty, though largely rebuilt in the astonishingly short space of three years after the Great Fire, in attracting all its former inhabitants back; the west was smarter, and though the new houses in the City were a great improvement on those that had been burned, they were also more expensive and not all could afford them. One gets the impression that London's vitality was busiest in the area between the City and Westminster, around Fleet Street (1708: 'a very publick and spacious street of excellent Buildings ... which fetch great Rents (one house having been let near Temple Bar for £360 per annum ... In this street are 19 Taverns, as many Booksellers, and many Linen Drapers; I find it recorded that one James Farr, a barber ... was in the year 1657 presented by the Inquest of St Dunstans in the West for making and selling a sort of Liquor, called *Coffee,* as a great Nuisance and Prejudice of the Neighbourhood etc. And who would then have thought that London would ever have had near 3,000 such Nuisances, and that *Coffee* should have been (as now) so much Drunk by the best of Quality, and Physicians ...')

From these coffee houses the clubs were later to develop (pp. 149-50), and some were already famous virtually as such — like Will's, near Covent Garden, where the greatest poet of the Restoration period, John

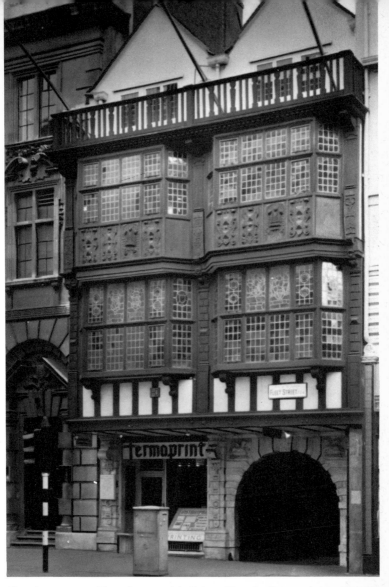

Temple entrance, Fleet Street, with Prince Henry's Room above, 1610/11.

Dryden, was glimpsed as he held court there by a small boy who was to become the greatest poet of the early 18th century, Alexander Pope. But one or two were to develop rather differently: one, Jonathans, in the City near the Royal Exchange, with a clientèle of stockbrokers, was the seed of the Stock Exchange.

Running from the Thames to the north, between Covent Garden and the City, there was also the amenity offered by the congregation of legal fraternities known as the Inns of Court. These were already long-established, since the lawyers moved into the area when the Knights Templar moved out: they were a sort of combined guild and university of the legal profession (and still are its main examining authority). They found physical expression in a complex of courts centring round great halls and chapels, closely comparable to university colleges, and these survive in an enchanting meander of courts, alleys, huge sweeps of lawn and majestic trees, enclosed yards with perhaps a fountain, that stray up from the Thames to Fleet Street (Inner and Middle Temples); thence up between Chancery Lane and Lincoln's

Lincoln's Inn, New Square. Unusually complete and well-preserved, of c. 1685-97. Dickens worked here as boy clerk.

Inn Fields (Lincoln's Inn); interrupted again by the busy traffic divide of Holborn but continuing in Gray's Inn. Much altered through the centuries, hideously blitzed but on the whole well restored, their architecture reflects predominantly a classical idiom, apart from the chapels, especially Temple Church (p. 25); Lincoln's Inn Gateway, 1518; the great halls (pp. 22-23); the Jacobean gateway on Fleet Street and the Elizabethan façade of Staple Inn (p. 62). Most of the surviving older fabric is 18th and 19th century, but in King's Bench Walk, Temple, there is a very handsome range designed by Wren, 1678, in stately brick with handsome doorways. This whole sequence of collegiate buildings and gardens forms an extraordinary and refreshing anomaly in the heart of a great capital city.

In the Covent Garden area the theatre had taken root, after its banning by the Puritans, and Drury Lane was already famous for drama. The movement of London is charted minutely and brilliantly in Samuel Pepys's *Diary* in the 1660s, which conveys the feel of ordinary life, and miraculously transposes the ephemera of almost minute-to-minute existence into an enduring and living monument.

But other monuments survive in substantial brick and stone, not only from the rebuilding of the City after the Fire, but also from the resumption, after the Restoration of 1660, of the Crown's expansion and remodelling of the royal palaces. In the City, as we have noted,

King's Bench Walk, Inner Temple. Includes rare and fine late 17th-century domestic houses, as here, some ascribed to Wren.

the rebuilding of domestic houses and shops was astonishingly fast; though the richer and grander had mostly migrated for ever to the west, and though there was the initial reluctance of some lesser people to return (in 1673 nearly 3,500 houses in the rebuilt City were empty), gradually the streets filled up. Reconstruction of the major institutional buildings also proceeded; the Guildhall, of such symbolic importance to the City, had been gutted but the shell remained; the Royal Exchange, burned to the ground, was rebuilt, adhering generally to its former design, with arcaded courtyard, though with Baroque flourishes (burnt in its turn in 1841). A rare survivor is the brick College of Arms of 1671-88 above Queen Victoria Street, but the original eaves and pediments of this were subdued into decorum by parapets in the 18th century; it is proper, however, that this building has continued as have the Heralds whom (together with a remarkable genealogical library) it houses. The Heralds' functions, concerned with the ritual of state ceremonies, the correct drawing-out of heraldic arms and the authentication of anyone's right to arms, is one of the more strangely archaic, though splendidly picturesque, continuations of medieval habit.

The City Livery Companies (45 of their halls were destroyed) were not backward in rebuilding, though economically they had been heavily hit by losses in the fire; these were relatively simple buildings, but the Companies were fond of a Dutch opulence, especially in the wood

Trade sign, Fish Street Hill. Late 17th-century inn sign, carved in wood, of the former Peterboat and Doublet tavern.

carving of the interiors, with which to enrich the basically Italianate idiom. A number were rebuilt before the 20th century, and then the Blitz took a terrible toll of the City halls; only five remain with much of their original 17th-century character—Apothecaries, Innholders, Skinners, Tallow Chandlers, and Vintners. Halls and staircases tend to be of massive magnificence (and many Companies have wonderful collections of plate), but the Companies are still private bodies and their halls are rarely open. Nevertheless, set back from the street, generally with a small forecourt, they offer the passerby tantalizing but picturesque glimpses (the Apothecaries off Blackfriars, Skinners and Tallow Chandlers Halls, both off Dowgate Hill); their exteriors, however, were all much altered in the 18th and 19th centuries.

What have survived in quantity are the new churches of post-Fire London, and of these especially the spires. As we have seen, the Monument records the loss of 89 churches in the City. Fifty-one were rebuilt, a number of parishes having been amalgamated. They were financed by a tax on coal, built under general authority of three Commissioners, and master-minded by a Surveyor-General, who was Sir Christopher Wren. It is the City churches, above all, that evoke Wren's delicate yet sturdy ghost. Though the Blitz of the Second World War wrought havoc with them, some fifteen survived in fair shape, and there are remains of many others, especially their towers and

Apothecaries' Hall, Blackfriars Lane. A City Company Hall, basically of 1670 and 1786.

spires. (One, St Mary's Aldermanbury, gutted to a shell in 1940, has migrated to Westminster College, Fulton, Missouri, where, restored, it serves as a memorial to Sir Winston Churchill.) The pressure of building was staggering—it has been reckoned that, at the peak of the rebuilding, about thirty were in progress simultaneously.

Wren was thirty-four when the Fire created for him a *tabula rasa* offering opportunities of a scale that few architects in history have been confronted with. An Oxford graduate, he had been previously concerned with matters mathematical and scientific, and only somewhat incidentally with building. But he was an inner member of a circle of men of remarkable and most various genius, characterized by high intellectual interests fired by unremitting eager curiosity and tempered by a most English pragmatism. This was the group from whom the nucleus of the famous Royal Society formed: it was the generation of Newton, of Boyle, of Locke, devoted to relentless rational enquiry into the fundamental laws of existence, yet always within the framework of a devout Christian faith. Wren had, before the Fire, designed buildings at Oxford and at Cambridge; he had also, in 1665, spent some months in France where he certainly saw not only the classical churches of Paris, but also the literally palatial expression of royalty in Louis XIV's grandiose building programme. In Paris Wren also met, if briefly, Bernini. Thus he was not entirely unversed in the practice and study of architecture; but he was certainly not an architect of mature experience when he took over so much of the re-creation of London. Frail-looking but wiry, he was fortunately endowed with tenacious stamina, and by the time he died, in full possession of his faculties, at the age of 93 in 1723, he had to his credit not only the City churches plus those he built outside the City, but ambitious royal works carried out for four monarchs, a major theatre (Drury Lane) and, his crowning achievement, one of the great cathedral churches of Europe, St Paul's, devised, built and completed within his lifetime. One of the essential qualities of Wren's genius, but one about which we known relatively little, must have been an extraordinary ability for mere mundane administration and with it a rare talent for delegation. In the pressure of work, this inevitably meant a great variation in quality, both in plan and in detail, of the dozens of churches associated with his name, but it is also true that the controlling genius, everywhere apparent, is of an exceedingly high order. The Wren style is very English, eclectic and pragmatic, developing from the severe Palladianism of Inigo Jones towards the full Baroque of contemporary European practice, yet never as rigid as the former or taken to the spectacularly full-blown extremes of the latter. Throughout his career, moreover, Wren was happy to play variations on forms drawn from traditions that might seem alien to the main line of his development (Dutch or Flemish, even Gothic) in a way that would have been inconceivable to the logic of French or Italian architects, or to mix, in a single building, disparate elements—for example, in the deliberate playing off of the very ingeniously developed Baroque movement of the western towers of St Paul's against the serenity, the calm magnificence, of the dome that looks back to the High Renaissance, to Bramante rather than to the surge of Michelangelo in St Peter's.

It is a truism that Wren worked to a classical mode rather than a Gothic one, yet this needs stressing, for he had, in his City churches, virtually to create an English classical church style. The previous century had seen very little church building in London, or indeed in all England; examples such as St Katherine Cree (p. 81) were very few, and there was no established tradition to develop, though Inigo Jones's efforts in Covent Garden and at St James's Palace (pp. 69-70) gave a lead. This involved much more than purely formal questions; fundamental problems of function remained to be satisfactorily resolved, particularly the relation of the new churches to the liturgy of the Reformed Religion. At the Reformation, superficial elements connected with Catholicism had been (disastrously) swept away—all imagery, involving figured glass, rood-screens, altar-pieces—but the Protestant clergy had no choice but to go on using the actual existing buildings of the church. The body of the church, however, no longer acted as theatre for the mysterious spectacle of the Mass; right at the end of his life in a famous memorandum, Wren summed up his idea of the principal needs a modern Protestant church should meet—'that all who are present can both hear and see'. Romanists might be content to 'hear the Murmur of the Mass and see the Elevation of the Host'; Protestant churches on the other hand 'are to be fitted for Auditories'—

▷

St Mary-le-Bow, Cheapside, by Wren, 1670-83. Bow bells (replaced after the Blitz) called back Dick Whittington to London, and a true Cockney technically is one born within hearing of them (see p. 104).

essentially almost lecture halls. The logical formal answer was therefore the hall church, a bare, preferably centrally planned, space with
the plain altar and the pulpit near the middle for optimum 'seeing and
hearing' by the congregation. In practice, such churches are rare in
Wren's work, probably because both clergy and congregation needed
the consolation of the known, traditional longitudinal form with which
they had been brought up. But the variety of the solutions that Wren
produced is both enchanting and bewildering; it is due not only to
the suppleness of Wren's mind, but to the nature of the sites he had
to work on, generally constricted and often pre-conditioned to very
odd shapes by the old, pre-Fire, demarcations of property. Held tight

London (the City) from Richmond House by Canaletto, c. 1746, showing the original effect of Wren's spires about St Paul's.

PP. 100/101

St Paul's as it is now, in the reconstruction of the City after the devastation of the Blitz.

in the pressure of surrounding commercial and domestic building, most of them could not be designed externally as monuments to command and dominate a three-dimensional space. Often all that is easily visible of the exterior of the body of the church is a somewhat pinched façade on the street. For the external expression of each church's individuality Wren concentrated generally on the towers or spires, and these, thrusting to heaven high over the relatively low roofline of the streets, were deliberately conceived of as a stunningly variegated *corps de ballet,* disposed in homage about the great central feature of the City, the dome of St Paul's. The effect was delightful, the lyric ejaculations of tower and spire, in luminous white of Portland stone

Royal coat of arms, St Margaret Pattens, Eastcheap. Superb example of the quality and virtuosity in decoration of Wren's churches.

or sombre dark of lead, saluting the majesty of the dome: it can be seen still in certain painted panoramas of London (especially Canaletto's), but no longer by the London perambulator, and less so each year as the modern multi-storey blocks reduce the spires to dwarfs. But all is not loss, for on occasions an individual spire, set now against a cliff of concrete and glass, and reaching only half-way up it, can tell most strikingly, like a hollyhock against a high wall. In form these spires range through simple square tower (St Andrew-by-the-Wardrobe); tower with pinnacles (St Mary Somerset, of which only the tower remains); almost purely Gothic restatements (St Margaret Pattens); towers with lantern or dome (or both, as on the very Dutch brick box of St Benet Paul's Wharf); spires ending in an obelisk (a wonderful one at St Magnus)—to much more elaborate conceits, like the 'wedding-cake' spire of St Bride's Fleet Street (still, with its diminishing

▷

Font cover, All Hallows Barking, Tower Hill. One of the finest examples of free woodcarving in the style of Grinling Gibbons (1689).

St Magnus the Martyr, Lower Thames Street, by Wren, 1671-85. T. S. Eliot's 'inexplicable splendour of Ionian white and gold'.

octagonals, a dominant gleaming accent in the view of the City from west London); the ingenious virtuoso pieces at St Stephen Walbrook, St James Garlickhythe and St Michael Paternoster Royal; the majestic splendour of St Mary-le-Bow, with its colonnade. Much admired by architects is the very simple-seeming spire of St Vedast, with its beautifully subtle play of concave yielding to convex.

The interiors are often rich in ornament of carved wood, stone and iron, even though Defoe noted approvingly that the London churches were 'not adorned with pomp and pageantry as in Popish countries'. Dark wood pews provided a sonority of tone and, as it were, an anchor for the light-flooded upper air of the churches, with their white plaster and gilt. The altar was generally simple, with a huge board as reredos on which was inscribed in gilt the Creed: the centre of attention was in many cases provided, even more than by the altar, by the pulpit, often very lavishly carved, and with a great sounding board over it designed to push the eloquence of the preacher out into the church rather than up into the roof. Many churches were also provided with galleries, an innovation important for the church's functions as 'auditories', but most of these were removed in the 19th century. So too were the pews and further great losses happened in the Blitz.

Almost all City churches have their own individual charm and an unexpected surprise and to 'collect' them is a rewarding hobby but a time-absorbing one (most City churches open only and for differing periods, around the lunch times of weekdays). In the space available, I can only recommend a handful for special attention. St Mary-at-Hill (1670-76): partly for its siting, slotted into the warren of fish-scented alleys on the slope of the hill from the river above Billingsgate; it has a square-domed centre resting on four Corinthian columns, and gives perhaps the best idea of Wren's interiors as they were for its floor is still serried with the great box-pews (though some of these are Victorian alterations, the later work is consonant in both style and quality with the old); pulpit (and sounding board), lectern and west gallery also all survive. Just south of this, almost in Billingsgate, St Magnus (1671-85), its air exotic with incense, after the reek of the market; through the Ionic-columned, tunnel-vaulted, gloom a pale gleam of white and gold. Its porch used to accommodate part of the approach to London Bridge, and its sturdy splendid spire, already mentioned, uses the towering wall of a bleak modern building behind as foil to great effect. St Mary Aldermary (finished 1682), in Queen Victoria Street, is often claimed as the earliest Gothic revival building in England, as Wren's instructions here were to follow the design of the original; it has typical late Gothic fan-vaults, but in plaster not stone. St Mary Abchurch (1681-87), hidden away off Abchurch Lane, a positively cosy little church on a minute open space with a minute, most delicate, lead spire, but opening inside into a room of contrasting grandeur, with painted dome, on a very irregular site so that one pillar props the dome in asymmetrical fashion—here a splendid altarpiece by Grinling Gibbons himself (his receipt survives) with swags and garlands in his characteristic manner and of highest quality. St Margaret Lothbury (1686-1701), a rich church (the parish church indeed of the Bank of England over the road) with correspondingly rich fittings, further increased—to the point that it is a veritable museum—by accumulation of furniture discarded from destroyed Wren churches elsewhere; especially the chancel screen (one of the only two surviving Wren screens); the font with its carved reliefs; pulpit and reredos; good monuments, including a rare early 17th-century bust (Sir Peter le Maire, 1631, perhaps by Le Sueur) and 18th-century ones by Nollekens (Mrs Simpson, 1795) and Banks (Alderman Boydell, 1791). The interiors of St Mary-le-Bow and of St Lawrence Jewry (the Guildhall's church) were of great splendour, but were gutted by the Blitz, though now restored. The most ambitious of Wren's churches, however, is St Stephen Walbrook (1672-77), next door to the Mansion House, and

PP. 106/107
St Magnus the Martyr. Tower and steeple finished 1706.
St Bride's, off Fleet Street. Wren's highest spire 1701-3.

St Stephen Walbrook. The most subtly complex and ambitious of all Wren's City churches, built 1672-77.

often described as a preliminary working-out, on a reduced scale, of ideas for St Paul's; it is indeed one of Wren's most purely Baroque conceptions, and a wonderful marriage of Roman form to the needs of the Anglican liturgy—of the marriage of a dome to the traditional longitudinal church plan. The cross-shape is marked out by the Corinthian columns, out of whose capitals the dome modulates with brilliant ambiguous ease—nave and aisles are there, yet it is also a centralized building under its dome. It also has wonderful woodwork (though the pews have gone), reredos, organ gallery, and a pulpit with stairs and sounding-board whereon delicate *putti* dance. It is full of light and air, and the dancing children on the pulpit are characteristic of much of the mood that prevails through Wren's churches; they speak not of decay and corruption, but—in the harvest festival of swagged fruits carved by Grinling Gibbons and his colleagues, in the

▷

St Mary Aldermary, Queen Victoria Street. Rebuilt by Wren, finished 1682, following the Gothic of the earlier church.

lucid if sometimes playful ordering of space, the gleam of white and gold—of a hopeful and reasonable well-being in the midst of life, of a confidence that life too is in the midst of death.

We should also mention churches built by Wren outside the City: notably St James's, Piccadilly, built for Lord St Albans' St James's Square development, for here Wren had a clear site, and built the church that to him seemed his best (though blitz-gutted, very well restored), and also St Clement Danes in the Strand. But the great focus of his career was, of course, St Paul's Cathedral, from the time of the completion of his first design for it in 1670 almost until his death in 1723—nearly half a century. In the building there were inevitably difficulties. The second design, for an immense Roman monument, in principle much as St Peter's, was a theoretical and intellectual project, and, though perfectly buildable (the wooden model survives in St Paul's library), was not acceptable as a church to the Anglican tradition. Accordingly, Wren produced the plan known as the Warrant Design (1675), a strange hybrid with a dome at the crossing, surmounted by a cupola in turn surmounted by a spire not unlike that of St Bride's. It was according to this design that building began, but the Royal Warrant authorizing it specified that the architect might make alterations as work proceeded, a clause of which Wren took full advantage. By 1698, the building was finished except for the dome and the west front; these were done by 1709, but by then Wren was falling out of the changing fashion of popular favour, and was indeed dismissed from the office of Surveyor-General in 1718. The building had been virtually completed the previous year by the addition of a balustrade round the parapets, against his wishes ('Ladies think nothing well without an edging').

In plan, the cathedral is essentially traditional, very reminiscent of a Norman cathedral, with long processional nave, transepts and chancel, yet the realization, as building progressed, modulated harmoniously to marry into the serenely central emphasis at the crossing under the dome. Externally, this was done by shaping the building to a uniform roofline as a coherent platform to answer the mass of the dome above; this involved some sheer illusionism, or what might seem illusionism, for the aisles adjacent to the external walls are not in fact as high as the main vaults of the building. Thus the two-storey elevation of the exterior is in a sense fake—there is nothing behind the façade of the upper storeys, yet on the other hand they are structurally vital, their weight acting as anchor to an almost Gothic structure of flying buttresses that support the main vaults. The external elevations depend basically on Inigo Jones's Palladianism, but greatly enriched, not only by copious carved ornament of great quality, but by the magnificent very Romanly Baroque columned porches at the north and south transepts, the Baroque movement being preserved again in the two-storey portico over the main entrance at the west, and in the western towers. Above this, the dome seems to float in a pure serenity, seeming (though it is not quite) a perfect hemisphere, and lacking the vertical emphasis given to Italian domes by ribs.

Inside, there is an expansive mood of ordered and calm space, of cool colour and great richness and quality of texture, provided by the furnishings. The three bays of the nave, with their saucer domes, move irresistibly with heightening suspense towards the great surge of the dome at the crossing; there are chapels off the aisles. The drum that carries the dome is visible, and then the inner surface of the dome itself (painted—again against Wren's wishes—by Thornhill;

St Paul's dome, completed 1710. Wren's masterpiece, second only to St Peter's in Rome, 365 feet high, and still dominant even in the new post-war 'vertical' City.

Wren wanted mosaic); but here there is illusionism. The inner dome is pierced at its centre, and up through this opening one can see into what seems a second outer dome but is not. In fact, Wren built a huge brick cone from the rim of the inner dome, and then, on wooden ribs stretched from the outer surface of the cone, floated the outer dome that we see today. This characteristically 'ingenious' device enabled him not only to sustain the serenity of the ribless hemisphere outside, but also to carry on top of it the lantern and the golden ball and cross that crown the whole with a perfectly judged accent.

Enjoyment of the interior comes not only from the pleasure of observing the slow and massive movement of space as the spectator moves, but from the detail of the furnishing. Wren was unexpectedly blessed (for the quality of earlier artisans in England is nowhere near as high) in his masons, woodcarvers and ironworkers. The genius among the carvers was Grinling Gibbons, Dutch-born; the virtuosity of his style is most apparent in the doorcase in the south transept, the choir stalls, and the organcase (the organ is by Schmidt, 1694). The greatest of the ironsmiths was also an immigrant, Tijou, and to him are due notably the screens in the chancel. But throughout, the quality is superb. The monuments are another matter—the floor was kept clear until the end of the 18th century, and then, following the erection by public subscription of statues of four intellectual heroes of the nation (Dr Johnson, Joshua Reynolds, Howard the prison reformer and Jones the great orientalist) at the corners under the dome, an invasion of generally over-rigid and aggressively naked statues in chill white marble began—mainly of military and naval heroes of the Napoleonic and later wars. Among them (nave), the memorial to the Duke of Wellington, an equestrian figure by Alfred Stevens, is much more in keeping with the church. Through the 19th century, indeed, St Paul's became, like Westminster Abbey, a Valhalla for memorial effigies of national heroes. The actual burial place, however, is the Crypt, where Wellington and Nelson both lie. Nelson rests (under the dome) in a magnificent black marble sarcophagus made originally, 1524-29, by Benedetto da Rovezzano for a tomb intended (but never used) for Cardinal Wolsey. More remarkable than Wellington's tomb is his funeral carriage, designed by Gottfried Semper in 1852. But the best known is perhaps Wren's own—the almost anonymous plain black marble slab, offset by the famous inscription on the wall above it:

SI MONUMENTUM REQUIRIS, CIRCUMSPICE

In the Blitz, St Paul's sustained only one direct hit of consequence, but the area all round was laid flat. Once again, as in 1666, the opportunity existed of creating a setting that would reveal the cathedral in all its majesty, and once again the property values of commercial London made this impossible; St Paul's is still ringed about by mostly undistinguished buildings. Note, though, the Deanery on the hill south of the church, a dignified dark brick mansion, one of the few certain Wren domestic buildings.

Elsewhere in London, Wren was busy mainly on works for the Crown, which began again on Charles II's restoration to the throne in 1660. Neither as sensitive nor as learned as his father, Charles II had, however, in his long exile on the Continent, become aware of especially French ideas of royal palatial magnificence. Work was put in hand at Greenwich and at Old Somerset House, but the urgency of rebuilding the City after 1666 put all work on the royal palaces into long abeyance, and only in 1681 did the first major work start, with the foundation of Chelsea Hospital for the care of old soldiers. It is essentially a barracks, and composed austerely about a court in red brick, rather Dutch in feeling; grandeur, however, is supplied by the use of a giant Doric order in the great portico, with its pediment

▷

St Paul's, choir stalls by Grinling Gibbons. Typical of the splendid enrichment of the interior by Wren's craftsmen.

(top) *Royal Hospital, Chelsea, by Wren, finished 1692.*

(below) *Royal Hospital, Greenwich, by Wren and others.*
Queen's House (central) by Inigo Jones.

and cupola behind, and these were to have great influence on comparable institutional buildings in the next century. The Hospital has a central chapel and hall (in the former, a good altarpiece by Sebastiano Ricci); and, in the courtyard, a statue of Charles II by Grinling Gibbons. Set in its expansive lawns and gardens by the river, it still performs its original function, and its pensioner old soldiers, in their summer uniform of vivid red, clanging with medals, add an agreeable archaic and picturesque accent in the street life of one of London's most fashionable quarters.

The Hospital was still unfinished at Charles II's death in 1685. James II, in his brief and troubled reign, was interested mainly in Whitehall, where Wren built a new block at great speed; when England (with the full support of the City of London) ejected the Catholic James to exile in 1688, and welcomed instead Protestant William of Orange as William III, and his wife (James's daughter) Mary II as joint monarchs, royal attention turned to Hampton Court. The plan, initially under Mary's inspiration, was to demolish the entire Tudor complex (pp. 54-58) (except the Great Hall), and to build instead a modern

palace that could stand comparison with those that flowered in France in the régime of William III's arch-enemy, Louis XIV; Wren, in his designs, seems to have had elements from the Louvre and from Versailles in mind. The plan was carried out only in parts (the Park and Privy Garden façades, the architecturally rather overcrowded but charming Fountain Court), and few probably regret this, as Wren, over-hurried in his designing, produced, especially in the long Park front, a somewhat monotonous variation on the manner of Mansart. This is redeemed, though, by its relation to the beautiful formal lay-out of the gardens, and the admirable fittings, many of them by craftsmen, such as Tijou and Cibber who worked for Wren also at St Paul's. For those interestered in mural painting in England, Wren's interiors offer a wealth of the work of the immigrant Italian, Antonio Verrio. Just before Mary died, in 1694, she founded a hospital, in rivalry to that at Chelsea, but at Greenwich, for sailors. The plan for this was complicated, as it had to include the existing Queen's House by Inigo Jones, and another blocks (by Inigo Jones's son-in-law, John Webb) of the 1660s. Wren's final plan consisted of two blocks set wide apart on the river front, receding to two further blocks closer together and accented by two domes. The vista created by this recession is closed by the Queen's House, really too small to discharge its obligations as focal point. This plan, however, was not to be worked out by Wren himself, but was continued and much modified by his successors, Hawksmoor and Vanbrugh, with a remarkable colonnade. The Hall (1698) is Wren's, and is of great and grand simplicity, enhanced by the most successful large-scale wall paintings in England, featuring an allegorical exaltation of William and Mary on the ceiling, and on the end wall a welcome to George I and the Hanoverian dynasty. It took its painter, Sir James Thornhill, from 1707 to 1726. This group of buildings subsequently became the Royal Naval College (the Hall and Chapel are visitable), though Inigo Jones's Queen's House was incorporated in the National Maritime Museum (p. 227).

Long before that, fire had struck again, but this time in Westminster and not in the City; on 4 January 1698 the Palace of Whitehall burned to the ground, and with it perished not only great treasures of the Royal collection—including Holbein's wall-painting of Henry VIII and Bernini's bust of Charles I—but often-entertained plans for a grandiose palace central in London (Inigo Jones, John Webb and Wren himself had all built, on the drawing-board, that particular palace in the City). It is true that the destruction (the major survivor was the Banqueting Hall) in theory cleared the site for just such a palace, but William III had never liked Whitehall, and in the end the site was let out, in the 18th century, in parcels for private building.

William's attention was focused more on a new palace, on higher ground and clear of the river (he had asthma) at Kensington; this was (and is) relatively modest, originally a Jacobean house adapted by Wren in various stages between 1689 and 1696 and indeed not designated 'palace' but simply Kensington House. It consists of three courtyards, in warm brick, and proved to be not only William III's favourite residence, but Queen Anne's too. It was much occupied by George I and George II, for whom considerable alterations were carried out,

especially by William Kent (the staterooms are open to the public, and part of the house is the temporary abode of the London Museum; a third part is the residence of Princess Margaret and the Earl of Snowdon). The gardens were originally very Dutch in style, but were remodelled in the more free English landscaping manner by Charles Bridgeman from 1728—the basis of the present lay-out of Kensington Gardens, with the famous Broad Walk and the Round Pond. The most spectacular architectural feature is the Orangery (1704), a design said to be Hawksmoor's with modifications by Vanbrugh, and of beautiful dignity yet with the most subtle movement in the handling of its elevations. But in Queen Anne's time—the Orangery was made for her—Kensington was still a country village. It was not long to remain so, for major development of new areas in West London was soon to begin.

Georgian London

It might be thought that the concentrated effort put into the rebuilding of the City churches after 1666 had been exhaustive, and exhausting, enough to content London's ecclesiastical needs for a century or more. Not so, however; the effort had been mainly in the burnt-out area, and elsewhere in London new churches were needed both for the newly-developed areas and for those where the old neglected Gothic churches were no longer considered suitable. Thus, following an election in 1710 that brought in a High Church Tory government, an Act was passed providing for the erection (to be paid for, again, from a tax on coal) of fifty new churches 'of stone and other proper Materials with Towers or Steeples to each of them'.

Although nothing like fifty were built, out of the 1711 Act there did grow some of London's most famous, and most loved, churches. Wren was now an old man (St Paul's was virtually completed in the year the Act was passed), and the varying styles of the new churches represent both a development from, and a reaction against, his urbane eclecticism. The architect, who initially was the prime adviser to the

(far left) Kensington Palace. An old house, remodelled by Wren and others from 1689, as palace for William and Mary. Now the home of the London Museum, State Apartments, and Princess Margaret.

(left) Chiswick House, built for himself by Lord Burlington, impresario of the Palladian movement, from 1725.

Christ Church, Spitalfields, 1723-29.
One of the three monumental
churches built in the East End
by Nicholas Hawksmoor.

Commissioners for the Fifty New Churches, was James Gibbs, a Scotsman in his early thirties, and recently returned from prolonged study in Rome. And his first church, St Mary-le-Strand (begun 1714) is a purely, and successful, Roman Baroque church, small but of a massive movement and proportion that make it seem bigger than it is. Since 1910, when development of the Aldwych isolated it and its neighbour, St Clement Danes, it has been possible to appreciate it better than ever before—now, the two churches sail in gracious convoy down the middle of the Strand, and the lyric elegance of both spires is due to Gibbs, who added St Clement Danes's in 1719. Still better known, owing to its site in Trafalgar Square and its repute as a venue for fashionable weddings, is Gibbs's St Martin-in-the-Fields (though this owed nothing to the 1711 Act). In comparison with St Mary-le-Strand, this renounces the emotional appeal (no doubt distrusted as being of Popish flavour—Gibbs was incidentally a rather cautious Catholic) of the earlier building in favour of a more austere, more truly 'Roman' (i.e. Vitruvian) Christian temple with pedimented portico. It is a much-loved yet not entirely successful church (the spire appears to ride on the roof). But it was immensely influential on later church-building in London, and is also symptomatic of the somewhat doctrinaire and puritan (though precociously neo-classical) reversion away from Wren to the severer Palladianism of which Inigo Jones was held to be the great English master. This movement we shall return to later, but for the moment the opposing swing of fashion should be noted—the development of a full-blooded Baroque, which was brief but contributed some splendid monuments to London's fabric. Hawksmoor and Vanbrugh are the famous names associated with this, but the latter is hardly represented at all in London, whereas the former built considerably.

Nicholas Hawksmoor rose from humble beginnings in Wren's office

St Mary-le-Strand. James Gibbs's first London church, 1714-17. Wren's St Clement Danes is seen beyond, but its spire is by Gibbs.

to become a major architect in his own right. His version of Baroque is far from the Continental one; very English and with a unique character: a dour, almost clenched Baroque but with a mastery of control of mass and volume that generally surpasses Wren's. In Wren one often senses an intellectual delight at work, but only rarely the passion that in Hawksmoor seems to infect the heavy stone itself. One of his churches is in the City—St Mary Woolnoth; three are in Stepney, in what is now the East End but was then a prosperous development associated particularly with immigrant weavers: St Anne, Limehouse (1715), St George-in-the-East (1715), and Christ Church, Spitalfields (1723)—all bomb-damaged, and restored, but still standing with a commanding density and purpose of presence that make the modern multi-storey blocks that stand about them look as flimsy as paper. Then there are St Alphege, at Greenwich; and, on the then new development at Bloomsbury, St George, with its dramatic portico and its remarkable stepped spire based on Pliny's description of the tomb of Mausolos and topped by a St George statue as a salute to George II. A more Continental kind of Baroque was practised by Thomas Archer in St John's, Smith Square (1721); its exterior (it was gutted in the war) is still a declamatory ascension skywards, up through its four bold corner towers. It was held to offend against good manners and polite decorum, and was long ridiculed in London slang as the 'footstool church', according to a legend that Queen Anne had designed it by kicking over a footstool, and leaving it to lie with its four legs sticking in the air.

Archer's St John's remained something of an anomaly. Other churches built as a result of the Act bear a much closer relationship to the more sedate manner of Wren's St James Piccadilly and Gibbs's St Martin-in-the-Fields: for example, St George's, Hanover Square (another church celebrated for fashionable weddings) by John James (1721-24), or St

Giles-in-the-Fields (1731-33) by Flitcroft. Flitcroft was known as 'Burlington's Harry', a reference to his being one of the favourite protégés of the 3rd Earl of Burlington, an aristocrat of learning and taste who exerted a decisive influence through the 18th century, not only by patronage but by his own work as architect. It was Burlington who led the Palladian revival, and himself essayed it in London in Burlington House, Piccadilly, and in his 'party-villa' at his (then country) estate at Chiswick. Burlington House, with its great gateway on Piccadilly and the curved colonnades embracing the courtyard back to the façade of the house, was almost entirely remade in the 19th century, but the ground floor interiors, and some of the first floor ones, with paintings by S. Ricci and Kent, still show something of its original effect (it now houses the Royal Academy, p. 190). The Chiswick villa (1725), with its garden, remains one of the most delectable sights in London; it is, in a sense, a folly, designed for holding very grand parties in, and in form is a variation on Palladio's *Rotunda*, a square building with dome, tautly simple in exterior, densely complex and rich in ornament inside. The gardens, with the formal, statuary-studded, melting into the informal, are William Kent's. Further up-river is Marble Hill, another country villa in the Palladian manner (by Robert Morris, 1728) of the most charming dignity and restraint. This can be visited, but the villa where the poetic *genius loci* lived, the celebrated riverside house of the poet Alexander Pope with its grotto, which established the tone for these just-out-of-town Arcadian retreats, is long demolished.

The Palladian gospel was broadcast not only by the work of Burlington and his protégés but by their books, of which the most important were Colen Campbell's *Vitruvius Britannicus* and Giacomo Leoni's *Palladio* (1715-17), and then William Kent's *Designs of Inigo Jones* (1727). All three were Burlington men, especially Kent, and all left some mark on London. Burlington himself was involved in the urban development of west London at that time proceeding apace, as the great landowners one after another began to exploit their holdings in answer to the demand for houses of quality in the area, and for the increase of income. From 1715 on, Mayfair, as we know it, was gradually filled in. Burlington built the streets behind his own grand house (Burlington Gardens, Savile Row, etc.), and the three splendid squares which are such an amenity of Mayfair were building at much the same time: Hanover Square, about 1720; Grosvenor Square, from 1725; Berkeley Square from the late 1730s. Very little of the original or early houses of these squares remain — a few houses on the west of Berkeley Square as on the west of Hanover Square, almost nothing in Grosvenor Square — but their central green, and the splendour of ancient trees remain invaluable. In Berkeley Square the giant plane-trees, each in spring a glorious fountain of green and gold, are said to go back to about 1790, but they are not quite the oldest things in the square among the characterless building of the early 20th century — No. 44 is by William Kent, and has inside one of the most opulent hall staircases in England.

Grosvenor Square remains a great expanse of green (6 acres) with the Franklin D. Roosevelt statue in its midst, but has indeed been almost entirely taken over by the United States. The process begun in 1785 by John Adams, first American Minister to Britain and later President, when he came to live at No. 9 (still extant, with a plaque for Adams, in the north-east corner), was completed by the occupation in 1960 of the whole of the square's west side by Eero Saarinen's U.S. Embassy. Somewhat controversial, its rather ambivalent character is due to an

44 *Berkeley Square. One of the most sumptuous and ingenious domestic interiors in London, by William Kent, 1744.*

attempt to echo the Georgian rhythm of the old in the square, though this no longer existed when it was built. I have heard the square and the area about it referred to as 'Little America'. 'Mayfair' as a whole is now synonymous the world over with high-quality merchandise, but the old market, laid out to serve the domestic shopping needs of the western part of the area in 1735 (on the site of the old May fair from which the name comes), still remains, a tight little complex of alleys and minute squares: Shepherd Market.

Expansion was not confined to Mayfair. Neighbouring it on the north, on the other side of what is now Oxford Street, the Harley-Cavendish estates were in full development from about 1720. This was a grandly planned venture, with Gibbs apparently as architectural consultant and co-ordinator, and centred on Cavendish Square. Though the great town houses on the Square itself never materialized, there was a market building (demolished) and an elegant little church (St Peter's, Vere Street, by Gibbs) that survives, as do the family names attached to the regular grid of rather stately streets round about — Harley and Wimpole Streets (now the headquarters of the leading private medical consultants), Henrietta, Cavendish, Wigmore.

If the Harley-Cavendish plans failed to live up to their original inspiration, this was in part due to a very marked slowing down in the war-ridden middle years of the 18th century, and in part to the fact that the English aristocracy now tended to give full rein to ambitious imagination (and expense) in their country houses, rather than in their London abodes. Big, free-standing town mansions were becoming rarer, and have anyway now almost all vanished. South of Mayfair, the burnt-out Whitehall Palace area was leased for large houses, but the only survivors of these are later, Gwydyr House (Whitehall) and Dover House; there is, however, fronting elegantly on Green Park, Spencer House, by John Vardy (finished about 1765), a Palladian-minded mansion, with its pilasters and pediment, and bleached statuary on the skyline. The more characteristic urban texture of relatively modest terrace houses does happily survive in parts in that area — Queen Anne's Gate is still a delectable enclave of houses from about 1700 on, and the streets around the Baroque explosion of Archer's St John's Church in Smith Square date from about the same time as the church, in the 1720s, but in enchanting contrast — trim, compact,

Hampton Court, the façade which was built by Wren, reflecting his memories of Paris (1689); seen from the gardens (see p. 114).

in brown-brick with red-brick dressings — to the church's flamboyance. Here Lord North Street is almost perfectly intact, and the automobile seems a most uncouth intrusion. Smith Square and Queen Anne's Gate are all hard by the heart of Westminster, signalled now architecturally by the very belated addition of the two west towers to Westminster Abbey — added, rather unexpectedly and not entirely adequately by Hawksmoor in 1739 (though the Baroque accent of the Gothic is fascinating to decipher).

The importance of Westminster was further stressed by two events. First, the erection of Westminster Bridge, begun in 1739; secondly, the beginning of those institutional public buildings whose successors now house the great Whitehall bureaucracy of modern governmental administration. Halfway up Whitehall, St James's Park side, Kent built the Treasury, and the present day's Treasury façade on to the Park is still his. Near by, in a modest little road then called the Cockpit,

St Martin-in-the-Fields, off Trafalgar Square. James Gibbs's most famous London church, built 1722-26.

Greenwich, Royal Hospital Hall. Designed by Wren, 1698, with details by Hawksmoor, and painted between 1708 and 1727 by Sir James Thornhill with allegorical scenes celebrating the Protestant succession from the landing of William of Orange to that of George I. Perhaps the most successful ensemble of its kind in England. *(see p. 116).*

The Lord Mayor's Coach, built 1757;
still in use but only for Lord
Mayors' Days and Coronations.
Painted panels said to be by Cipriani.
It weighs nearly four tons and
is drawn by six horses, each with
a state harness weighing 106 pounds.

Sir Robert Walpole, whose powers were roughly the equivalent of those of a present-day Prime Minister, settled in in a likewise quite modest little house, today (vastly expanded) known as No. 10 Downing Street. A little further up Whitehall, Kent designed the Horse Guards, intended to house the Commander-in-Chief of the Army. This building arouses the scorn of architectural purists in its lack of proper relation of one part to another, but remains endearing to the public in its odd, jerky picturesque (much enhanced for the tourist by the presence of splendidly-accoutred mounted Horse Guards). Still further up Whitehall, the old Admiralty headquarters was already there, a rather tedious block (by T. Ripley, 1722-26) much improved by being partially hidden by an elegant stone screen added by Robert Adam in 1760. Thus the essential elements of government were established at Whitehall — Prime Minister and Treasury, with Parliament and the judiciary down in old Westminster Palace, and the might of arms supporting government in the Horse Guards and the Admiralty. At the same time the monarchy had withdrawn from its devastated Whitehall Palace to St James's across the Park and to Kensington, remote in the west.

Meanwhile the mercantile centre of London, the City, was flourishing and not immune to the Palladian influence as expressed in architecture. The City's building activities between 1735 and 1767 were supervised by the 'Clerk of the City Works', George Dance the elder, and institutions that had previously had no specially designed habitat were now given one. There was a new Corn Exchange and a market by the Fleet River; the Bank of England was given its first permanent abode, and the Lord Mayor of London also allotted his. The last, the Mansion House, is the only one of these that survives, designed by Dance; together with the Royal Exchange and the Bank of England, sited at a now traffic-jammed confluence of many ways, it constitutes a kind of hub for the City. The Mansion House (finished 1753) suffers from apparent constriction as if too big for its boots, and its façade, its squashed-in portico, almost in danger of abrasion by the passing traffic; inside, however, it has one enormous state reception room, the 'Egyptian Hall', which expresses, if without great finesse, something of the City's material pride and grandeur.

As it spread, the Palladian theme grew somewhat diluted and a little anaemic, breeding buildings of plain wholesomeness that tended towards monotony. But soon after the Peace of Paris in 1763, a new building boom started and went on till the beginning of the French Wars in the 1790s, and the architects who served and exploited that were very different. The two most famous were Sir William Chambers and Robert Adam, contemporaries but of very contrasting tempers. Chambers was a man of learning and of travel (not only in Italy, but as far as China); a serious professional, of academic bent of mind, and indeed the most influential member of the architectural profession in the founding of the Royal Academy in 1769. He was responsible for the Albany in its original form, but this was largely rehandled later into the form it is known in today — a strange, becalmed oasis of exclusive apartments at the heart of London (off Piccadilly), long beloved, as a London *pied-à-terre*, by eminent writers, from Lord Byron to Graham Greene. Chambers's major, and majestic, enduring contribution to the London scene was his rebuilding of the former

◁

Westminster Abbey — the west towers, seeming at first integrally of the Gothic vision, yet added by Nicholas Hawksmoor, 1735-40.

Mansion House, the Lord Mayor's official residence: Egyptian Hall, 1739-53.

Royal Palace of Somerset House, between the Strand and the river. When built by Protector Somerset in 1550, this building, as we have noted (p. 64), was the first in England to express something of the coherence of Renaissance principles. Chambers's façade on the Strand reflected something of what it replaced, discreet and not particularly noticeable today; the other front, however, is quite another matter. As the whole was built on the slope to the river, the river front is carried high on a massive base of rusticated arches — with rather Piranesian overtones, heightened by the pedimented open colonnades above that give access, as it were, to the sky. This façade, already extensive, is now over 910 feet long with later extensions carried out in successfully similar style (on the west, by Sir James Pennethorne,

No. 7 Adam Street, Adelphi, the urban vision of Robert Adam, c. 1772.

from 1856; on the east, the King's College (London University) extension by Sir Robert Smirke from 1829). The great central courtyard is of a rich, ornamented but somewhat unexcitingly sober splendour; the purpose of the renewed Somerset House was no longer as royal palace, but as home for a number of governmental offices — one of the earliest complexes of its kind. It was also the first home of the Royal Academy (p. 190) and its rooms still survive, but Somerset House now is best known as the great national repository and archive of wills and testaments.

Somerset House was begun in 1776, and was in rivalry to another great riverside enterprise — the Adelphi — a little further to the west, by Adam. Both were intended, praiseworthily, to initiate a river frontage worthy of the Thames, which then lapped at the basement arches of Somerset House though now it is banked far from it by the Victorian embankments. The Adelphi was a speculative development (1768-72) for private houses, in a great terrace raised, like Somerset House, on arches high over the tideway. Its style was very different: the river front was unhappily entirely demolished, but the Adam style can still be assessed from a few surviving examples in the inland streets of the development, notably Nos. 7-10 Adam Street.

The Palladian manner was an exercise within a strict grammar, the essential tenets of which were provided by the five orders, as re-interpreted by Palladio from the supreme classical authority of the writings of `Vitruvius, meaning, usually, a rusticated basement, a *piano nobile* within the framework of massive columns or pilasters carrying the entablature; to this exterior the interior had to answer with an echoing· logic. The style tended to the severe, to the rigid, to a cool solemnity. In contrast, Adam developed an exquisite decorative sensibility, which for his supporters seemed a proper, and greatly relieving, gaiety, both urban and urbane, but which was condemned by his opponents as vulgar, meretricious and even positively frivolous. The principle behind Adam's exterior ornament is, however, quite sound: it is that of cosmetics, an enhancement by colour and skilful heightening of accents by decoration, that works admirably on a dense city crowd of terraced house-faces. His interiors corresponded; the massive décor of, say, Kent, gives way to a filigree delicacy and sparkle of ornament, and Adam liked to design every detail down to door-furniture and carpets. The work of Robert Adam and his brothers (James and John — it is to them all as a team that the name *Adelphi,* brothers, refers) is happily, despite the Blitz and demolitions, still very richly represented in London. A few yards from No. 7 Adam Street, with its enchanting honeysuckle decoration, is a good example of Adam's graver institutional style, the Royal Society of Arts (8, John Adam Street, 1772-74) with fluted Ionic columns and pediment. 'Arts and Commerce Promoted', announces an inscription on the façade, and the Society was indeed founded (1754) 'for the Encouragement of Arts, Manufactures and Commerce', to some extent heralding an interest generally thought of as Victorian, that was to find full expression in the Great Exhibition of 1851 and the consequent founding of the South Kensington Museum (p. 217). The Society in Adam Street still flourishes, and has some elegant furnishings; its most famous possession is a series of large canvases by the gifted and manic Irish painter, James Barry — perhaps the most ambitious attempt at epic painting in Britain in the 18th century. They attempt a sort of progress of the human spirit and its achievement, from a state of savage ignorance to 'Elysium, or the State of Final Retribution': included are likenesses, in various guises, of many distinguished contemporaries such as Dr Johnson and Edmund Burke, and the paintings are indeed of great historical interest rather than of major artistic achievement (viewable by previous appointment). Examples of Adam's domestic style can be found also in Portland Place, a major development subsequently included by Nash in his great St James's Park to Regent's Park triumphal way, but since much dislocated by replacement and the Blitz; near Portland Place, Chandos House, a soberly distinguished urban house; or, at No. 20 Portman Square, a beautifully preserved house, both exterior and interior, with charming staircase and stucco work, and decorative painting by Angelica Kauffman. It now houses the Courtauld Institute of Fine Art, a department of London University. Other examples are No. 20 St James's

Square (its façade recently repeated on No. 21); Fitzroy Square. Some of the rooms in Apsley House (now the Wellington Museum, p. 228) preserve much of their original Adam delicacy of touch, and one room from a famous house, belonging to the great actor David Garrick, has been set up in the Victoria and Albert Museum.

Further out, but still easily accessible, are the grandest examples of Adam's style, his big houses built for noblemen, then country-houses convenient for town, though now absorbed into the spread of Greater London. One of the most beautiful is Kenwood (the Iveagh Bequest, p. 229) on the edge of Hampstead Heath, poised in white serenity over a majestic sweep of grass, woods and water, with a library by Adam that is one of the most elegant rooms in London. This was built for the great Lord Chancellor, Lord Mansfield; and for one of the oldest of English aristocratic families, the Percys (Dukes of North-umberland), Robert Adam rehandled an ancient house on the western reaches of the Thames, Syon House. Plain, almost dour in exterior, this has interiors of great fantasy and richness of decoration, especi-ally the pillared and be-statued Hall and the Ante-Room, a very individual, and magical, interpretation of the antique. The Percys still live at Syon, but it opens to the public, and its popular appeal is enhanced by its now housing, in the grounds, an ambitious horticultural centre (there is also, at the approach to the estate, the extensive and fascinating premises, littered in surreal fashion with stone gods, cherubs, and lead shepherdesses, with fountains and garden fur-niture, of the antique dealers, Crowthers). Also to the west is Osterley Park, like Syon once a quadrangular Tudor house, but remodelled by Adam from the 1760s; it is less successful than Syon, perhaps because the furniture and fittings belonging to the old owners (the Earls of Jersey) have all gone, though Adam's entrance is inspiring; it is now administered by the Victoria and Albert Museum.

Adam's style, though it may gallivant in decoration, rests within the Renaissance tradition, and the 'cosmetic' is always applied to a proper symmetry. There were other styles, witness to the rich variety of 18th-century taste. The Gothic revival was under way, and even if, as in Adam's case, this tends to be an application of ornament to a basically

Kenwood House by Robert Adam (from 1767), from Hampstead Heath. The house and magnificent art collection were bequeathed to the Nation in 1927.

The Pagoda, Kew Gardens. Chinoiserie folly, by Sir William Chambers, c. 1760, in the superb botanical gardens founded by Princess Augusta, 1759.

classical bone-structure, it is quite different. There was also the Chinese, but this really was limited to 'follies', decorative pavilions, such as the Pagoda that Sir William Chambers built to adorn Kew Gardens. This huge expanse (280 acres) has developed into the Royal Botanical Gardens, now one of the favourite (and, so far, cheapest) excursions for Londoners, and certainly one of the most attractive of government departments. Among the changing colours of the seasons that wash through the expanses of flowers and trees, Chambers' thin multi-twinkled roof minaret still emerges, but is not the only item of architectural interest. A small red brick early 17th-century house in the Dutch style is the most modest of all the Royal palaces, while the Palm House is the most ingenious, happily resolved of early Victorian ventures in curving glass and ribbed iron. The famous Gothic house of the 18th century lies also to the west and on the river: Strawberry Hill at Twickenham, the fantasy house built for that eccentric, acid-tongued, multifarious virtuoso and man of letters, Horace Walpole, between 1747 and 1776, in the cosily spooky mood of his famous 'Gothic' novel *Otranto*. It is not normally available to public visitors, and its fantastic conglomeration of furniture and bric-à-brac was dispersed in a sale in 1842 that lasted many days — but an idea of its interior can be glimpsed in a room from a very similar house (Lee Priory) preserved in the Victoria and Albert Museum.

These are but some examples of the grander buildings that grew up in the immediate vicinity of London, still rural retreats, but already threatened by the expansion of urban development, in spite of a relative slowing-down in the 18th century of the actual population: between 1700 and 1801 (when the first official census was carried out) the number of Londoners only increased from about 750,000 to some 860,000. In the first half of the century especially, the death-rate was phenomenally high (one modern authority indeed suggests 674,000 in 1700, and 676,000 in 1750), aggravated by disease of plague intensity

Queen Anne's Gate, Westminster. One of the best preserved enclaves of early 18th-century domestic architecture in London.

in the poorer, already slum, areas and probably by the Londoner's addiction to cheap and deadly gin (the effects of which are spelled out with appalling vividness in Hogarth's print, *Gin Lane*, see p. 202). Nevertheless the drift, especially of the well-to-do citizens, to the west away from the City increased, and after a lull in mid-century, owners of great estates resumed the development of their lands until again, in the 1790s, the pace slackened but by no means ceased, in the crisis of the wars with France. It picked up once more well before Waterloo in 1815. In the west, there were notable developments, particularly north of Oxford Street (which had by the end of the 18th century entirely displaced Cheapside, in the City, as the focus of London shopping). Bloomsbury was one — property of a family whose name is almost synonymous with London development, the Russells, Earls and then Dukes of Bedford. From the early 17th century when the Bedfords commissioned Inigo Jones to design the first square at Covent Garden, through to the mid-19th century, the family estate office was involved almost continuously not only in expansion, but in re-planning and re-building, and it is just that almost the only surviving intact 18th-century square bears their name — Bedford Square (begun about 1775), each side of which is treated as an architectural whole. In 1800, the Bedfords, realizing that the great aristocratic free-standing house was an anachronism, demolished Bedford House, and thence expansion northwards (hitherto inviolate in order to preserve the views of open country from the family grounds) opened up. Gradually the Bloomsbury that we knew till yesterday, that serene, most civilized sequence of regular streets and open squares — Bloomsbury, Bedford, Russell, Tavistock, Gordon and Woburn — developed. Further west, a comparable expansion by the Portman family produced Portman and Manchester Squares, and the still delightful terrace streets around Baker Street.

By about 1800 the character of modern London's lay-out was well

135

established. London is often cited as the classic contrast to Paris, scattered, open city as against planned, closed city. This is true to a certain extent, and the felicities of London often seem truly the result of happy accident, and tend to happen in the backwaters behind generally scrappy, often indeed almost brutally haphazard, façades of the great thoroughfares. But it is also true that much of London is an agglomeration, if unplanned overall, of nevertheless carefully planned (and carefully maintained) units, which are in themselves, like Bloomsbury, often of considerable extent. Hence that delightful variation of rhythm for the pedestrian sightseer in west London: the movement through a regular pattern of streets, opening ever and again into the expansion of a square, and then yielding to the denser, irregular pattern of what was once an outlying village — thus the meander of Marylebone High Street between the grid-like pattern of the Cavendish/Harley and the Portman estates. In fact the squares were not first thought of in terms of aesthetic refreshment, but more often as almost hygienic — as necessary 'ventilation'; their often delicious picturesqueness, the gardens, the great plane trees with their cascades of green — is due generally to a later rehandling of the earlier squares under the influence of the Picturesque movement in English landscaping, from about 1810 onwards, as is also the present so artfully 'natural' form of St James's Park.

The individual houses that comprised the long terraces of the new developments are still so familiar to, so accepted by, present-day Londoners that the astonishment of European visitors at their archaic quaintness merely astonishes the natives. For all the growth of modern blocks of flats, the Londoner still seems reluctant to accept horizontal living, but sticks to his narrow-fronted terrace house, two or three bays wide, with its never-ending up-and-down exercise on the stairs. The houses have their advantages, of privacy and self-containment. The grander ones, however, were built in terms of a rhythm of everyday living that now seems as formal and remote as a minuet, the rooms disposed and composed to suit certain dispositions of servants, of almost public entertaining. The Adam house at 20 Portman Square, with its elegant stairwell, is a superb surviving example of these, but such houses, of the very grand citizen, proved inflexible to adaptation by later changing generations — hence part of the reason that so few remain. But the great inherent problem of long streets of terrace houses is monotony. Though the proportions of the elevations of the individual units remained generally of high standard, the vitality of any street depended on the liveliness of the detailing and the accents of ornament (Queen Anne's Gate in Westminster, or Church Row in Hampstead, are delightful examples of surviving ensembles in which visual interest is constantly sustained by crisp accents of variegated detail and ornament). The tendency to a deadening monotony was strengthened, albeit involuntarily, by a series of Building Acts culminating in the famous one of 1774; these were all framed, entirely laudably, in the interests of public convenience and of countering flimsy jerry-building and fire risks. One of the results, however, was an increasing standardization of houses. Projections were banned, and the face of London became ever more plain and wholesome, and ultimately boring — especially in the cheaper areas, where the need for economy struck first by cutting

▷

Syon House, Isleworth. The Ante Room. One of the most brilliant and ambitious of Robert Adam's interiors, 1762-69.

Apsley House, Piccadilly; the Waterloo Gallery added by the Duke of Wellington in 1828, to hold the annual Waterloo banquet.

apparently superfluous decoration. This applied even to shops, though not so drastically, but the bowed windows tended to shrink in, and the picturesque clutter of hanging sign-boards vanished. It is difficult now to visualize the shopping streets of that period, as few old shops remain, all swept away by time and the retail traders' insatiable need for novelty; but here and there individual façades remain with a doll's-house charm, such as Fribourg and Treyers' tobacco shop in the Haymarket, or Lock's Hat Shop at the bottom of St James's Street and a famous shop front in Artillery Lane. Some good examples are preserved in the Victoria and Albert Museum; a fine, rather later, sequence is Woburn Walk in Holborn, off the Euston Road. But the magical survivals are the arcades — Burlington Arcade (1819) between Piccadilly and Burlington Gardens, a famous tourist attraction of fabulously pretty and mostly equally expensive luxury shops; the Royal Opera Arcade (by Nash and Repton, 1816-18) behind New Zealand House by Haymarket, with mini-doors and bow-fronted windows. (The Piccadilly Arcade between Piccadilly and Jermyn Street is a modern but most elegantly successful pastiche of Regency style.) Though there was surely glitter and sparkle in the shopping areas, the great blocks

Apsley House — the Waterloo Gallery. The standing candelabra of Siberian porphyry, given to Wellington by Emperor Nicholas I of Russia.

of housing, especially north of Oxford Street, with the help of a decade or so of London soot, soon reached that stage of dreary monotony that so appalled later visitors like Heine or Taine, particularly on a raining London Sunday. Long canals of streets, all brick. Brick was the great London building material, grey or red (the red more expensive, the 'grey' often tending to yellowish, roofed (from about 1770 on, when the Welsh quarries began to be exploited) by slates, with their grey-green or purplish sheen).

In the last quarter of the 18th century, however, a remarkable change overcame London's expression, its physiognomy, in certain quarters. This came from the introduction of 'Roman cement', or stucco, as popular cladding material for brick houses. This was originally used perhaps almost as *ersatz*, poor man's masonry, and the skin of plaster, painted white or cream, was scored regularly to look like stone-work. Adam had used stucco at times; No. 9 Conduit Street (by Wyatt, 1779) is the earliest surviving stucco façade, and very smart it looks still today (helped by scrupulous maintenance as Dior's London head-quarters); but its use is above all associated with the work of John Nash. Nash — a curious figure, rather like a Roman gnome (see his

Kenwood House, Hampstead Heath.
Built for the Earl of Mansfield,
Lord Chief Justice, from 1767.
The library is one of Adam's most
exquisite creations, with plasterwork
by Joseph Rose and ceiling
decorations painted by Zucchi.

Lancaster House, begun by B. Wyatt 1825, completed by Sir R. Smirke and Sir C. Barry. A focus for Victorian high society.

bust in his church, All Souls, Langham Place) — came late to success, in his fifties, after a somewhat disastrous early career. Veiled with mystery, following marriage to a woman often said to be the mistress of the Prince of Wales (later George IV), he became an intimate of the brilliant circle about the Prince. On the elevation of the Prince to Prince Regent in 1810, the two men became involved in the most ambitious scheme of town-planning in the grand manner that London has ever known. This was aided by an economic upswing towards the close of the Napoleonic wars, and sparked by rivalry with Napoleon's

Paris and specifically by the reversion of the lease of what is now Regent's Park to the Crown.

The Prince Regent was the most artistically sensitive and artistically ambitious English monarch since Charles I; from 1787, he had built an admirable new classical palace for himself, designed by Henry Holland: Carlton House, on the north edge of St James's Park between the Mall and Pall Mall. Now he aimed to develop Regent's Park in a startlingly dramatic way — with a 'National Valhalla' in the middle, rich villas in wooded grounds about a lake, and the whole contained

at the perimeter by lofty terraces. To link the two royal projects, Carlton House and Regent's Park, a triumphal way over a mile long was planned, south to north: Regent Street. Along this route, between 1817 and 1823, grew a processional of shimmering painted stucco houses; yet, though truly processional, it was characteristically English in its rejection of pomp, its picturesque and its pragmatism. No attempt was made to cut through a straight avenue, like, say, the Champs-Elysées; instead, a relatively short avenue (Lower Regent Street), immediately north of Carlton House, came to abrupt closure at Piccadilly Circus; from there, on a slow handsome curve to the west and north (the Quadrant), it came into the straight of Regent Street proper, which drives north, over Oxford Circus, to a second climax marked by the endearingly pretty little church — as though a mini-temple with snuffer as spire — of All Souls, Langham Place (its emphasis now lost in the rotund modern presence of the B.B.C. building behind it). Here it sidestepped to the west again, and thence northwards Nash took in what had previously been the most elegantly grand of London streets, Adam's Portland Place. At the end of this, Nash supplied splendid columned twin crescents, their arms opening out to the grass and trees and flood of sky of Regent's Park beyond.

The Park itself was only partly developed according to the original plan, some seven villas only within, but the terraces that fringe it have become one of the most loved of London urban landscapes. Whether seen half-hidden by the foliage of summer trees, or gleaming pale in a winter sun, Nash's Regent's Park terraces become almost dream-like. They are often justly compared to a stage-set, but — although notoriously jerry-built behind their princely façades and not responding well to close inspection for either architectural precision or quality of detail — they work, creating a floating suspense of illusion. They range round three sides of the park, the most spectacular being Cumberland Terrace with its floating statuary topping the skyline. To the north, the park is closed by the Zoo, established in 1827; and even if the cultural seeker turn up his nose (possibly literally, as the odour of lions is not acceptable to all), the Zoo is agreeably picturesque, with some remarkable architectural fancies, ranging from Decimus Burton's original Lion-House to Tecton's inspiredly spare penguin parade pool (one of the few pieces of first-class architectural engineering produced in London between the wars) to Lord Snowdon's recent open tenting of wire netting for an aviary. But the terraces are the enduring testimony of Nash to posterity: a classical dream to bewitch the Mediterranean yearnings of Londoners under their grey northern skies. Other isolated original elements of the scheme can be found — Adam's Portland Place, interrupted by later insertions, the church of All Souls, and, at the southern end of the route, on Haymarket, the Haymarket Theatre with its columned portico closing the admirable vista from St James's Square to the east, and the present American Express building alongside, behind which the *cul-de-sac* of Suffolk Street preserves, in spite of some bomb destruction, an impression of the serene dignity of Nash's intentions. The rest London has typically destroyed in its voracious, ruthless onward march, and replaced by modern commercial architecture; and stylistic coherence has evaporated. One of the *raisons d'être* of the whole project vanished with

◁

Burlington Arcade, Piccadilly. The first shopping arcade, built 1819, by Samuel Ware: a centre of tourist attraction.

All Souls, Langham Place, by Nash, 1822-24. Broadcasting House beyond.

unexpected suddenness; Carlton House itself, almost before the scheme was complete, was demolished in 1826 as a result of a financial crisis arising from Nash's translation of Buckingham House into yet another palace. Thus Regent Street sweeps and winds grandly southwards, to collapse at the end down a flight of steps into St James's Park. Yet the steps are grand in their way, and they are not only marked by the great column bearing the statue of George IV's brother, the Duke of York (1834), but flanked by two of Nash's most spectacular terraces (Carlton House Terrace), built as though to make good the loss of Carlton House itself.

Nash's genius, in his old age, was inexhaustible, though the full realization of all his plans eluded him, inevitably in view of the over-optimistic ambition behind them. Though Buckingham Palace was to become the main London residence of succeeding monarchs till today (the monarch's presence or absence being signalled by the presence or absence of the Royal Standard floating from the flag pole above it), it has never been considered an architectural success. Nash's elevations on the garden front are in substance the original, but never seen by the public, while the present familiar and somewhat tedious façade at the end of the Mall is an 'improvement', slapped on by Sir Aston Webb

Cumberland Terrace, 1826, most spectacular of Nash's Regent's Park terraces.

in a matter of months after the coronation of George V. Fragments of Nash's work remain, but dispersed. The famous Marble Arch, now translated to the north-east end of Hyde Park, was part of an intended grand entrance, and the elegant columned screen and arch at the entrance to Hyde Park at its south-east end was meant originally as an element in a grand route from the Palace to the Park. Designed by Decimus Burton (not by Nash) it is now a charming folly, too small in scale for modern traffic.

The Buckingham Palace development was intended to link up west of the Regent Street one, on the hinge of the Mall in St James's Park. Similarly, to the east, Nash devised Trafalgar Square, as the anchor of another projected grand throughway to link St James's and Whitehall with the British Museum and Bloomsbury. The plan is Nash's but none of the buildings are, though characteristically fragments, from incompleted or demolished projects, can be found there — the columns of the National Gallery, salvaged from Carlton House; the equestrian statue of George IV (by Sir Francis Chantrey) intended for the top of the Marble Arch.

Trafalgar Square is much altered — the National Gallery (see p. 192), on the north, and the old College of Physicians building (by Sir Robert

Smirke, 1824-27), on the west, indicate the kind of colonnaded grandeur that was envisaged, while St Martin-in-the-Fields, which Nash's plan released from concealment in a clutter of old housing, forms with its handsome spire the focus of one of the best vistas in London, to the east from Pall Mall West. An older survivor is at the bottom of the Square (in the roadway, as if advancing on Whitehall where he met his death): the equestrian Charles I, modelled by Hubert Le Sueur in 1633. The centre point of the Square is of course the famous Nelson Column, which supports a statue of Nelson, itself some 17 feet high, 145 feet in the air. The statue is by Edward Baily, and round the base are the famous lions modelled by Sir Edwin Landseer between 1858 and 1867: the unusually spirited bronze reliefs on the base are also worth looking at.

The Square proved on the whole a success, not only as the junction of a number of famous roads — Fleet Street, Whitehall, Pall Mall, Charing Cross Road — but as a national forum for mass meetings. Before it, the junction had been marked only by a slight widening in the road, known as Charing Cross (the Cross, a 19th-century version of one of the crosses erected to mark the resting places of Queen Eleanor during her long funeral procession from Lincolnshire to Westminster Abbey in 1290, stands 100 yards to the east, rather forlorn in the courtyard of Charing Cross Station). It was at Charing Cross that, earlier, Dr Johnson had sensed the full tide of life — there, apparently, rather than in the City, or the coffee-houses round Covent Garden or near his own habitation off Fleet Street (p. 231). Intellectual and fashionable life moved indeed inexorably westward.

The quick stir of that life is still evoked vividly through the witness left by the artists and writers of the 18th century. After Charles II's

Carlton House Terrace, 1827-32. Built by Nash to replace the Prince Regent's demolished former palace, and to flank St James's Park and the approach from the east to the new residence, Buckingham Palace.

death in 1685, the court lost its sparkle and, under the Georges, grew dull. There developed a bourgeois literature, impatient not only of royal patronage but of all aristocratic patronage, and delighted to take as its subject matter the fascinating social comedy of London: Steele and Addison in the *Spectator*; the great early novelists, Fielding — also closely concerned, in his role as magistrate, with the realities of public behaviour — and Samuel Richardson. Fielding lived in Bow Street; Richardson lived a little to the south and east, over the other side of Fleet Street, in Salisbury Court. Then Boswell, laying his life bare in frankest detail in his only recently-published *Diary*; and through Boswell, the archetype of the English man-of-letters, of the humour, asperity and high pragmatism of London intellectual society: Dr Samuel Johnson, a clubbable man. Visually, the social scene was recorded as never before or since with the vivid loving indignation of Hogarth; and the master-portraitists, Reynolds and Gainsborough, Romney and Sir Thomas Lawrence, flourished. Canaletto, arriving from Venice, saw London sharp and clear, jewelled with light (see p. 98). Male society, from informal and ephemeral sites of the taverns and coffee-houses, developed into one of the most famous and enduring London institutions: the clubs. In St James's Street, as prime examples of the surviving clubs of the 18th century: Boodle's (No. 28, built in 1775 by John Crunden); White's, a famous Tory stronghold (No. 37); Brooks's, a very elegant and well-preserved example of Henry Holland's classic style and with a fine Nollekens bust of its patron saint, the great Whig statesman, Charles J. Fox (No. 60). These were designed basically in terms of fairly grand private town houses; a grander, more institutional form came into fashion in the great club boom that followed the end of the Napoleonic wars in 1815: the United Service

The Athenaeum Club, Waterloo Place, by Decimus Burton. Founded 1824; refuge of bishops, civil servants and others of the 'Establishment'.

Club, in Waterloo Place on Pall Mall, part of the Nash rehandling of the bottom of Regent Street when Carlton House was demolished, though somewhat altered from its original appearance; the Athenaeum, opposite it, on Pall Mall, by Decimus Burton, very Grecian with an Athenian frieze — the haunt of bishops, top civil servants, of the 'Establishment'; and next to it, along Pall Mall, two famous works by Sir Charles Barry, the Travellers and the Reform Clubs, moving out of the antique manner into the Renaissance, both brilliantly successful transpositions of Italian palazzos into harmony with a London street-front.

For more popular relaxation, there were the famous pleasure-gardens: Vauxhall, south of the river; Ranelagh, west towards Chelsea. Both utterly vanished, though Roubiliac's marble statue of Handel, once at Vauxhall, now presides, plucking a mute lute string, over the Costume Court at the Victoria and Albert Museum. Religion was less success-fully served in the later 18th century; new churches were relatively few, and tended to be rather chill and heartless, showplaces for the congregation, perhaps, rather than for God or the divine liturgy. Exceptions are the light, elegant, almost witty, All Hallows, London Wall, well restored after the Blitz, by George Dance the Younger (1765-67); and perhaps St Pancras Church, Euston Road (by W. and H. W. Inwood, 1819-22). But a charitable concern for physical health was manifested in the building or rebuilding of some splendid hospitals: St Bartholomew's at Smithfield's, with its superb hall and staircase (with a rather strange painting by Hogarth); Guy's at Southwark; the now-demolished Foundling Hospital. There was also great concern for the correction of faults of society, and this produced one of the most spectacular monuments of 18th-century London, Dance the Younger's great fortress of Newgate Prison, with Piranesi-like magnificence. It was burned out in the greatest London disturbance of the 18th century — the Gordon Riot of 1780 — but, rebuilt, survived till 1902; the present Old Bailey (Central Criminal Court), that floridly handsome scene for major criminal trials, stands on its site and incorporates some of its stone under the towering gilt figure of Justice that is a landmark of Ludgate Hill; the road opposite is widened because the public scaffold, on which hundreds died, was there, and there had to be room for spectators.

But Newgate is typical of the City's endless rehandling of its institutional buildings. Many were built in the 18th century but almost all have gone, the major exception being, as noted, the Mansion House. Thus it is that the work of one of the greatest of English architects, Sir John Soane, is hardly represented any more in the City. Though there he built his masterpiece, the Bank of England (finished 1808). To get a glimpse of this strange and original genius, one must visit his old house in Lincoln's Inn Fields (p. 201), or go south to Dulwich Picture Gallery (p. 192). The present Bank retains only part of Soane's austere girding wall; within, it has pushed monstrous columns skyward (by Sir Herbert Baker, 1921-37), an overpowering specimen of the City's manic urge to express itself ever bigger, and to exploit more fully the confined sites of very valuable land.

Victorian London

For a student of London who considers the history of the metropolis from a detached viewpoint, the metamorphosis of the first half of the 19th century is so vast and dramatic as to be almost incomprehensible. The greatest writer of fiction of the Regency, around 1800, was Jane Austen; by 1850, it was Charles Dickens. Their subject-matter seems to be drawn from essentially different worlds, as do their styles. The spare, elegant and ironic prose of Jane Austen is comparable in its rhythm to that of the terraced streets and squares of the development of west London; in Dickens, the shape of the city dissolves in the eddying London fog, in which teeming human life finds temporary lodgings in structures already corroded with decay. Slums and docks; the tears as copious as the laughter; the emergence of the urban *petit bourgeoisie*, and of the poor.

The teeming life that Dickens reflected so vividly was no fiction. Between 1801 and 1840 the population exploded from under a million to almost two million; by 1900 it was somewhere between four and a half and six million, depending on where one estimated London's boundaries to lie. From the City and Westminster, the tides of people welled out, submerging the surrounding countryside, annexing villages, towns even, in the inexorable growth of what Cobbett years before had accurately diagnosed as the 'Great Wen'.

The huge inflation was the result of that extraordinary shift in tempo of manufacture and commerce generally known as the 'Industrial Revolution' — the acceleration of technological innovation that transformed England from an agrarian country to an industrial and urban one; steam and steel, gas and electricity, the invasion of the machine. The geographical spread of London would have broken down without improved means of transport, to get men to their work: this was provided first, in the 1840s and 1850s, by the horse-drawn omnibus, and, from the 1860s, by the invasion of the railways almost into the heart of London, and by a complex web of suburban lines, supplemented from 1863 (when the first section of the Underground opened) by the subterranean lines. The growth was far from steady or consolidated. Parallel with the population of outlying suburbs came the depopulation of the City, whose residents dropped from 128,000 in 1801 to 27,000 in 1901 (and by 1950 formed a mere caretaker body of 5,000); it became almost purely an arena for work, with tens of thousands of commuters flooding in and out at morning and evening. But in the 19th century, not all could afford high transport fares, and so in the inner suburbs, indeed as close in as St Giles-in-the-Fields, the slums festered; the weaving industries at Spitalfields in the East End decayed as Lancashire took the lead, and the resultant close-packed misery of poverty was appallingly vulnerable to disease. Already by 1830, while the mortality rate for well-to-do infants was one in ten, for the children of the poor it was one in four.

Disraeli, in a famous phrase, had spoken of the 'Two Nations' — the rich and the poor. The rich, however, were not all complacent, and the Victorian conscience fought through the century a devoted battle for reform, voiced by Dickens, Ruskin and Morris, illustrated factually by classics such as Mayhew's *London Labour and the London Poor*, and implemented materially by vast planning operations that changed part of the face of London. Such were the cutting-through of major traffic arteries in the West End — Victoria Street, Charing Cross Road, Shaftesbury Avenue — part of a big slum-clearance operation from the 1850s onwards, and more importantly, the embankment of the Thames from Westminster to Blackfriars, and then west as far as Chelsea, which was tied in with a massive rationalization of London's whole sewage system. These were made possible by the belated creation of a responsible administrative body for London outside the City in 1856: the Metropolitan Board of Works, which in 1888, when London was defined as a County on its own, became the London County Council (now the Greater London Council).

The visible heritage, in brick and stone, in iron and glass, that the Victorians left to posterity is often thought to be in a Gothic idiom. The transition was relatively gradual. The last of the major developments of great central estates, that of the Grosvenor family, was built between 1820 and 1845. It continues and amplifies the theme of Nash, within the Georgian tradition, gleaming with stucco — the area west of Buckingham Palace, known as Belgravia, and initially supplying the great servants of the royal court, now newly centred on Buckingham Palace, with convenient residences. Much of Belgravia remains externally as it was, very opulent seeming, with generous width of road, and a bland grandeur of presence; it was well and solidly built, much of it by the great entrepreneur, Thomas Cubitt, who was also involved in Bloomsbury. It has since, especially its greatest square (Belgrave Square), become a home of embassies, one of the few kinds of establishments that can sustain such expensive premises. In some of Belgravia's later parts, such as Lowndes Square (finished 1849), there begins to appear an impatience, which is Victorian, with the inexpressive

▷

Travellers' Club, Pall Mall; library, by Sir Charles Barry, 1832. Founded 1819 for travellers of 'not less than 500 miles' from London.

All Hallows, London Wall. The most elegant, by George Dance the Younger, 1765-67, of the rare churches of the later 18th century.

Georgian symmetry, expressed with almost Jacobean motifs. But more significant for the future of Greater London was another development, this time to the north-west of Regent's Park, the Eyre Estate at St John's Wood, where the delightful villas began to express themselves, though in the Georgian mode, in semi-detached units among their gardens — forerunners of tens of thousands of 'semis' in the outer suburbs. Also, east of Regent's Park itself, a late essay by Nash himself, about 1824, in a Picturesque that was to have a huge following — Park Villages East and West, a series of villas, some almost doll's-house scale, dispersed among gardens and in fanciful styles — Gothic, Italian, even near-chalet.

In fact, variety of idiom rather than Gothic is dominant through Victoria's reign. A great deal of institutional building was carried out in Classical or Renaissance style, and it is to this that the architectural coherence, such as it is, of Whitehall is due. Indeed, there was a famous battle of the styles over Sir George Gilbert Scott's Foreign Office (1868-73), designed by Scott originally as a Gothic building; over-ruled by Palmerston, the Prime Minister, he was forced back to the Italianate, a florid building with arched and very copious figurative decoration. Elsewhere the classical columned portico continued in great demand — for the rebuilding of the British Museum (p. 199), for the new National Gallery (p. 192), as for the third rebuilding of the

154

Sir John Soane's Museum, Lincoln's Inn Fields. Built by Soane, from 1812, for himself, and bequeathed to the nation.

Royal Exchange in the City, in 1841-43 by Sir William Tite, after it was burned out yet again. Nevertheless, an official seal of approval to the Gothic was given by the competition for a replacement of the Parliament buildings, also burned out (16 October 1834) in a grandiose conflagration at night which moved Turner to some of his most spectacular studies. The competition was won by Charles Barry (till then known for his exercises in classical or Italianate manner); he took on as collaborator A.W.N. Pugin, the most passionate apologist of the Gothic revival in England. Between 1835 and 1860 that majestic fretted silhouette of the present Houses of Parliament emerged against the skyline of Westminster, a masterpiece born of the tensions between two minds of genius, or at least near-genius, who were of almost diametrically opposed convictions yet who managed to collaborate until Pugin died insane. Barry was the planner, the brilliant resolver of the complex demands of Parliamentary procedure into a superbly logical design, and still an unswerving believer in classical 'regularity and symmetry'. Pugin believed in irregular Picturesque as a tenet

PP. 156/157
St Bartholomew's Hospital, Smithfield, by James Gibbs 1730-59. The staircase, with Hogarth's Pool of Bethesda *and* Good Samaritan.

155

(above) Westminster from the air.

(below) The Houses of Parliament from the river.

of moral faith, and, in a famous remark, once dismissed the whole great building as 'All Grecian, Sir; Tudor details on a classic body'; he was responsible above all for the wealth of invention that enriches the ornament, down to the door-furniture, even to inkstands. The result is a building that is both sensible and highly picturesque (with the two major but very dissimilar verticals of the Victoria Tower at the west end, and of Big Ben — with its world-famous clock, and fantasticated crowning fretted cap with the light that shines when Parliament is in session).

Together with Westminster Hall (p. 30), which survived the fire, alongside and tied in with it, and the great bulk of the Abbey over the road, the Houses of Parliament make a wonderful ensemble. The interior (visitable generally on Saturday afternoon) is relentlessly splendid. The visitor follows the logic of the constitutional chain of command, entering to the west at the Victoria Tower, through the Monarch's robing room, the Royal Gallery, the Princes Chamber to the House of Lords; the Peers' Lobby, the Central Lobby (where the two Houses, Lords and Commons, meet, and off which is St Stephen's Hall,

site where the old Commons met). Thereafter, unfortunately, the quality sinks into commonplace, as the present House of Commons is a starved rebuilding after its destruction in the Blitz of 1940. This progress takes the visitor down the spine of the building, through an astounding richness of polychrome decoration of high craftsmanship, dazzlingly successful within its own terms of reference — except for the many large wall-paintings. The rebuilding was considered a golden opportunity to revive the more or less defunct English school of mural painting, and competitions (1843-47) were held, but the general result confirms in the main that the epic style in English painting really was dead. An exception is Daniel Maclise's work in the Royal Gallery (*The Death of Nelson,* and *The Meeting of Wellington and Blücher*).

The fire at Westminster devoured also the several law courts that had functioned in the area before, and these were, somewhat later, rehoused on a new site in the Strand. The competition for this was won by G.E. Street, and the building went up between 1868 and 1882. This again is Gothic, but a very different Gothic from that at Westminster — an exercise in English 13th-century Gothic rather than the Tudorish effect of the Houses of Parliament. As housing for a function, it has never been loved by its occupants, the lawyers; as street frontage, however, it has magnificence and constantly changing interest, with towers, turrets, and movement of proportions, while the detail is of high craftsmanship — see especially the iron-work. Inside, the Great Hall is astounding, a superb expanse 250 feet long and 82 feet high — worthy of a cathedral, and surely ecclesiastical rather than legal. One can understand the frustration of the lawyers, for all the rest of the interior is dependent, and very awkwardly so, on this Great Hall, though its function is only that of foyer. For the visitor, however, it is a fine visual bonus.

There were other Gothic institutional triumphs, some of them almost as extravagant-seeming in their disdain of mundane function. Such is St Pancras Station: here Sir George Gilbert Scott, thwarted of Gothic in the Foreign Office, let go in an assault against the sky with turrets, a curious if triumphant salute to the revolution of the railways — but this is only the street-front, built (1874) as hotel frontispiece to the real workplace behind it, a great shed of iron and glass (by W. H. Barlow, 1865) over the platforms, purest and grandest of all the London terminals. This engineering looks to the future as the hotel appended to it does not, and the junction, almost crash, where the two meet, uncompromising one with the other, is eloquent of the Victorian difficulty in reconciling the needs of traditional 'fine arts' with those of the new technologies. St Pancras's frontage remains as folly, but a spectacular one and vital as a monument to vitalize that area of London's skyline. But an equally fine monument, almost alongside, demonstrates in turn that a Victorian railway station could have both aesthetic dignity and functional appositeness — King's Cross: twin sheds answered on the façade by two massive brick arches (by Lewis Cubitt, 1851-52).

On a more domestic scale, Gothic caught on briskly, and with the reintroduction of the gable came a fretted skyline to many of the endless streets stretching into suburbia; but the message that emerged from

◁
Houses of Parliament, the throne in the House of Lords, designed about 1846 by Pugin, who was responsible for most of the rich and colourful detail of the interior.

(above) St Pancras Station, by Sir George Gilbert Scott, 1867-74
(right) The Law Courts, Strand, by G. E. Street, 1868-82: the Hall.
(below) 33-35 Eastcheap, by R. L. Roumieu, 1877 - Gothic abandon.

St Luke's, King's Road, Chelsea, by J. Savage, 1824.

slightly Gothicized streets for the poorer classes is that debased Gothic
built to minimal budgets is as debased as the Georgian mode in comparable circumstances. On the other hand, when built with care and
money, the movement produced splendid eccentricities of which a
number still survive, like the celebrated Nos 33-35 Eastcheap in the
City (by Roumieu, 1877).

But Gothic served most naturally for ecclesiastical purposes: the
revival of the 'national' style for the national religion, even if the
national religion had only begun, in the first place, with the Reformation of the 1530s, after the last great churches in the original Gothic,
built to serve the Catholic faith, had been completed. The 19th-cen-
tury Gothic churches of London are a specialist's subject, but they are
widely scattered (none in the City) to serve the expanding suburbs,
and here one can only indicate a few landmarks. One of the earliest
is St Luke's, Sydney Street, Chelsea (by J. Savage), 1820-24, a somewhat
dry, almost pedantic exercise in Gothic Perpendicular structure, as if
built from a rediscovered 15th-century blueprint. (Dickens was married
there, when it was still new, in 1836.)

The church architect who really transposed the Gothic theme into a key
at once entirely Victorian and entirely personal was the formidable
William Butterfield, using modern materials — marble, Minton tiles,
glazed brick, terracotta — to create harshly splendid interiors. His
masterpieces, such as All Saints, Margaret Street (1849-59), are Victorian in their relentless, often very hard, ornament but also in their
practical piety — he was a devout Anglican, imbued as was Ruskin
with the passionate belief that architecture was faith in action, a moral
affair even more, perhaps, than an aesthetic one. The results — though
he tends to be saluted by modern onlookers as the master of

St Augustine's, Kilburn, by J. L. Pearson, 1870.

passionate ugliness — exert a strange compelling fascination. Other notable church architects include George E. Street (of the Law Courts), as at St James-the-Less or St Mary Magdalene, Paddington; John L. Pearson (St Augustine's Kilburn, Paddington, 1870 — a somewhat bleak but splendid handling of space, with an unexpected bonus of good early Italian paintings, ascribed to Crivelli, Filippino Lippi and Titian, given by Lord Northcliffe), and many others.

A new element in religious building was provided by the emergence of the Catholics from the centuries of deprivation of the full rights of citizenship. In due course they proclaimed the old faith in two major buildings in Inner London. The first was the Brompton Oratory, South Kensington, and here they reverted confidently to full Italian Baroque (by Herbert Gribble, 1884), nave with side chapels and no aisles, and the proud assertion of a noble dome borne on a drum at the crossing: here too a particular bonus from Italy, the spectacular Baroque marbles of the Apostles by G. Mazzuoli (1680-85), once in Siena Cathedral. Outside, a monument to the great leader of the convert English Catholic movement, Cardinal Newman. Later came the Catholic Cathedral at Westminster, Ashley Place off Victoria Street (by J.F. Bentley, 1895-1903), Byzantine, a long red-brick structure, striped with stone courses, and with a dominant, elegant campanile some 293 feet high. The progress up the 390 feet of the interior to the apse is one of the most splendid offered by any church in London — but the Cathedral is still

PP. 166/167

The Roman Catholic Westminster Cathedral, designed by J. F. Bentley from 1895 in the Byzantine mode of Constantinople. The pulpit, with its lavish marble decoration, is by C. A. Leonori, 1899.

Selfridge's clock, designed by A. D. Millar with Gilbert Bayes, 1931. In bronze, gold, polychrome faience and mosaic: the Queen of Time.

incomplete. Its interior was planned to be clad by polychrome marbles from all over the world, and this work proceeds ruthlessly to the regret of many who prefer the stark majesty of the brick.

From the examples mentioned already, the Victorian delight in variety might seem to be adequately illustrated. But the list is far from complete. There was, for example, a French manner, exploited from the 1860s in the Grosvenor Hotel that flanks Victoria Station or the former, multicellular, Langham Hotel that is now part of the B.B.C. building standing opposite in Portland Place. Through the century, the tendency for larger units in building grew inexorably, as the commercial firms, expanding, needed more and more room, and many of these late 19th-century buildings still provide dominant accents in the London townscape — like Alfred Waterhouse's immense dark brick pile housing the Prudential Assurance Company in Holborn (1879). The manner tended towards a kind of inflated Baroque, often referring back rather coarsely to Wren. Thus Nash's Regent Street all came down by degrees, and was rebuilt from 1900 on; the Quadrant, with the allied Piccadilly Hotel, are emphatic examples of this manner, especially the Hotel (by Norman Shaw, 1905) with a screen of colossal columns borne high in the air — dramatic, still supremely confident architecture hinting not at all at *fin-de-siècle*, and only to hindsight redolent of *fin d'Empire*. It is a kind of rhetoric that works best when most brash, and the first of the enormous Oxford Street stores, Selfridge's (begun 1908; the consultant

The Crystal Palace, by Paxton, 1851, as re-erected at Sydenham before its destruction by fire in 1936.

was Daniel Burnham of Chicago), is a specimen that age has not shrunk, and from the example (and commercial success) of which the vast department stores, catering for shopping crowds in thousands, descend. The style is still all over the City and the West End, in the work of Blomfield, Lutyens, Aston Webb, Herbert Baker and many others. It affected institutional as well as commercial buildings — the War Office in Whitehall; the Port of London Authority building in Tower Hill with Father Thames gesturing eloquently over the river; the Aldwych. Out at Egham, in Surrey, a millionaire built a mansion that has been compared, in size as in style, to the Château de Chambord (Royal Holloway College, now part of the University of London).

Many of these buildings seem planned from outside in, or to be a shell expressive of high art bearing scant relation to the function, and, when using the new materials provided by the new technology, generally hiding them or attempting to work them into shapes of traditional design in stone. Thus the Ritz Hotel, on Piccadilly, has a steel frame but is dressed in pink granite. The more honestly functional structures are rare: mainly the railway stations, or at least the glass, iron-ribbed sheds of the stations, for the frontispieces, as we have noted at St Pancras, are ornamental expressions of high art often latched with little reason and no rhyme on to the sheds. Then there are the markets — the meat market at Smithfield; the charming Leadenhall market that survives magically in the midst of banks and insurance offices in the City; and there are the great greenhouses at Kew and Syon. It is these last, perhaps, that will give a better impression of the great lost prototype of glass-and-iron building than the others, for that was designed by a gardener (also a constructional genius), Sir Joseph Paxton — the celebrated Crystal Palace, now so thoroughly vanished that illustrations of it seem as remote and enchanted as a fairy story castle. It was designed to house the Great Exhibition of 1851; the result was as if one had transposed the idea of a cathedral, with nave, transepts, and chancel, into terms of curved iron ribs and glass. It was magical; it was also a major break-through in technological construction. It had to be built fast, inside a year, and yet it was a third of a mile long; it had to be light, for it had virtually no foundations; and it had to let in light everywhere, for there was no way yet of safely illuminating it with artificial light. For it, Paxton invented a system of prefabrication — it was made in standard component parts in factories, not on the site — that has really only been caught up with in recent years. It worked, the Exhibition was an enormous success, and its task done, the Crystal Palace was transplanted to Sydenham where ultimately it crashed to ruin in a great fire, in 1936, and entered London mythology. From the hard cash profit it made, grew the great complex of museums in South Kensington, discussed in the chapter on London Treasures (pp. 186ff). This tremendous spate of building and rebuilding through Victoria's reign and up to 1914 was part of the expression of enormous wealth. In the 19th century, London was overall the most important manufacturing town in England. Even more was it the centre of distribution, fed from all over the world by a great series of docks, spreading east for miles downriver from London Bridge; and perhaps the most typical of the new London scenery were the docks (for example, Telford's massive buildings at St Katherine's Docks hard by Tower Bridge, now translated, in part, imaginatively into artists' studios); the huge systems of warehouses that still lend a Piranesi-like drama to the south bank of the river in the City, though many are now coming down. And not least, the warehouses in which to stack the poorer members of society; these, grim and inhumane though they now seem, were in their time advanced rehousing for the poor cleared from the slums, and were financed by a long line of benevolent philanthropists from the 1840s on, including the American Peabody (whose effigy can be seen seated near the Stock Exchange) and the English Waterlow (whose effigy, standing in bronze with bronze frockcoat and bronze umbrella, presides over Waterlow Park, Highgate). Examples of these can be found not only in the East End in places like Bethnal Green, but unexpectedly off Charing Cross Road and even in Mayfair (south of the west end of Oxford Street). But they lead in turn to the first municipal attempts at large-scale rehousing, the Millbank Estate (by the Tate Gallery) built by the London County Council between 1897 and 1902 to accommodate 4,500 people, and still, with its trees, its relatively humane and decent design, an acceptable amenity.

Other great steps forward were in communication: not only trains, buses, trams, but the consolidation of the roads, and the introduction of gas-lighting (still surviving in 1970 at least in parts of Westminster, while a strange relic can be found in Carting Lane off the Strand, a specimen of Webb's 'Patent Sewer Lamp' designed to burn off gases

▷

Clink Street, Southwark. Spectacular Victorian warehouse landscape, now fast-disappearing, of the south bank.

*Albert Bridge, Chelsea. Built to Ordish's 'straight chain suspension system',
1873; the prettiest survivor of the Victorian suspension bridges.*

from the sewers, in this case those coming from the Savoy Hotel). With
the sudden sprawl of London over regions south of the river came a
corresponding increase of bridges. Westminster and Blackfriars Bridges
were added to London Bridge in the 18th century; in 1811, a famous
and very beautiful bridge was built at Waterloo (replaced in 1939-45 by
an equally successful, sleek, beauty by Sir Giles Gilbert Scott), and in
1823 the old London Bridge too, that had been for so many centuries
a symbol of London itself, with its picturesque burden of houses (though
these had been cleared before), gave way to a new one. Thereafter the
bridges multiplied down to as far west as Hammersmith — almost all
now replaced, though a very pretty and delicate survivor of the
suspension type, Albert Bridge, remains at Chelsea. But the bridge that

The Pool of London, looking downstream towards Tower Bridge, with Hay's Wharf on the right.

has replaced old London Bridge (the revised version of which was sold, rather over-cannily, to America for almost a million pounds in 1968/69, while its replacement — the third on the site — is due to open in 1971) in the affection of Londoners is Tower Bridge, and it, with its unmistakable silhouette, has too replaced London Bridge as a visual symbol for London the world over. It is a daring amalgam of High Victorian Gothic with high precision engineering, beautifully detailed in both its architectural finish and its mechanics: in appearance it marries with, and marries together, the greatest antiquity in London, the Tower alongside, Telford's dock buildings, the gaunt skyline of the warehouses and the dipping beaks of the cranes. It has, also, the necessary sheer size with which to live up to its importance: it is nearly 163 feet high, with a dizzy pedestrian way across the top (long since out of use owing to fear of suicides) and the main roadway below. The roadway splits open when ships come through, and it is claimed that the machinery that heaves the huge weight into the air has never failed since the bridge was finished in 1894: a thousand tons of bascule is raised in a minute and a half. The design is the work of Sir J. Wolfe Barry and Sir Horace Jones.

By 1914, much of the pattern of London today was established — the depopulating City, in which, though Wren's spires were still visible, the lavish architecture of the banks was already the predominating common factor; the river tamed by the embankments, the artery of Fleet Street given over to the newspaper offices; the shopping centres sited firmly in the west, for mass selling on Oxford Street, for specialized highly individual selling in Mayfair, and Knightsbridge already busy (*art nouveau* is relatively rare in London, but one of the best examples is the Meat Hall in Harrods department store in Knightsbridge, while another variant, celebrating the triumph of the motor-car in coloured tiles, still further west at 81 Fulham Road, is in the fantastic building that the Michelin Tyre Company opened in 1910). St James's was the home of the clubs, the clubmen and the specialist shops that served them; Whitehall was already almost solid with the big ministries of bureaucracy. In affluence, the theatres blossomed in the new Aldwych and along the Strand, near the traditional leader, Drury Lane, and opera at Covent Garden. Drury Lane is the only surviving interior Georgian theatre design in London (by Benjamin Wyatt, 1810), but its exterior impressiveness is due to the rhythm of the colonnade added in 1831 — and it has, ironically, become the traditional home of the spectacular American musicals; the Opera House is a nice pair with the Floral Hall of the Market, and both are by the same architect, E.M. Barry But theatre spread as far as Shaftesbury Avenue, which has come

The Mall, Chiswick; riverside road dating from the 18th century.

to stand for London theatre as Broadway does for New York's, and though much of the lavish Edwardian décor of theatre interiors has gone, there are survivors — an excellent one is the Globe on Shaftesbury Avenue. The music-halls, the great popular participation entertainment of the '90s, have altogether vanished, but some pre-1914 pubs survive — the Salisbury, in St Martin's Lane, with elegant touches of *art nouveau*; the Red Lion, with its glitter of cut-glass screens, in Duke of York Street, St James's. Soho, serving the theatre and music-hall district north of Leicester Square, had been since the late 17th century international in flavour, a babel of many tongues, and still was, full of tailors (serving the high-class trade the other side of Regent Street, in Savile Row), prostitutes, cheap lodgings and restaurants catering for the tastes of all nationalities. The police, founded by Sir Robert Peel in 1829, had settled into their famous home, New Scotland Yard on the Embankment (by Norman Shaw), a bold baronial brick fortress that seems likely to be demolished.

But the most extraordinary phenomenon was invisible from inner London — sheer territorial sprawl. South of the river, fed by the bridges, the inner suburbs expanded south and west. On the river front eastwards into dockland the terrible slums festered through Southwark into Bermondsey, as on the north bank from Stepney through Poplar to Bethnal Green, Shoreditch and beyond. South and west, the once charming villages that had long been gentlemen's country retreats were swallowed up by the advancing tide of brick. North of the river, to the west, Chelsea was only annexed after the creation of Belgravia (which had been insalubrious marsh land, a problem solved by Cubitt filling it up with earth scooped from the excavation of the docks the other side of London), and still retained a village-ish atmosphere, much loved by artists and writers, from Carlyle to Whistler, Rossetti, Wilde. Beyond Chelsea, endless monotonous second-class citizen housing through

Cheyne Walk, Chelsea, where Rossetti, Whistler and George Eliot lived.

Fulham; then the surrounding of the pretty riverside villages at Hammersmith and Chiswick. Kensington was built up in many styles, stucco but also warm red brick — tall, opulent houses often in tree-lined roads that ought, it may seem, to be canals. The area by Holland Park became a favourite residence for the successful High Victorian academicians, with a very special kind of big villa in big garden, such as Lord Leighton's (p. 231). Paddington was endless stucco, with one surviving area of enchantment — grave, pale houses dreaming over the waters of the canal, inset like a quotation into the context of railway tracks and now of tower blocks as slum clearance proceeds, and popularly known, not entirely unjustly, as 'Little Venice'. Highgate and Hampstead, the beloved country retreat of John Constable, who liked to paint swift studies of sky and cloud on Hampstead Heath. Mercifully, the tide did not flatten these villages, and most of them preserve at their heart elements of their old quality — Hampstead the most famously picturesque, with its paths climbing up and down the hill.

London, in its size, had become one of the wonders of the world. For all its extremes, its shifting contrast of extreme wealth, of flaunting imperial power, of raddled slum and teeming misery that bewildered, appalled yet fascinated almost all its visitors, its size nevertheless was overall a reflection of an enormous accumulated national capital, built in a hundred years of peace from major wars as the centre of the greatest trading nation in the world — a peace secured by Trafalgar and Waterloo, by Nelson and Wellington, whose images and names recur again and again in honour through Victorian London. It was a peace that, in spite of the disasters — but remote disasters — of the Crimean War and of the Boer War, Londoners had got so used to that it seemed a condition of life — until 1914. It was, though, also peace which gave opportunity for reflection, not always without smugness, on the country's past, and it was partly in that mood that the splendours of the great national historical and art collections, that were consolidated through the century, took real root and flourished.

Twentieth-Century London

The wounds inflicted on London by the 1914-18 war were on human flesh and blood rather than on the brick and stone of the city, casualties recorded in the endless black columns of the newspapers through four years. Over London itself, the Zeppelins passed, but the damage was relatively slight (Lincoln's Inn was one of the monuments hit). The monuments subsequently raised all seem inadequate to encompass the memory of the millions of dead — the Cenotaph (by Sir Edwin Lutyens) in Whitehall, a simple stele, with flags limp; the immense Artillery Memorial (by C. S. Jagger) at Hyde Park Corner, more potent; but of all these, the simple slab, beneath which rests the Unknown Soldier, at the West Door of Westminster Abbey, is the most moving.

Afterwards, in what now seems the respite of the '20s and '30s, London's face changed little in character. The fundamental revolution in architecture associated with the names of Gropius and Mies van der Rohe, with Frank Lloyd Wright and Le Corbusier, was then very largely ignored, and London continued serenely to rebuild on itself in the vein very much of late Edwardian Imperial Baroque right up to

▷

Big Ben at night. A light kindled at the top of the tower signifies that the House of Commons is in session.

1939; the commercial value of the sites soared ever higher, and so did
the buildings on them. The depopulation of the City proceeded apace,
but so — a new factor — did that of the West End and Mayfair,
where the domestic citizen could rarely afford to live; correspondingly,
the outlying suburbs swelled. Some of this suburban expansion was
controlled: an excellent example, in the Garden City tradition, was
Hampstead Garden Suburb, designed for relatively high income groups,
free-standing villas in generous gardens; another, for lower income
groups, was the enormous development at Dagenham, Essex, to house
some 100,000 people, tediously sound in building yet, after early
teething troubles, a considerable success sociologically. Much more of
the expansion was uncontrolled, speculative building, reaching out
down the by-passes in ribbon development, often in a strange semi-
detached style christened 'by-pass Tudor', with black and white gables.
An attempted halt to this was called by the establishment of the
'Green Belt' in 1938, when a tract of agricultural or generally rural
land, ringing the extremes of London, was established as inviolate —
but the suburbs merely leapfrogged that into the country beyond. The
pattern of suburb established by the early railways was relatively close-
knit, nodules of housing clinging round each station. But the popular
introduction of the automobile made a much wider pattern possible,
and the gaps between the railheads filled up in suburbs of often
widely spaced individual houses, in which a new strain of urban
neurotic loneliness began to breed.
There are scattered examples of 'modern' building from the '20s and
'30s in inner London, but none of international seminal importance.

Royal Albert Hall, Kensington Gore. Built 1867-71, designed by Captain Fowke, with a terracotta frieze of the Triumph of Arts and Letters; seats 8,000. The foot of the Albert Memorial on the left.

Good examples of commercial building are the Peter Jones department store in Sloane Square, Chelsea, and Simpson's clothing shop in Piccadilly. A major symbol, seminal in a different sense, was the building of the federal centre of the University of London, the Senate House (by C. Holden), 1933 just north of the British Museum. This plain building, with its effect of a rather timorous skyscraper, signals the beginning of the takeover of one of London's most famous districts, Bloomsbury, by two institutions, the British Museum and the University. London, very unlike Paris, fostered its own university late; the earliest college in Bloomsbury was University College (in an elegant building by the architect of the National Gallery, William Wilkins, 1827-29) at the north end of Gower Street, but the great expansion did not begin till the 1920s. Now it is one of the greatest universities in the world, and is rapidly taking over the whole of northern Bloomsbury.

In 1940, war at last came home to Londoners for the first time for centuries. 'We would rather see London laid in ruins and ashes than that it should be tamely and abjectly enslaved...' — those words of the greatest Londoner of the 20th century, Sir Winston Churchill, found a solid answer in the citizens of London, but when peace came to a London still unenslaved, in 1945, no small part of it was indeed ruins and ashes. The extent of the catastrophe was unassessable; the opportunity for rebuilding an ideal city was even greater than after the Great Fire of 1666. The City and the East End (close to the target of the docks) had suffered particularly grievously, but bomb-damage was everywhere throughout Greater London. As after 1666, so after 1945

Tower Bridge at night. The
easternmost bridge over the Thames,
finished 1894, and the river gateway
to London. A remarkable
marriage of Gothic detail with
high-precision steel engineering,
its silhouette is known all over
the world as a symbol of London.

PP. 182/183
The view from the air over the
bridge and the beginnings of the
great 19th-century dock system
that extends mile upon mile down
the estuary, but which is now
falling into disuse in favour
of the new container systems
far to the east.

the attempt at a rational solution has failed, perhaps for the good reason that ideal cities are impracticable in a most unideal world, but also for many of the specific reasons that were operative even in 1666: limitations of money and difficulties over property demarcations, plus hideously more complicated problems of administration and of bureaucracy.

It may be too early to judge, for the process is still in progress; however the quality of the change is assessed, there can be no argument but that London, in the twenty-five years after 1945, changed more swiftly and fundamentally than ever before in her history. From being a horizontal city, she is becoming a vertical one, and everywhere in the centre the skyscraper blocks go up. In the City, this is especially marked, but in the City too a deliberate attempt is being made at repopulation, notably in the vast Barbican development north of St Paul's, where a twin programme of commercial development (along London Wall) and of housing (Barbican) will go through its testing time in the 1970s. Even the old medieval street pattern begins to break down, as elevated pedestrian ways, piazzas at various levels, are built across it. Whether the new pattern will help to breed a successful community remains to be seen: one of the most aesthetically handsome of post-war housing estates, not merely in London but in Europe, that at Roehampton to the west, has yet to prove that good architecture helps to produce good citizens.

Yet, after the shock of the war, after the long post-war period of grey austerity, London has emerged in a new release of vitality. As she ceased to be the hub of an empire, and yielded in world political primacy to Washington and to Moscow, the fundamental political, economic and emotional revaluation that that involved seems to have charged new energies. Like all old cities, London is torn with argument about the problems of the 20th century — of using and not being enslaved by technology, of adapting to the present without losing too much of the past. The preservationists join battle with the developers; frequently, the whole city appears to be on the point of suicide through self-strangulation by the automobile, and the trunk roads, ploughing into the centre of the city, begin to cause almost as much disruption as did the railway stations when building in the 19th century. The fog that Dickens knew, that T.S. Eliot still knew, yellow, dense, clinging, has evaporated; in its place there is a less palpable smog, perhaps more lethal. After creating an underground railway system that was the wonder of the world, Londoners can find it paralyzed because twelve men have gone on strike. But these problems are common to all modern urban civilization; in London they are offset not only by the traditional amenities peculiar to her — the great sequence of parks no less than the strange ways of democracy in debate in the House of Commons — but by new ones that promise well. If the docks withdraw from central London in the 1970s, the Thames may come back into its own as playground; already much of the big cultural centre on the South Bank, bringing together music in the Royal Festival Hall, the Queen Elizabeth Hall and the Purcell Room; painting and sculpture in the Arts Council Gallery in the Hayward Gallery with its great loan exhibitions; cinema in the National Film Theatre — is completed and in action and the chances seem brighter than they have ever been that the National

London Wall, the southern commercial sector of the Barbican, keying the new skyline of the City of the 1970s.

South Bank — Festival Hall, Queen Elizabeth Hall, Purcell Room, Hayward Gallery — with the City seen beyond Waterloo Bridge.

Theatre will actually be built on the same site. In fact, London is in a state of transition — though this particular state be more violently fundamental than ever before, this may well prove a sign of health, for the alternative to being in a state of transition, for a living organism, is death, and in that condition London is still even less interested than Queen Victoria was in defeat.

London Treasures - Museums and Galleries

Though the decoration that enlivened the interiors of London's dwellings is even more subject to change and decay than the fabric itself, nevertheless the collections — scientific, learned and artistic — that London can now show to the world are not to be surpassed in their overall variety, richness and quality by those of any other city in the world. The beginnings, as noted in Chapter I, were not promising: the artefacts of Roman civilization, whether made here or imported, were ground into dust or at best fragments in the remorseless movement of time — and were anyway of provincial rather than metropolitan

quality. The fragments, surfacing in the ceaseless churning of London's subsurface as it builds and rebuilds itself, are collected together in the British Museum, the London Museum, the Guildhall Museum, and are sources of fascinating interest for the antiquarian, the archaeologist, the historian, but generally less so for their aesthetic quality. This holds even more for the newer fragments of the Saxons and the Danes. In the Middle Ages, a great wealth of beautiful objects must have accumulated, above all in the churches and the monastic foundations. Then the quality of English workmanship was often very high, sometimes outstanding in European terms, as, for instance, the illuminators of the twelfth century, or the embroiderers of *opus anglicanum* which was famous through Christendom till the close of the Middle Ages. Throughout Britain, this rich heritage was deliberately destroyed in the two ruthless iconoclastic movements in religion, in the Reformation of the mid-16th century, and the Revolution of the Puritans a century later. Thus in 1644 a mason called Wilson was paid £7 16s. 0d for taking down the altar in Henry VII's chapel at Westminster; that altar was a masterpiece of High Renaissance sculpture by Torrigiani. Thousands of records of such payments for destruction survive, as the objects themselves do not. In the City of London specifically, the destruction of the Middle Ages' heritage was completed conclusively by the Great Fire of 1666.

To find unmutilated medieval sculpture, therefore, you have to soar through binoculars into the heights where the iconoclasts could not reach — thus you can still find rewards, such as the radiant Chartres-like angels in the spandrels of the transepts at Westminster Abbey. But there is one type of exception. Tombs, or at least tomb-effigies, generally were spared by the iconoclasts; though angels and attendant saints were chopped brutally from their settings, the figures of the great English dead were often left intact. They were not 'images of superstition', but witnesses to values of lineage and blood that remained valid. Thus in areas spared by the fire, there survive some medieval tombs of very distinguished quality, most notably of course the royal ones that circle the shrine of Edward the Confessor in Westminster Abbey (p. 39), but also elsewhere, in Great St Helen's, for example, and in Southwark Cathedral. English medieval painting has almost vanished (survivals can be seen in Westminster Abbey); though the work of the illuminators, more portable and easier to conceal, can be seen above all in the British Museum, and the famous work of the 15th-century alabaster carvers (some of which was saved by surreptitious export to the Continent) in the Victoria and Albert Museum, where the splendour of *opus anglicanum,* faded yet still of great magnificence, is also displayed.

Works of art generally survive best, of course, when associated with an institution whose function endures, rather than with the fickle fortunes of an individual owner and his descendants; but the wealth of early treasures in the City institutions, the Guilds, was largely destroyed again by the Great Fire of 1666. The one 'private' institution that survived was the monarchy, and indeed the **Royal Collection** stands today as perhaps the richest private collection in the world. In Henry VIII's time it was more an accumulation of exotic, valuable, even barbaric, treasures to jewel, as it were, the concept of kingship, rather than a collection informed by any guiding taste. But Charles I was one of the first true connoisseurs of art in England, and he bought, through his agents abroad, with intelligent and sensitive acumen, his major coup being the purchase en bloc of the great collection of the Duke of Mantua. He adored Titian; he imported the best living artists he could find, most notably Van Dyck, and even though, after his execution in 1649, much of his collection was sold off (and many of the stars of his collection are now to be found in the Prado and the Louvre), a considerable proportion was recovered. Though the Royal Collection also underwent a great fire, when Whitehall Palace burnt in 1698, its holdings are still staggering. They are now dispersed through the various palaces, and on Charles I's foundation his successors have built, often haphazardly, but sometimes with informed delight (George III's Venetian pictures, especially Canalettos, George IV's Dutch pictures, and the 'primitives' acquired precociously by the Prince Consort). The main parts of the collection generally open to the public are, most importantly, at Hampton Court and the staterooms at Kensington Palace: Windsor, with its matchless Van Dycks, and Canalettos, the miniatures, and the major wealth of Old Master drawings (most notably perhaps the great Leonardo series and the Holbeins) and the Royal Library itself, is somewhat less accessible. Buckingham Palace is never open at all, unless you can get invited, but the enlightened establishment of a public picture gallery there in 1962 has made the riches of the Royal Collection far better known; in it are shown temporary exhibitions drawn from the collections in all the Royal palaces, not only those in the London area.

London has not been lacking in other private collections of great quality and there are still some remarkable ones, though almost all are open only by personal introductions. On the whole, however, London, with the tremendous pressure on its space, has extruded the private mansion which is the natural habitat of such collections, and the great families that still retain their handed-down possessions keep them almost all in their country-houses. It was these collections, including the Royal one, which, being open not only to connoisseurs of high social rank, but also often to artists, helped establish a standard

The National Gallery from Trafalgar Square with one of Landseer's lions at the foot of Nelson's Column.

of taste, which was fostered further, from the 17th century on, by the inveterate habit of the English aristocracy in making the Grand Tour — an excursion on the continent of Europe that could be spun out for years. Thus, in the 18th century particularly, wealthy English collectors refined their knowledge through the collections, public and private, of Europe, and bought vigorously to bring their own collections up to a comparable standard. Relatively few of these remain, and they are rusticated to the country; yet the effect was to build up an incomparable reservoir of pictures of high quality which has since nourished not only the great public collections of Britain but those of other countries, especially the United States.

By the mid-18th century an active and informed interest in the visual arts·was very much part of a London gentleman's normal equipment. Pictures could be seen in artists' studios, aristocrats' houses, and in the art sale rooms, well established in London long before the famous Christie's opened their (still open) doors in 1766. More formally organized exhibitions did not come till later. One of the earliest was associated with a charity, the **Foundling Hospital**: both Hogarth and Handel were closely linked with this, and though the Hospital itself is now demolished, the old Court Room has been reconstructed in its modern offices (off Brunswick Square), and there is a small collection, including not only some masterpieces but also engaging trivia, such as Hogarth's punchbowl of Lambeth Delft. It has a unique and charming atmosphere, and in it can be seen Hogarth's greatest formal portrait, of the Hospital's founder, Captain Coram (and a brilliant humane transposition of the court style of Van Dyck into rubicund bourgeois mode); also his large *March of the Guards to Finchley,* showing Tottenham Court Road as it was and is not at all any longer; and other fine paintings mostly presented by the artists, including one of the most enchanting of early Gainsboroughs, a little roundel view of the entrance to the Charterhouse; some interesting sculpture includes work by Roubiliac (bust of Handel) and Rysbrack. In the 1740s, the Foundling Hospital became as a result a great attraction, 'general resort, and rendezvous, for people of all classes'; this indicated how popular exhibitions might be. Following it, various groups of artists organized exhibitions, but these were accompanied by much professional quarrelling, and the long-felt need for a properly established national Academy was met only in 1768, when the **Royal Academy** received its royal charter, and was set up to answer various functions — to establish the artistic profession, to maintain a school for teaching, and to offer artists an annual exhibition which was also a market. These functions the Academy still fulfils. Though in the 19th century its exhibitions became notoriously reactionary, so that many of the more enterprising original artists abstained from them, and relied rather on dealers' exhibitions, the annual exhibition is now much more catholic in selection, and has always remained a great event of the London social season. The Academy has also its own permanent collection. Its first President, Sir Joshua Reynolds, in his opening Discourse to the students, indicated that it was to be 'a repository for the great examples of Art'. So a collection has grown up: part came with the original house (including four large mural paintings commissioned about 1715 from the Venetian Sebastiano Ricci by the 3rd Earl of Burlington, and a sort of apotheosis of Inigo Jones painted by William Kent), but most from two kinds of gifts — one, the depositing of an example of his own work by every Academician, known as his Diploma Work, and two, by benefactors. Thus from Sir George Beaumont came the greatest treasure,

Bronzino's Venus, Cupid, Folly and Time *(National Gallery). Coolly erotic Florentine 16th-century mannerist art at its most polished.*

the early Michelangelo marble *tondo* of the *Madonna and Child with the Infant St John c.* 1505 (the Leonardo cartoon having gone to the National Gallery). But other works range from a rare set of drawings by Stubbs to excellent paintings by Reynolds, Gainsborough, Turner and Constable's great *Leaping Horse.*

A general public awareness of the arts and of learning helped precipitate the foundation of the first major public collection, the **British Museum,** created by Act of Parliament in 1753. The nucleus of the British Museum's fabulous riches was provided by a wealthy Chelsea physician and virtuoso, Hans Sloane, who accumulated '5,497 mineral specimens, 804 corals, 8,426 vegetable specimens, 3,824 insects, 3,753 shells, 568 birds, 54 mathematical instruments, 20,288 coins and medals, 2,666 manuscripts and other objects amounting in all to 53,000 items'. On his death this was offered ('to the manifestation of the Glory of God, the Confutation of Atheism and its consequences, the Uses and Improvement of the Arts and Sciences and benefit of Mankind') to the nation at a nominal price of £20,000. After some hesitation, Parliament decided in favour, and bought as well, for good measure, two great private libraries of books and manuscripts, formed by Robert Harley, Earl of Oxford and Sir Robert Cotton. With these collections, the omniverous nature of the British Museum was set, and also the pattern of purpose of these collections, very much of the Age of Enlightenment — the support of faith by reason and empirical experiment; of learning not only for its own sake but in the cause of the education, both factual and moral, of the public. But the emphasis on the arts was relatively slight. To see collections of old masters, students and connoisseurs were still dependent on the private collections and the auction rooms. Another great doctor collector, Dr Mead, opened his remarkable collection (including perhaps the first Watteaus to come to England) to students, and the Duke of Richmond also encouraged artists to work in the sculpture gallery in his Whitehall mansion. The idea of a National Gallery of art, however, was still fairly remote from reality, though John Wilkes promoted it strenuously in a Parliamentary debate in 1777 when one of the finest English collections, Sir Robert Walpole's, was sold en bloc to Catherine of Russia (now in the Hermitage, Leningrad). It took almost fifty years more, and the threat of losing another great private collection (that of John Julius Angerstein) to the Continent, to crystallize the National Gallery into reality in 1824.

The National Gallery was, however, not the first public picture gallery in London. That honour belonged to the unique institution, **Dulwich College Picture Gallery**, some miles out from the centre of London, south of the river, and still very rural when opened in 1814. It is peculiar in that it is both mausoleum — a shrine for the bodies of its founders — and picture gallery (the two united into fascinating coherence in a remarkable building, blitzed but restored, by Sir John Soane). The pictures came from two sources — early English ones, mainly portraits of historical interest (including a self-portrait of Shakespeare's actor-colleague, Richard Burbage) and an extremely important art collection built up by a French dealer, Desenfans, for the King of Poland in the late 18th century, which came to Dulwich (an important public school) by bequest through Mrs Desenfans and an English painter, Sir Francis Bourgeois. It includes a remarkable Dutch representation — two Rembrandts, Cuyps, Elsheimer, Hobbema, Ruisdael; admirable works by Rubens and Van Dyck; Claude and several superb Poussins; Watteau; Italian paintings from Raphael to Tiepolo and Canaletto.

This was perhaps a magnificent eccentricity, very English even to its French accent. The **National Gallery** was more orthodox, except that, unlike the vast majority of the great national collections of Europe, like the Louvre or the Prado, it did not have the rich foundation of an expropriated royal collection to build on, owing to the conservative British habit of (generally) retaining their monarchs. It has, however, not been inhibited by that lack, and has on the contrary, since its foundation, built itself a collection which has no peer in the world for both concentration and range of high quality. The Angerstein collection, the foundation stone, bought by the nation for £60,000, had thirty-eight pictures only — but five were by Claude (the darling of the English 18th-century aristocrats, who even remodelled their own parks in the likeness of his arcadian vision), and six were Hogarth's great series Marriage-à-la-Mode. Great masterpieces followed: Titian's Bacchus and Ariadne in 1826, then Sir George Beaumont's magnificent gift, including the Rubens Château de Steen and Canaletto's supreme work, The Stonemasons' Yard.

Arnolfini and his wife, *by Jan Van Eyck, 1434 (National Gallery).*
A major masterpiece of early Flemish realism, and one of the most
famous paintings in the world.

Thus far, little or nothing was earlier than the High Renaissance, but
this was rectified by a Director of genius, Sir Charles Eastlake, whose
acquisitions ranged from Van Eyck to Velasquez, from Piero della
Francesca to Veronese. The collection, of course, has gaps, for no
collection is perfect: some older masters, for example Georges de la
Tour, or, to an extent, El Greco, were recognized at their true high
stature too late for the modest budget of the National Gallery to be
able to compete with the bottomless purses of the first generation of
the great American collectors; there are superb late 19th-century
French paintings, but not the wealth that is to be found in the major
museums of the United States. French painting of the 18th century
(though it has Chardin, Watteau, Boucher) the National Gallery is content mainly to leave to its London neighbour, the Wallace Collection.
But overall, the representation of the European schools, from Duccio
(and earlier) to the beginning of the 20th century, is breathtaking.

(above) St George and the Dragon. *An unusual work by a rare master, Uccello (1397-1475).*

Many galleries boast labels with great names; it is the virtue of the National Gallery that the paintings over the labels so often show the great masters' work at its peak of quality, condition and representativeness. Thus the Van Eyck *Arnolfini* double portrait, that haunting, minutely particular description of a marriage pair, ineffably mysterious, ineffably tender, is the quintessence of Van Eyck's art; Titian is shown

Nativity *by Piero della Francesca (active 1439-1492).*
The National Gallery's representation of early Italian painting is probably the best outside Italy.

(above) Titian Noli me tangere. *(right)* Rembrandt A Woman Bathing.
There is a formidable sequence of 16th-century Venetian painting in the
National Gallery, and 23 Rembrandts, ranging through his entire career.

extended through his triumphant range, and the two Vermeers con-
centrate the Dutch painter's ultimate silence like pearls in their shells.
Rembrandt is there in his copious wealth, majestic in his earthy
humanity; there are great pageant pictures by Veronese, as by Van
Dyck and Rubens; Raphael is serenely represented, Leonardo has the
Virgin of the Rocks and the sybilline smiling of the *Virgin and St Anne*
in the cartoon, and the unfinished Michelangelo of the *Entombment* is
an endlessly fascinating tension of subject and form. The Claudes, the
great Poussins: the unique Velasquez nude. The fantastic erotic concoc-
tion, in enamel-like blues and ivories, Bronzino's *Allegory*, to be contrasted with Botticelli's equally but entirely differently magic vision
of *Mars and Venus*. The wealth is all but infinite, and the visitor who
succumbs to it will return again and again and never exhaust it.
British painting is relatively sparsely shown — from not earlier than
Hogarth to not later than Wilkie. The display includes, though, major
masterpieces — Hogarth's *Shrimp Girl*, a fine range of Reynolds, and
Gainsborough from the exquisitely matter-of-fact Arcadian of his early
Suffolk period *Mr and Mrs Andrewes* to the very late sophisticated
floating dream in colour of the *Morning Walk*. There are magnificent

Constables, and some of the most famous Turners. The National's range, in all schools, reaches not much later than the close of the 19th century — 20th century art is the province of the Tate Gallery.

The building, dominating Trafalgar Square with not quite enough authority of presence, is by William Wilkins (1834-37), but the inner rooms are later (some by E. M. Barry). A further extension to the north, accompanied by the completion of air-conditioning throughout the building, is likely to disrupt through the 1970s the old disposition of the paintings.

Wilkins' design, inevitably at that period, evokes an aura of classical shrine or temple of the muses; all over Europe the museums were going up in this mode. The National Gallery (with its pillars re-used, for reasons of economy, from the Prince Regent's Carlton House, then recently demolished) is, however, more elegantly, Corinthianly, relaxed in mood, than the massive sobriety of the majestic colonnaded Ionic structure into which Sir Robert Smirke was remodelling the **British Museum** from 1823 on. From its very beginnings, the British Museum had attracted objects of all kinds like a magnet; that its reconstruction to cope with its swelling contents should be in the shape of a temple

Vermeer, Girl at the Clavichord *(National Gallery).*

had been made ever more inevitable by its acquisition of the most celebrated sequence of classical sculptures in the world: the marbles from the Parthenon, salvaged by Lord Elgin in a long saga that reads like a first-class adventure story. Till then, the British Museum had not been greatly concerned with art as such, but more with the increase of learning, and although the artistic impact of the 4th-century BC masterpieces from the Temple of Athene was undeniable, the Museum remained, until quite recently, relatively indifferent to the aesthetics of display (there is, significantly, no easy equivalent of the French '*mettre en valeur*' in English).

This has changed; though the Elgin marbles are housed in a shrine with uncomfortable overtones of grandiose 1930s cinema-décor, the new arrangement of other Greek and Roman antiquities (including world-famous objects such as the *Mausolos* from Halicarnassus, and the *Demeter* from Cnidos) is breathtakingly successful in its tact and spaciousness. Inevitably, though, much of the British Museum is hidden away, available only to the student: for many, probably most, Departments this cannot be otherwise — Coins and Medals (perhaps the greatest Coin Room in the world); Manuscripts; Prints and Drawings — these, let alone the Library, form archives or reservoirs from which only token showings are possible for the general public. But changing exhibitions continue in the gallery of Prints and Drawings (here also

Oriental art); in the 325 feet-long King's Library (books, including usually a Gutenberg Bible and a Shakespeare First Folio, Oriental books, music, also postage stamps) and the Magna Carta Room (illuminated MSS, including Magna Carta and the famous Lindisfarne Gospels). Other Departments include Egyptian antiquities — an enormous, often colossal, wealth based on Napoleon's collection of antiquities surrendered by the French at Alexandria in 1801, and vastly expanded since by a series of celebrated pioneering British Egyptologists; western Asiatic — Assyrian, from Nimrod, Persian, Syrian, Hittite, Mesopotamian; British and medieval, a great range from the Mildenhall treasure, the Battersea Shield, to a rich collection of ingenious clocks: Oriental — China, Japan, India, art of all kinds. 'Primitive' art — the cultures of Africa, the Americas, Polynesia — was collected very early on by the Museum; its administrators were buying Aztec in 1823, and in 1865 acquired the fundamental collection of the pioneer in this field, Henry Christy. This art, though it has had such seminal and revolutionary influence on western art in the 20th century, is still classified by the British Museum as 'Ethnography', but the cream of it is now displayed (removed from jam-packed cases in the Museum) in an annexe to the Museum in Mayfair (in Burlington Gardens).

Then there is the Library; unique among such major institutions, the Museum still houses in its one institution both the national museum and the national library. The problems of the library (6 million volumes — or 7 or 8 millions? who knows?) are indicated by the fact that its intake demands each year another mile of shelving: apart from other acquisitions, it receives, by law, a free copy of every book published in Britain. Its public focus is the great circular Reading Room (created in 1857 by roofing the inner courtyard with the second largest dome in Europe). The pressures of space have been the subject of acrimonious controversy since 1945, but it now looks as if the area between Smirke's colonnade and Oxford Street will be developed for the Museum through the 1970s, and the Library moved into that. (Then Bloomsbury will be a solid hive of learning, as the University of London takes over more and more of the area north of the Museum). The Museum has already long-since been freed to separate some of its collections; as early as 1881 the Natural History collections, now quite separate, moved to South Kensington (see below), and in 1904 the newspaper section of the Library was established almost out of London, at Colindale.

After the foundation of the National Gallery, there was a momentary pause in the breeding of new museums. But one of the most eccentric and charming of them, the **Soane Museum**, was founded by bequest in 1837, when the great architect, Sir John Soane, left his house in Lincoln's Inn Fields, and its contents, which remain today very much as they were. They include his private gallery, with its world-famous Hogarth series — *The Rake's Progress* and *The Election;* works by Watteau, Canaletto and Turner; a vast collection of drawings — Piranesi, Clerisseau, but especially architectural drawings by Thorpe, Wren, Chambers, Adam, Dance and Soane himself; and a supremely magnificent Renaissance illuminated manuscript by Giulio Clovio. Sculpture (Flaxman especially), casts, models, Soane's personal furniture, the Sarcophagus of the Pharaoh Seti I (about 1370 BC), a Shakespearean shrine, and a mock-Gothic tomb to Mrs Siddons' dog, Fanny. As a whole, in its personal atmosphere, its concentration of the interests of a highly cultured man of about 1820, it is unique, and has its own *frisson* to be found nowhere else.

GIN LANE.

Gin Lane, *engraving by Hogarth (British Museum). Scathing comment on the havoc wreaked by cheap gin in 18th-century London (see p. 135).*

There is, though, opposite the Soane Museum on the other side of Lincoln's Inn Fields, another museum that may shock a delicate sensibility more profoundly than the charming contrivance of Soane — the museum of the **Royal College of Surgeons**. The nucleus of this is the former private collection (blitzed, but now reconstituted) of a great pioneer in the history of surgery, John Hunter (d. 1793). Essentially it is a scientific museum, for some aesthetic palates too packed with pickled extracts from human viscera, but it includes a number of interesting other things, notably brilliant paintings by George Stubbs, commissioned by Hunter as descriptions of certain exotic animals for scientific purposes, but far more than that as executed by Stubbs. Admission is only by previous application to the Secretary of the College, but should the visitor penetrate, he should also look at the extraordinary recently restored, hieratic cartoon, by Holbein, of Henry VIII seated like a royal, rather Oriental juggernaut, among the Barber-Surgeons.

The impetus for the next major national museum was provided by the famous Great Exhibition staged in the even more perennially famous, though long demolished, Crystal Palace, by Sir Joseph Paxton, in Hyde Park in 1851. This enormous demonstration of Victorian confidence in British commerce, art and empire was largely inspired

British Museum. The Portico, built by Sir Robert Smirke, 1842-47, with sculpture in the pediment by Sir Richard Westmacott.

by the Prince Consort, Albert; it produced, among other things, a profit, and out of the profit and Prince Albert's earnest didactic concern for the spiritual and moral edification of the nation at large, plus his equal concern for the raising of standards in especially the applied arts, grew the Victoria and Albert Museum. About this nucleus in South Kensington, where land was available, there subsequently developed perhaps the most remarkable museum complex in the world — Englishly haphazard in comparison with the logic of the old *Museuminsel* in Berlin, but packed with collections of enormous and diverse riches, and mingled with great teaching institutions.

It may be helpful to survey this South Kensington area briefly as a whole. It lies on the slope south of Hyde Park, a big triangle approximately, its base on the Brompton Road and its climactic northern apex actually in Hyde Park: the elaborate, Gothic-canopied mammoth memorial to its prime instigator, Prince Albert, erected by his widow, Queen Victoria, after his death in 1861. The architect was Sir George

PP. 204/205
The Elgin Marbles, 448-432 BC, from the Parthenon. Details.

Mexican head, Xipe Totec. British Museum, Ethnological Collections (Burlington Gardens).

Gilbert Scott, and the overall effect is of a hugely magnified piece of Gothic church furniture, a pinnacled and gabled shrine, ciborium even, in which a seated colossal bronze of Albert presides in pious meditation over the great cultural organization to the south — the book open on his knees, however, is the Catalogue of the Great Exhibition and not the Bible or a catalogue of the Victoria and Albert Museum. The attendant sculpture speaks symbolically of empire, of great men, of the triumphs of art and industry, and is technically of high proficiency; the whole, long held in anathema as the nadir of Victorian taste, is now held in affection, respect and perhaps in envy of the lost national confidence of which it is redolent.

Immediately opposite (on the other side of Kensington Gore) is the great domed oval amphitheatre of the **Royal Albert Hall** (1867-71, by an engineer, Captain Francis Fowke), with a terracotta frieze celebrating the Triumphs of Art and Science. This is one of the major focuses in London for mass celebration and spectacle (it will hold about 8,000 people) for meetings, boxing, demonstrations — but held dearest in London's affection as the home of the Promenade Concerts (founded by Sir Henry Wood) every summer. To the east of the Albert Hall is the **Royal Geographical Society** (founded 1830, building by Norman

▷

Head of a Queen Mother. Nigeria, Benin (Iyoka) bronze, life-size. 16th century (?). British Museum, Ethnological Collections (Burlington Gardens).

Shaw, 1874); this has a major map library, and a good small museum —
relics of great explorers. West of the Albert Hall are the **Royal College
of Organists**, and the **Royal College of Art**; the latter which now has
university status is one of the great forcing-houses of English art since
the war — it has sporadic, lively exhibitions in its Gulbenkian Hall.
Immediately sout of the Albert Hall is the **Royal College of Music**
(founded 1883), the leading English musical seminary; its concerts by
students are well worth watching for, and it has an interesting collection of musical portraits plus a varied and important collection (the
Donaldson Museum) of musical instruments (Handel's spinet, Haydn's
clavichord). South of this again, now almost entirely rebuilt but retaining a dominant Renaissance campanile (by T. E. Collcutt), is the hive
of activity of the Imperial College of Science and Technology (affiliated
to London University) and then, more or less cheek by jowl, the
Geological Museum, the Science Museum, the Natural History Museum,
and the Victoria and Albert Museum.

The **Victoria and Albert Museum** (commonly known as the V & A)
has burgeoned from a foundation originally known as the 'Museum of
Ornamental Art' (1852) and then as the 'South Kensington Museum'.
The present building (by Sir Aston Webb) was opened in 1909, a florid
Edwardian structure with a crowning cupola like a very grand wedding
cake. Its purposes, typically Albertian, were 'the application of fine
arts to objects of utility' and the 'improvement of public taste in
design'. In fact, its art collections, European and Oriental, have grown
to such richness and variety that its task as pure museum — of conserv-
ing, categorizing, describing, and displaying — now seems paramount,
yet it is still loyal to its original didactic purposes, and is a great
teaching institution and instrument of learning, enlivened by the
constant presence of students. Over the years, it has become the home
of several major national collections: of post-classical sculpture (but not
20th-century sculpture, which is in the Tate), of British miniatures,
and of watercolours, and its great library is the National Art Library.
In other categories, it often seems to share territories with the British
Museum, but it is at the V & A that visitors will find best and most
copiously shown early medieval art; Renaissance art (sculpture, bronzes,
ivories and furniture); the ceramics, bronzes and paintings of the
Orient and of Islam; tapestries and carpets; costume (a bewitching
circular arcade, like a shopping centre extending backwards through
time); metalwork; musical instruments (with tapes to play); one of the
greatest collections of ceramics in the world, (the finest of all, indeed,
of English ceramics); a great Prints and Drawings Room. It has
magnificent inconsistencies — it no longer acquires oil-paintings, but
has the seven monumental cartoons (lent by the Crown) commissioned
from Raphael by Pope Leo X for tapestries for the Sistine Chapel, as
well as a curious collection of pictures due to various benefactions.
Thus, to see Constable you go to the V & A for the artist's family
collection; an endless wealth, especially of these sketches and studies,
vivid as the sun flying in the wind, is there. But there also, offering
delightful surprise, are pictures ranging from Crivelli through a Le
Nain, a Boucher of Madame Pompadour, Delacroix, Courbet, Degas
(Ionides collection) to an important 19th-century British collection
(Sheepshanks).

▷

Girl wearing a tunic-like gurment over a chiton.
Etruscan c. *500* BC. *British Museum.*

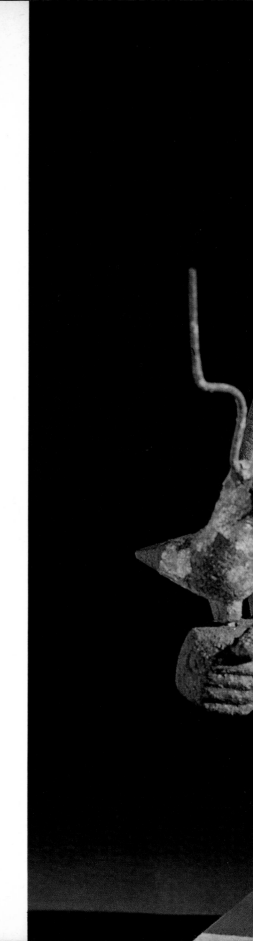

*Bust of a woman holding a
horned bird
Etruscan. c. 600 BC
British Museum.*

Bronze cat with gold earrings.
Egyptian. Late Period 600-300 BC.
British Museum.

The V & A is enormous, comprising well over a hundred galleries, but alleviated by ever-improving display, two restaurants, and a helpful division of the galleries into two kinds. These are, firstly, the Primary Galleries, in which the best from almost all the collections is brought together in harmonious ensemble and sequence, so that you can follow through the development of European art in all media chronologically — and similarly English art. The English sequence, for those fascinated by the changing domestic texture of London, includes some complete period rooms from long-demolished London houses (notably from the Old Palace, Bromley-by-Bow, 1606; Clifford's Inn, c.1686, Henrietta Place, 1722-25; Hatton Garden, 1730; the great music room from Norfolk House, St James's Square 1756; a cosy mid-18th-century room from Great George Street; the glass drawing-room from Northumberland House at Charing Cross (most elegant Adam décor), and a room from David Garrick's house in the

The Portland Vase, British Museum. Roman glass amphora, 1st century AD *(?); the design cut in relief through opaque white casing.*

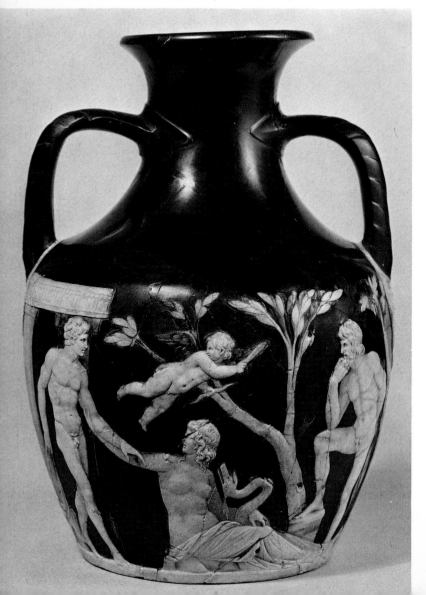

Adelphi. These are all outfitted with furniture, objects and pictures of the period. (Elsewhere in the Museum, of special London interest, is a kind of anthology of architectural details — doors, stairways, windows — preserved also from demolished houses; they include old shop-fronts, and the whole façade, of splendid picturesqueness, of a celebrated late Elizabethan house, Sir Paul Pindar's, from Bishopsgate of about 1600.) The Primary Galleries are the essential route for the visitor with limited time, but for the addict of the 'V & A', and for the student or connoisseur, the secondary, or Departmental Galleries, are inexhaustible. These contain, shown much more densely than in the Primary Galleries, the full range of the holdings of each Department, so that if you want to see, say, English Delft in depth or 'Nottingham' alabasters, or church plate, or domestic silver or jewelry or textiles or whatever, the relevant Departmental Gallery (sometimes slung dizzily high in the roof, it seems) is where to go.

Thomas Baker, by Bernini, c. 1638, the lace probably studio work.
Victoria and Albert Museum.

The collections have indeed progressed far beyond the original concept of 'ornamental art', and, while it is for the lover of 'antiques' an encyclopaedia materialized into tangible objects, for which in the general context of the arts, the epithet 'applied' is sometimes very misleading, it houses many world-famous masterpieces of the human visual imagination: the *opus anglicanum* (the Syon cope, the Butler-Bowden cope — both early 14th century); the four 15th-century French 'Hunting Tapestries' once at Chatsworth; miniatures by Holbein (the *Mrs Pemberton*) or Hilliard (especially the famous *Young Man among Roses,* the visual epitome of Elizabeth melancholic love), I. Oliver and S. Cooper; the Chinese Han jade horse; a brilliant series of Indian miniatures; the 300 drawings by G.B. Tiepolo. But perhaps the most impressive category is the sequence of European sculpture, from Byzantine to Gothic (Riemenschneider, Veit Stoss), and a most remarkable representation of Italian — the prophetic, doom-laden head of *Haggai,* one of the very few works of Giovanni Pisano outside Italy; four exquisitely expressive reliefs by Donatello; work by Antonio Rossellino (including a celebrated startlingly vivid bust of *Antonio Chellini*), by the della Robbias, Desiderio da Settignano; a minute but immensely potent wax figure probably by Michelangelo; bronzes by Riccio and Antico. There is also the big dynamic Giovanni Bologna marble, *Samson and a Philistine,* leading on to the full swirling Baroque of the great Bernini group (the biggest outside Italy), *Neptune and a Triton;* there is a famous Bernini bust, *Mr Baker,* and in similar but much coarser mode — though a triumph of characterization — H. Pellé's *Charles II.* Later sculptors include such as Houdon, Clodion and Canova, and there is a very full representation of sculptors working in Britain, especially Grinling Gibbons and brilliant terracotta studies by Rysbrack and Roubiliac. In addition to all this, you will always find, in the V & A, temporary exhibitions, whether drawn from the Museum's own collections or major loan exhibitions (often organized by the Arts Council).

Ambitiously, perhaps, the institution from which the V & A grew, the South Kensington Museum, attempted for a long time to house both the arts and sciences, but in 1909 the two were separated, and the National Museum of Science moved into its own premises, still neighbourly (over the other side of Exhibition Road) but, more significantly, now almost physically tied in with the great academic scientific establishment to the north, Imperial College. From very humble beginnings (the original science collections were primarily educational, at artisan level, including, for example, displays of apparatus — with price lists — for teachers) the **Science Museum** has become one of the most sophisticated and fascinating museums in the world — and one of the most popular. Its aim is to demonstrate visually the fundamental principles of pure science, the history of scientific thought and its application in applied science, now better known as technology. The demonstration begins (at basement level) imaginatively with a room for children, in which a series of ingenious toys (all workable by the clientele) engage children (and adults) into enquiring as to how and why. This is one of the best places in the world to take children on a wet day, but, while most parents may feel that the fact that the exhibits demonstrate eternal scientific verities is dispensable in favour

◁
Yakshi *from a Jain shrine (India). Red sandstone, 2nd century* AD. *Victoria and Albert Museum.*

of pure pleasure, the fact remains insistently there. For the adult much of the story told is that of the harnessing by man for his own purposes of the natural resources of power; implicit in it is the uncertainty of his grasp of those forces. There is the story of the conquering of land, sea and air; of the investigation of the more intimate parts of the atom — of procedures that lead to man's landing on the moon or more mundanely to the fact that New York is now only some six hours from London, but also to atomic fission and the mushroom cloud over Hiroshima. The display techniques are constantly being improved, and much of the immediate appeal of the museum lies in its rich provision of working models — for adult as for child, to press a button and provoke a spectral happening in swirling mercurial light is pure bonus; even if the adult mind fails to grasp the principle that the happening illustrates, he can pass on with easy mind, knowing it is all educational. South of the Science Museum and west of the Victoria and Albert, there stretches along the Cromwell Road an enormously long, rather ecclesiastically-mooded building, buff terracotta striped horizontally with cool blue-grey, a dour vision of Byzantium (by Alfred Waterhouse, 1873-81). It is not an exterior one would expect for its content, for it is the third of the great national institutions in this area, the **Natural History Museum.** It was, as indicated above, part of the British Museum, but is now entirely separate, though its origins lie in the rich cabinet of specimens collected by the virtual founder of the British Museum, Hans Sloane, supplemented notably by a formidable botanical collection bequeathed by Sir Joseph Banks in 1820. In 1881, when it moved here, it was constituted of five basic departments: Zoology, Entomology, Palaeontology, Mineralogy and Botany. Near its main entrance there brood, in benevolent if austere wisdom, statues of Charles Darwin and of his great apologist, T. H. Huxley; and inevitably the museum, as indeed nature itself, is an illustrated encyclopedia of the principles and processes of natural evolution, supported by (though these are not visible to the ordinary visitor) a formidable range of working research laboratories. The time range in the exhibition galleries seems enormous, from the fossils, from the giant reconstruction of the Dinosaur *Diplodocus,* 150 million years ago, onwards; the variety is no less overwhelming: the variety, in fact, of life in all its forms, from the stuffed elephants and gorillas, to the birds (including their evolution from the reptile, the mechanics of flight, the structure of the egg, the mysteries of migration); from corals to arachnids; fish, plants (including, incidentally, a very practical herbarium of English wild flowers, on folding screens so that you can check your queries). If much of the message seems to be that nature is indeed red in tooth and claw, it is at least safer than the Zoo, for everything is stilled in death for your calmer contemplation; the Museum also offers visual splendours, some of the dioramas, mute conversation pieces — or the huge spectacle of the Whale Gallery with 98 feet of Blue Whale suspended above the visitor.

The last museum in this South Kensington galaxy of great national institutions is the **Geological Museum** (next to the Science Museum in Exhibition Road), subtitled as 'of Practical Geology'. This was opened here only in 1935, but goes back to collections instigated by the Geological Survey about 1837. This, essentially a demonstration in detail of the physical structure of the globe we live on, provides a sobering context, for its neighbouring treasure houses, of the globe's ephemera, with its built-in insistence on the shortness and insecurity of the tenure of man himself, as of all his works. This earth is far too

Sir Paul Pindar's house, formerly in Bishopsgate; c. 1600. V. & A. Museum.

little solid — shrinking on itself, subject to wilful erysipelas by earthquakes as is a teenager's skin by acne, constantly decomposing (note here a demonstration of what London's alleged 'air' does to stone statues exposed to it). But, more immediately helpfully, it illustrates the endlessly fascinating structure of the world, region by region (for those interested in London's fabric, a section on the building stones used in it); as bonus, there is a celebrated series of cases that display a huge selection of the precious stones of the world, their names — lapis lazuli, amethyst, ruby, sapphire — often as lyrical as the glowing hearts of their intense colour.

This whole South Kensington area must be one of the most rewarding concentrations in the world for the visitor of intellectual and artistic curiosity (music is not excluded; apart from the Albert Hall and the Royal College of Music, there are excellent Sunday concerts in the enchanted setting of the Raphael cartoons in the V & A). The urban sector in which it is set is in key with the airy spaciousness of Hyde Park as its open boundary to the north, the great shopping area of Knightsbridge — with not only the magisterial matron of London department stores in its midst (Harrods) but many excellent antique shops and art dealers too — along the road to the east, and its own agreeable local shopping centre around South Kensington Underground station (though the character of this is threatened by a proposed multi-storey hotel development); the station is, incidentally, connected to the four main museums by a long tiled subterranean passage of almost Piranesi proportions. Much of the charm of the area is that it is still very much a residential area, with a population much leavened and quickened by the presence of youth in the often picturesque shape of students.

This necessarily consolidated consideration of this unique complex has, however, diverted me from a chronological account of other museums in London. One of the oldest of the national institutions came in the same fruitful decade, and in much the same mood of confident and optimistic belief in progress, moral, spiritual and material: the **National Portrait Gallery** (to be found just behind the National Gallery, in Charing Cross Road). Founded in 1857 (though now in a handsome Italianate palazzo of 1895), it is in a genre peculiar to the Anglo-Saxon races — a picture gallery not of great portraits, but of portraits of great men. The idea behind it is historical, commemorative and for edification. The visitor who looks there for great art is likely to be baffled, for, though he will find some of the most splendid portraits ever made in Britain, he may feel they are swamped by those of mediocre quality — great men and women unfortunately often fail grievously to choose a good artist to depict them. The gallery has, however, become a uniquely rich repository of the history of British art which, perhaps notoriously, has always concentrated on portraiture. For the art-lover, there are such splendours as the Holbein cartoon; magnificent icon-like Elizabethan portraits; a full representation of the Baroque portraitists (except — so far — Van Dyck himself), Lely, Kneller, and Riley; Hogarth (a famous *Self-portrait,* painting the Comic Muse), Gainsborough, a richly sonorous range of Reynolds, including some of his most formidable representations, the great hulk of *Dr Johnson,* the superb ease of *Warren Hastings,* the embottled visage of *Boswell,* and other major examples of this consummate artist who raised the habit of English face-painting to such a rare pitch of imaginative art. There is Sir Thomas Lawrence, painter of Regency bravura, in strength; the Victorians, especially G.F. Watts (who painted often with the Portrait Gallery specially in mind) and so up to the moderns — Sickert (his *Winston Churchill*), Augustus John. But many minor, less often publicly seen, artists are represented here by work of great charm, such as Cornelius Johnson or Joseph Highmore (his domestic vision of the novelist *Samuel Richardson*). The miniatures are often very fine (the Hilliards, Olivers and Coopers), and drawings and portrait sculpture are much in evidence (the Roubiliac of *Hogarth,* the Nollekens of *Laurence Sterne,* are among the finest busts in London).

But — and sometimes even for those of fastidious eye — it is the concatenation of legendary sitter with perhaps unknown artist, mingling by happy chance into an unforgettable image, that may most haunt the memory — such is the almost miniature portrait of *Sir Thomas Browne and his wife,* redolent of domestic love; or Branwell Brontë's supercharged, rigid, view of his three famous sisters — or even the wishy-washy pudgy view of *Jane Austen* that her sister Cassandra

The 'Chandos' portrait of Shakespeare, National Portrait Gallery.
The only painting of Shakespeare that has substantial claims to be an
authentic likeness from life.

perpetrated: a daub, but the only authenticated likeness to survive. One of the most famous of all is the painting by an unknown artist, the 'Chandos' portrait of Shakespeare, the only painting with any substantial claims to be considered as an authentic one, from the life, of the greatest imaginative genius of western Europe. The purpose of the Gallery was to record the likenesses of the men and women who had created England through the centuries and with them to inspire the onlooker to go forth and emulate their achievement: it was long hung as a traditional picture gallery, and the impact of so many serried faces could only too easily be deadening, but in the last few years the display has been revolutionized, so that it now tells, as it were, a story. Simultaneously the Gallery has become celebrated for a series of brilliantly imaginative thematic temporary exhibitions. It prides itself on being also virtually a research institute, and has a huge archive of photographs.

In context with the Portrait Gallery, another institution, commercial this time, with many parallel interests, may be mentioned. Often dismissed by highbrows as sensationalism for children and tourists, it is not only a considerable historic curiosity, but has its own unique, surrealist scalp-prickling aura — **Madame Tussaud's,** the London home of the waxwork. Certainly it has its sensational side (the famous

Chamber of Horrors and, now, a very sophisticated set-piece of the Battle of Trafalgar complete with thunder of battle and smell of salt sea and cordite), but it is far older than the Portrait Gallery, going back to the wax-modeller, Madame Tussaud herself, who established it in 1802, after her escape from the Revolutionary Terror in France, and some of whose original moulds still exist. (Allied to Madame Tussaud, in unexpected conjunction, is a vast Planetarium, where the mysteries of the celestial heavens — in both hemispheres — reveal themselves, with commentary, several times daily.)

The last major additions to London's galleries in the second half of the 19th century were in a single year, 1897: the Wallace Collection and the Tate Gallery. The Wallace Collection is a virtuoso ensemble of objects of art of all kinds, unified by a wonderful consistency of discrimination of quality and by a French (as it were) *Leitmotiv;* the collection was formed from the late 18th century on by the third and fourth Marquesses of Hertford, and the latter's natural son, Sir Richard Wallace. It was bequeathed *en bloc* to the nation, with its containing house, a large mansion of rather pompous but not disagreeable tedium, on Manchester Square. Thus it retains to some extent something of the feel of an individual collection within a domestic habitation (the parquet floor creaks: a clock may strike), and, being a 'frozen' collection (meaning that it may not be added to), has a reassuring stability in a world in which museums, or large parts of them, tend so much to be invisible because they are so busy being re-arranged, repaired, improved, enlarged. The overall impression is of a lavish luxury of taste, of a polite and elegantly formal vision, a polish — sustained by the 18th- and 19th-century French furniture, all of the highest quality and refinement (and the envy of many Frenchmen), as by the green and yellow enamel fragility of the Sèvres porcelain. the lambent Renaissance bronzes, and especially by the very numerous masterpieces of French 18th-century painting. These include the two vast Boucher decorations (once Madame de Pompadour's) on the stairs, and many other Bouchers (among them a celebrated portrait of the Pompadour), one of the most famous Fragonards (*The Swing*), Greuze in several examples, no less than four Watteaus of supremely fine quality, major stars in a constellation, that elsewhere would itself seem major, of Paters and Lancrets. Much of the sculpture too is French — Coysevox, Houdon. Yet, though some of the English specimens even have a French accent (*Charles I* is by Roubiliac, and Bonington — the English-born painter who worked mainly in France — is copiously represented), France by no means excludes other nationalities. Good early paintings of other schools will surprise and delight (mainly on the ground floor) — a Bronzino of the *Grand Duchess of Tuscany,* a Crivelli, and Memlinc; Canaletto and Guardi; Cima da Conegliano, Andrea del Sarto, Foppa and Luini; there are fine Renaissance *objets de luxe* apart from bronzes — waxes, majolica, terracottas, and, rather unexpected, a vigorous armoury (incidentally the most important collection in England, apart from that in the Tower). The Dutch cabinet pictures also include masterpieces (on the first floor) — Steens, Terborch; Hobbema, Cuyp and J. van Ruisdael, with a singularly still and bewitching Pieter de Hooch. There are five Murillos and there is a rather sweet strain of female portraits by the great English 18th-century masters (with a predilection for portraits of royal mistresses), but these include one of the most subtly, shadowily magisterial studies of women that Reynolds ever painted — his *Nelly O'Brien.* But none of these — except the Watteaus — is really quite of the order of the truly universal masterpieces which would qualify the Wallace Collection as the national gallery in not a few other capitals of the world — the great late Titian *poesia, Perseus and Andromeda,* painted for Philip II of Spain; the Velasquez *Lady with a Fan;* two wonderful Rembrandts, *The Centurion Cornelius,* and the artist's son, *Titus;* a great sweep of Rubens in his *Rainbow Landscape* (and other Rubens too). Further you will find stately Van Dycks, Poussin, Claude, and (the best-known picture of all) Frans Hals's *Laughing Cavalier,* in which virtuosity of execution is so brilliant that at first it dazzles the fact (to this writer's mind, at least) that the sitter is of remarkable unpleasantness. Leave him, and contemplate instead Gainsborough's aerial, tenderly delicate vision, insubstantial and magical as a dream, of *Mrs Robinson.*

The Tate Gallery (its foundations due to one collector and benefactor, Sir Henry Tate) began primarily as a national home for British art; it has grown, however, into a triple function — it holds the national collection indeed of British painting, but also that of 20th-century modern painting of all schools, together with that of modern (19th- and 20th-century) sculpture of all schools. This has tended to strain (to

The Tate Gallery portico, Millbank, with the new Vickers skyscraper seen beyond.

put it mildly) the resources of its building and also to inhibit a logical sequence of display. The building was once the butt of ridicule — Edwardian rather than Victorian: a somewhat clumsily realized accumulation, with grandiloquent pillared portico and steps, of Renaissance motifs — but has now flowered (like other objects of the same period) into positive public affection against the bare monotony of its surrounding post-war buildings. (It was designed by S.J.R. Smith, opened in 1897 — built on the site of a celebrated prison.) In the 1960s public opinion successfully opposed the loss of its portico, and further land at the east, across the road, has been promised for an extension instead, to be built some time in the '70s when the Military Hospital now on the site has ceded to it. At present it shows its collections in two distinct main sequences of galleries: British painting, chronologically, in one, up to about 1914; all modern art, painting and sculpture, British and foreign, in the other. The British section is somewhat deprived in essentials by two factors: first (for the 16th and 17th centuries) by the lack so far of representation of the two figures who, though neither is British, are in different degree the source and inspiration of the British school — Holbein and Van Dyck. (It may be conceivable to imagine the Tudor painters without Holbein, but to understand the Stuart painters, deprived of Van Dyck, is impossible.) Secondly, for the so-called Golden Age of English painting, from Hogarth to Turner and Constable, the great masterpieces are mostly held in the British room at the National Gallery, and the richest representation of Constable, as indicated above, is in the Victoria and Albert Museum. (Miniatures are also in the V & A — the Tate does not collect these, though in Tudor painting they are the finest achievement in quality.) This proviso does not really apply, however, to the work of J.M.W. Turner: true, his most famous pictures — *Rain Steam and Speed,* for example — may be in the National Gallery, but Turner himself took care that his representation in the national collections should be at least adequate. On his death in 1851, he bequeathed an enormous collection of his own works, paintings and watercolours, to the nation; the great bulk of the paintings ultimately went to the Tate, the watercolours (some 20,000) to the British Museum. The wealth is such that, even though a handful of masterpieces remain in the National Gallery, there are many others of comparable majesty for the Tate.

In fact, the first two centuries of post-Renaissance British painting are dominated by European-born (and often trained) artists. Holbein was followed by Hans Eworth, a Flemish mannerist, and then by Lowlanders such as Gheeraedts. George Gower is an interesting native-born painter, and the finest of them, Nicholas Hilliard, though above all a miniaturist, is represented by a lifesize head and shoulders of *Elizabeth I* drawn with a jewelled, brilliant precision, that is confidently ascribed to him. But even the foreigners took on, so to speak, an English accent: the slender, relatively linear characterization of Gheeraedts is quite different in atmosphere from the work of Flemish portraitists. So, too, even Van Dyck was to reflect the silvery English light in his English work, and his followers — the Dutchman Sir Peter Lely, the German Sir Godfrey Kneller (who dominated English portraiture between 1650 and 1720) can ultimately be diagnosed, in their version of Continental Baroque, only as English.

But the emergence of a more purely native strain comes really with Hogarth, in his portraits as well, but also in his conversation-pieces and his dramatic pictures — an art that can no longer be considered as provincial, but one acknowledged throughout the Continent as a major contribution to the main European stream. He is well and variously represented at the Tate; the greatest portraitists, though, Gainsborough and Reynolds, do not on the whole rise here to heights comparable with their work at the National. Stubbs, however, the unique 'classical' painter of the English horse, is here — a major master at last recognized at his true stature. For the explorer of minor painters and relatively uncharted byways of painting, the Tate reveals moments of great charm — the masters of the conversation-piece, Arthur Devis in his silvery domestic bliss; the neo-classic strain in Romney, J. H. Mortimer. To foreigners, the work of John Crome (particularly the *Slate Quarries*) may come as an agreeable shock in its mastery of tone and its relished quality of paint, though the rather Claude-ian landscapes of Richard Wilson may seem to them perhaps to have too much of Claude. But it is to the major figures that one reverts — to William Blake, that unique English visionary (a very rich collection, though now relegated to the basement floor of the Gallery, among drawings and watercolours): this, for a foreign visitor, offers the (perhaps inexplicable, and certainly not easily exportable) quintessence of a certain kind of 'Englishness' in art, essentially linear, and at once ideal and passionately particular. Then there are the Turner rooms, in which the whole of his long career — his early deliberate rivalry with established Old Masters to the revolutionary, luminous incandescence of his later work, nature created in fluid light and colour — is set out in detail. The fresh, immediate-seeming vision of Constable in landscape is also well represented, while in the later stages of 19th-century art, the brilliantly-jewelled paintings of the Pre-Raphaelites (Millais, Holman Hunt, Madox-Brown and Rossetti) may startle visitors from abroad with an attack on the eye to which there is no exact Continental parallel.

The art of the 20th century is now well shown at the Tate, vastly improved over the last decade in both display and coverage, though still relatively weak in Expressionism especially (which was long unacceptable to the English artistic palate). The task is enormous, for not only is European art involved but now the American too. It is no disparagement to say that the overall effect is close to that of any first-rate museum of modern art, for modern art now tends to speak an interchangeable international language. The history of the isms is shown — Cubism, Purism, Futurism, Dada, Surrealism, up to the Abstract Expressionists, Op and Pop and way beyond. The unique English accent is effected by some contributions — of the Vorticists, Wyndham Lewis, William Roberts and David Bomberg, with their own development of Cubism and Futurism; there was, around 1907, a sort of private mini-Fauve movement by Augustus John; then, later, came the major contributions by Henry Moore (a huge gift of his work is destined for the Tate), Ben Nicholson and Graham Sutherland, followed by Francis Bacon. The whole period is under constant re-assessment, as the incredibly swiftly changing explorations in contemporary art find not only their own new images but reveal unsuspected relevances in earlier movements; in sympathy the display is bound to be very fluid. But certain artists, certain works have already established themselves as great classics of the 20th century, and they no doubt will always be visible — Picasso (a good sequence, recently enriched by the purchase of the very important *Three Dancers* of 1925); Matisse, especially a superb paper cut-out, *L'Escargot,* and the four reliefs of *Le Dos;* Braque, Gris and Léger; Klee and Arp; Brancusi and Giacometti. The Tate also overlaps, for the earlier artists, the representation in the National Gallery, so that Cézanne is shown in both, also Van

Gogh and others, though the brilliant sculpture of Degas is well to the fore in the Tate. There is a very rich representation of Rodin, as of Epstein, and in later developments British sculptors play a leading exploratory role — Paolozzi, Caro. Among these, a peculiar insular English quality persists in idiosyncratic artists like Stanley Spencer (often as though a latter-day more earthy William Blake). The Tate also offers major retrospectives and thematic exhibitions, and has, as *bonne bouche,* an agreeable restaurant with wall paintings, by Rex Whistler, on the theme of rare meats.

The national museums have increased, since the 19th-century foundations, somewhat hesitantly and sporadically — primarily historical ones. The **London Museum,** founded in 1911, has been refused a proper home for generations; its housing in domestic-scale rooms in Kensington Palace (p. 116) lends it a certain wilful charm, and it is tight-packed with visual witness of London's history, but its contents cannot be properly shown there. It is especially rich in costume, in theatrical history, and has remarkable association pieces, such as the stately chess set given by Pepys to James II, and a great collection of topographical material. Its function is shared by the Guildhall Museum, also in unsatisfactory temporary quarters on London Wall, but the two are destined to unite at last in a new building promised (further to the west on London Wall) for some time in the 1970s.

The **Public Record Office Museum,** first established in 1902, is designed to show some of the most spectacular of the huge mine of official records in the Office itself. Access to the students' room there is for scholars only, but the Museum itself is open freely and presents crucial moments in British history with a most forceful immediacy for all the immunization of its glowing showcases and controlled atmosphere. Here is the actual Domesday book, and a worn scrap of paper on which Shakespeare scratched his name, or another, in which the wavering ink is almost faded from sight, Philip Sidney's last letter. Drake writes to Walsingham of success at sea against the Spaniards; Marlborough, after Blenheim, confesses battle-fatigue ('I am so very much out of order for want of rest etc. . . .'); Wellington announces Waterloo. The Museum is sited on a long-gone medieval chapel, but preserves some of its monuments, most notably and startlingly an admirable Renaissance effigy of Dr John Yong, Master of the Rolls (d. 1516), convincingly ascribed to Pietro Torrigiani.

The **Imperial War Museum,** opened in 1920, was intended as the most serious of war memorials, devoted to the memory of the sacrifices of the 1914-18 war. Human folly has compelled it since to enlarge its scope to comprise the 1939-45 war as well, and again, in 1953, Korea. In it, quietened, tethered, tamed are shown the instruments of war on land sea and air, but it includes also the strange harvest of art winnowed from catastrophe by two generations of war artists — notably Augustus John, William Orpen, Paul Nash, C. R. W. Nevinson in the First World War; Stanley Spencer, Sutherland, Moore in the Second. It has fine Epstein busts. Its specialist library is unique, and it has a remarkable film archive much drawn on by television. It is housed south of the river at Lambeth, ironically in a strange, truncated, over-domed building, a fragment, designed in part by Sydney Smirke in 1846, of the premises to which there was removed about 1815 the Bethlem Royal Hospital for the Insane, better known as Bedlam. The early history of the army will be illustrated when the **National Army Museum** is moved from Sandhurst in Surrey to a new building designed for it in the precincts of Chelsea Hospital (due to open in 1971). This will

King and Queen, *bronze by Henry Moore, 1952-53. Tate Gallery.*

match the well-established (and superbly housed) **National Maritime Museum,** whose buildings are centred on Inigo Jones' Queen's House at Greenwich; it was founded in 1937. For the maritime enthusiast, a visit is essential; it includes ship models, a navigation room, a hall eloquent with ships' figureheads and strewn with gilded state-barges (the former Rolls-Royces of the Thames), and an intensely detailed celebration of Nelson, including the bullet-holed Vice-Admiral's coat that he wore at Trafalgar. It is also not only a maritime version of the National Portrait Gallery (including a Hogarth masterpiece, *Lord George Graham in His Cabin,* an interesting row of early Reynoldses, and fine Lelys and Knellers), but also a gallery of great sea pictures, with remarkable series especially of Van der Velde drawings. Other museums include the fascinating, nostalgic **British Transport Museum** (railways, buses, extinct trams) at Clapham, but a doctrinaire bureaucracy seems determined to disperse that to the provinces; and the

Commonwealth Institute, showing the products of the British Commonwealth, in an enterprising tent-like structure in Holland Park.

For the lover of great art, however, there are several relatively recent, fairly small but highly concentrated collections now made public. These tend to be overlooked by the hurried visitor, and are somewhat off the main track: they should not be neglected. The richest perhaps are the **Courtauld Institute Galleries** (Woburn Square), where you take a ponderous lift to a Gallery that still has the atmosphere, relaxation (sofas, carpets) and intimacy of a private collection. The Courtauld Institute (see p. 132) is the University of London school of art history; that it is blessed with a collection of such quality is due to Samuel Courtauld (d. 1947), the leading English collector of French Impressionism. Here are Degas, Renoir, Bonnard, Monet; five major Cézannes, particularly the magisterial *Lake at Annecy,* and one of the versions of the *Card-Players*: one of the Van Goghs is the famous *Portrait of the Artist with his Ear Cut Off;* the Gauguins are from the dream-laden Tahitian period; and Pissarro's view of *Penge Station, Upper Norwood* translates London suburbia into a masterpiece of painting. This breathtaking, collection is supported by perhaps lesser collections — but it includes Bellini, Goya, Rubens, Tintoretto; the Gambier-Parry bequest has great Renaissance objects, and the Roger Fry collection is a curious mirror of Bloomsbury taste. There is further a wide-ranging collection of drawings.

Offering equally intense calm pleasure is another institution, also part of London University and also, it seems, almost concealed though only a few minutes walk away, 53 Gordon Square, the **Percival David Foundation of Chinese Art,** a major collection of Chinese ceramics. Then there is, at the very beginning of Piccadilly at Hyde Park Corner, in a house long known as 'No. 1, London', **Apsley House,** the **Wellington Museum.** This too is not easy of access (islanded in swirling traffic), and may further arouse apprehensions of proving a shrine to a national military hero, not to the taste of all. It is indeed a shrine, and is filled with relics and portraits of the conqueror of Napoleon. But it is also (apart from being housed in a most urbane and delightful house) a collection of paintings that includes major works. These are loot, captured from Joseph Bonaparte, King of Spain, after his defeat at Vittoria in 1813. The Duke of Wellington, an upright English gentleman with strong views about the sanctity of private property, offered to return them to the Spaniards, but they held to the belief that the spoils of war were justified, and insisted he keep them. So it is that the general's house owns the best representation of Spanish painting in England (apart from that in the National Gallery) — three Velasquez as well as Ribera and Murillo. There are also good Teniers, and Italian pictures including a darkly luminous gem by Correggio of *Christ in Agony on the Mountain.* The Duke himself was also fortunate in his own painters: compare the virile handsomeness of his portrait by Lawrence with the equestrian portrait by Goya. The English pictures include especially fine paintings by Wilkie, and the furniture and fittings are rewarding — most spectacularly, the 'Waterloo' table service made for the Duke in Portugal, and, in the well of the stairs, a colossal nude marble statue of the great antagonist, Napoleon, by Canova.

Apsley House is rare in its preservation of the collections and personalia of its greatest inhabitant. Most of the surviving great town houses — Lancaster House, Marlborough House — are more interesting for their architecture than their contents, and this is true of the outlying country houses now engulfed by Greater London, such as **Osterley** (p. 133).

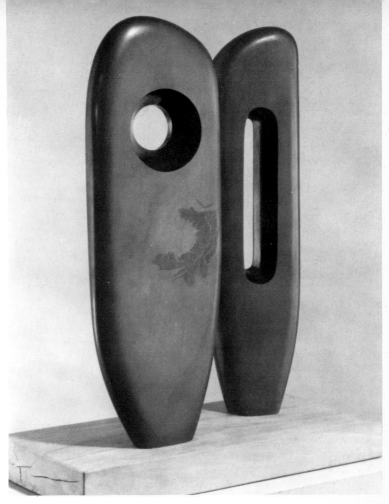

Two Figures *(Menhirs)*, by *Barbara Hepworth, 1964. Tate Gallery.*

Ham House at Petersham, some miles to the west of central London, is an exception — now run by the Victoria and Albert Museum, it preserves much of the character given it when the Duchess of Lauderdale enlarged it in 1673-75. The rather heavy but exuberant Anglo-Dutch Baroque style swirls through furniture and pictures alike, the latter mainly portraits, including fine works by Lely and J. M. Wright. **Syon House** — still the property of its ancient family, the Percys, Dukes of Northumberland, though it opens to the public — is not only (like Chiswick or Osterley) one of the grandest of Robert Adam's creations (mainly of the 1760s, p. 133), but has its superb furniture, decorative statuary, and a range of portraits mostly closely linked with the house's history, including Van Dyck, Lely, Reynolds and Gainsborough. Syon is at Brentford, Middlesex, away to the west though not as far as Ham. Another exceptional house is easier to reach, **Kenwood,** poised on its shelf-like terrace high on Hampstead Heath overlooking London from the north. This is again in part by Adam (see p. 133), but its most remarkable strength lies in the collection of paintings — not part of the original collection, but installed by Lord Iveagh early in the 20th century. It is not large; rich in Reynolds, in Gainsborough (his shimmery pink whole length of *Lady Howe* is the masterpiece of his Bath period) and Romney, as also in Van Dyck; a brilliant Hals, a Cuyp, a Van der Capelle, and a delightful view of *Old London Bridge* in 1639 by an otherwise little known Dutchman, Claude de

Ben Nicholson, White Relief, *1935. Tate Gallery.*

Jongh. It is not these though that most visitors come especially to see, but a little light-enchanted *Guitar Player* (the only Vermeer generally visible in London outside the National Gallery) and, even more, what has been to my mind rightly described as the greatest of all Rembrandt's late self-portraits. The ensemble of Kenwood — with its lawns dipping away to the lake, on the far bank of which there is an orchestra shell, from which music at summer concerts echoes across the water — offers rare arcadian enchantment for Londoners.

Another category of museum in which London is rich is comprised of houses, often quite modest, once inhabited by great men in British history, and now preserved or reconstituted as personal memorials to them. The Wellington Museum, already mentioned, is one such, but distinguished by its artistic collections. Others have artistic connections: **Hogarth's House,** at Chiswick, is an agreeable, small 18th-century house, though strangely set now, on the edge of the thundering Great West Road, almost swallowed by a boot polish factory — but it has

a selection of Hogarth prints and associated items. **Leighton House,** in Kensington, is a vivid evocation, exotically lavish, of the artistic life and context of a grandly successful Victorian academic artist: the Olympian Lord Leighton (d. 1896) was President of the Royal Academy, and a good selection of his work, now beginning to be valued again, is to be seen there. (The **British Theatre Museum** also has temporary headquarters here, pending the hoped-for establishment of an ambitious National Theatre Museum.) **John Wesley's House,** deep in the traffic of City Road (and opposite a historic cemetery, Bunhill Fields), has relics of the founder of the Wesleyan movement; and **Water House,** far to the east in Walthamstow and once one of the homes of William Morris, is now a museum devoted to his arts and crafts and those of his contemporaries. Others are mostly of literary associations, with relics, and portraits: **Dr Johnson's House,** hidden away in Gough Square in the maze of little alleys north off Fleet Street, is where he wrote the famous Dictionary around 1750, a delightful 18th-century survival among towering commercial building; **Dickens's House,** at 48 Doughty Street, was lived in by him only briefly (1837-39) but is the only survivor of the various houses in London which he had — a modest, simple early 19th-century terrace house. **Keats's House,** Hampstead, with relics of the poet and his contemporary, was once a simple little village street (now Keats Grove) house; but he lived and worked there in the zenith of his brief life, 1818-20, and the mulberry tree in front is said to have shaded the writing of the *Ode to a Nightingale.* But the most vivid of these houses is that in Chelsea, in Cheyne Walk, again a modest terrace house; but during his long sojourn there, from 1834 till his death in 1881, in an armchair still there, that forceful Scottish historian, praiser of great men and prophet, **Thomas Carlyle,** seems to have impregnated it so resolutely with his quirky, bristling character that one expects him to come in at the door at any moment. For years now the L.C.C., now the Greater London Council, has carried on the happy practice of signalling to the passer-by the houses in which great men once lived, or the sites on which these houses once stood, by a blue commemorative plaque, but, please note, these plaques do *not* mean that any house so marked is open to the public.

London as a whole also serves as museum for the connoisseur of English sculpture, indoors and outdoors. Indoors are mainly the churches, and above all Westminster Abbey, and, for a specialized neo-classic taste St Paul's, but other sites are rewarding — the Guildhall; the Houses of Parliament for Victorian sculpture. Of post-Renaissance work, besides Torrigiani and the colourful Elizabethans, there is fairly complete representation of the most important sculptors till the early 20th-century in Westminster Abbey, though the crammed medley may tax even the most discriminating eye. The work of the 17th-century English-born Baroque sculptors is generally disappointing in quality, though Grinling Gibbons' studio seems to have matched his own high standard of virtuosity in the City churches. In the 18th century the standard was lifted high beyond the provincial by immigrant sculptors, Scheemakers, M. Rysbrack, and Roubiliac, especially the last two. All are well represented at the Abbey: Scheemakers by the celebrated *Shakespeare* statue, in the area known as Poets' Corner; Rysbrack by, among others, his *Newton* monument, and Roubiliac by several masterpieces of dazzling virtuosity — the *Argyll, Mrs Nightingale,* and *Handel* monuments especially: Roubiliac, a French Huguenot, now ranks among the most distinguished of 18th-century sculptors in Europe. This standard was maintained by Nollekens, Flaxman and Banks among others, and by Sir F. Chantrey, but chills into somewhat frozen inexpressiveness in the 19th century. Neo-classic statuary, mainly of great military heroes of the French wars, began to invade St Paul's in vast set-pieces from 1790 on, but the *tour-de-force* in St Paul's is the fine *Wellington* memorial, in a fluent Renaissance style, by A. Stevens. But many other churches will surprise and delight the visitor with charming, if minor, monuments.

The outdoor monuments begin in spate only about the same time as the St Paul's invasion. In Whitehall, *Charles I* (p. 148) is an exception, as is the elegant *James II* (1686) outside the National Gallery associated with Grinling Gibbons (paired, rather strangely, with a cast of Houdon's *General Washington*). Other early ones are not of great

▷

J. M. W. Turner, Pilate Washing his Hands. *Detail, from one of the major Turners so richly represented in the Tate Gallery.*

Thomas Gainsborough, The Market Cart, *1786 (detail). Tate Gallery.*

quality, but there are some charming 18th- or early 19th-century examples, most notably the unusually informal equestrian *George III* (Cockspur Street; by Wyatt, 1836) and the belatedly rococo *William III,* also equestrian but about to stumble on the molehill that caused his death, among the great plane trees of St James's Square (by Bacon, 1807). In the 19th century the colossal figures of imperial statesmen and warriors began to collect in groves of fame in marble or bronze — most densely in Trafalgar Square, the Victoria Embankment, and Parliament Square, these ranging, from *George Canning,* very neo-classic, by Westmacott, 1832, through a version of Saint-Gaudens' *Abraham*

Lincoln in Chicago to *Jan Christiaan Smuts* by Epstein. But the most celebrated statues are elsewhere: *Peter Pan* (by Sir George Frampton, 1912), *art nouveau* vision of Barrie's hero, in Kensington Gardens; *Achilles,* in Hyde Park near Wellington's house, and said by some to be a portrait of him — but the first nude statue to appear in London (by Westmacott, 1822) — and the most famous of all, *Eros* at Piccadilly Circus, which has become almost a symbol of London, and is characteristically misnamed; it was made by Sir Alfred Gilbert, 1893, as the Angel of Christian Charity and memorial to the great Victorian philanthropist, the 7th Earl of Shaftesbury. Contemporary sculpture is rather

Francis Bacon, Seated Man with Turkey Rug, *1961. Tate Gallery.*

H. Matisse, The Inattentive Reader, *1919, Tate Gallery.*

P. Picasso, Woman in a Red Armchair, *1932. Tate Gallery.*

neglected though Epstein is well represented, not so much by his notorious *Rima* (Kensington Gardens), which was found so horrible when erected that it was tarred and feathered, but by other works, above all the beautifully tender *Madonna and Child* on the façade of 11 Cavendish Square, W.1. Henry Moore is represented high on the building over St James's Underground Station (as also is Epstein), and at the Time/Life Building in New Bond Street by a frieze and a fine reclining figure: at *The Times* (Queen Victoria Street) by a sundial, and on the Embankment by the Tate by two large bronzes. A superb Barbara Hepworth abstract *Meridian* is at State House, High Holborn.

PP. 238/239 Map showing principal monuments and museums of London. ▷

P. 240 Westminster Abbey; bronze by Henry Moore in the foreground. ▷

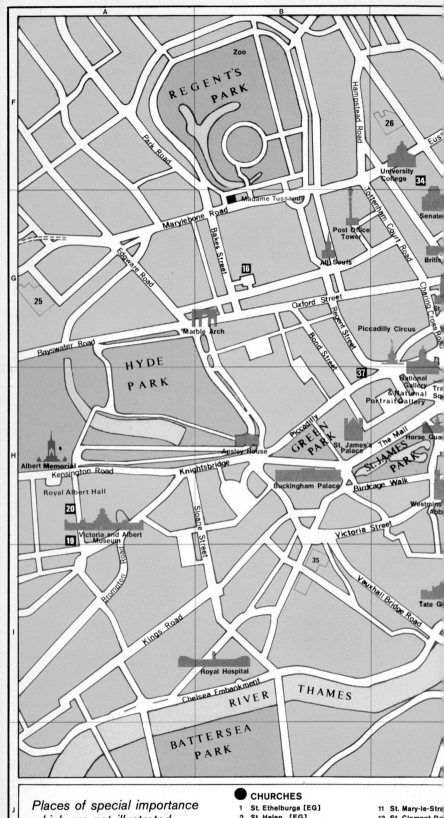

Map labels:

Zoo

REGENT'S PARK

Hampstead Road

Park Road

26

University College

34

Senate

Marylebone Road

Baker Street

Madame Tussauds

Tottenham Court Road

Post Office Tower

All Souls

Britis

16

Oxford Street

Regent Street

Bond Street

Piccadilly Circus

Chairing Cross Road

Eus

Marble Arch

Bayswater Road

Edgware Road

25

37

HYDE PARK

National Gallery & National Portrait Gallery

Tra Sq

Piccadilly

GREEN PARK

St. James's Palace

The Mall

Horse Gua

ST. JAMES'S PARK

Apsley House

Albert Memorial

Kensington Road

Knightsbridge

Buckingham Palace

Birdcage Walk

Royal Albert Hall

20

19

Victoria and Albert Museum

Sloane Street

Westmins Abb

Victoria Street

35

Vauxhall Bridge Road

Brompton Road

Kings Road

Tate G

Royal Hospital

Chelsea Embankment

RIVER THAMES

BATTERSEA PARK

Places of special importance which are not illustrated by architectural symbols with captions are indicated here by numbers with captions.

● CHURCHES

1 St. Ethelburga [EG]
2 St. Helen [EG]
3 St. Mary at Hill [EG]
4 St. Lawrence Jewry [DG]
5 St. Magnus [EH]
6 St. Mary-le-Bow [DG]
7 St. Bartholomew the Great [DG]
8 St. Benet [DG]
9 All Hallows Barking [EG]
10 St. Bride [DG]

11 St. Mary-le-Stra
12 St. Clement Da
13 St. Giles [DG]
14 Savoy Chapel
15 St. Mary Abchu

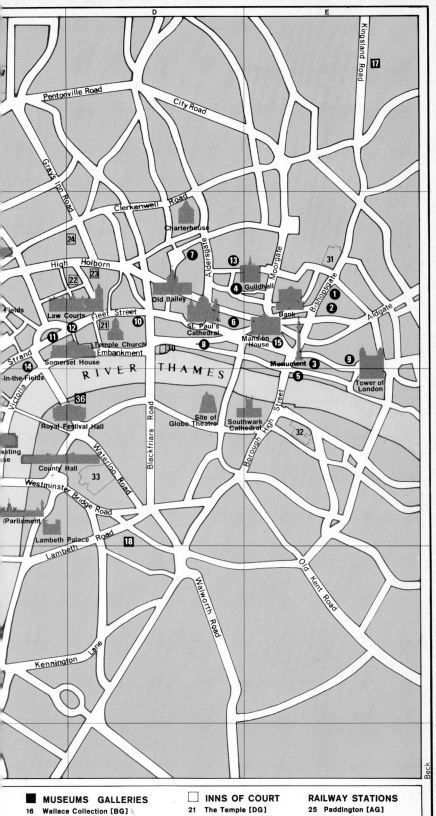

MUSEUMS GALLERIES

16 Wallace Collection [BG]
17 Geffrye Museum [EF]
18 Imperial War Museum [DH]
19 Natural History Museum [AH]
20 Science Museum [AH]
34 Courtauld Institute Galleries [CF]
36 Hayward Gallery [DH]
37 Royal Academy [BH]

INNS OF COURT

21 The Temple [DG]
22 Lincoln's Inn [DG]
23 Staple Inn [DG]
24 Gray's Inn [DG]

RAILWAY STATIONS

25 Paddington [AG]
26 Euston [CF]
27 King's Cross [CF]
28 St. Pancras [CF]
29 Charing Cross [CH]
30 Blackfriars [DG]
31 Liverpool Street [EG]
32 London Bridge [EN]
33 Waterloo [DH]
35 Victoria [BI]

Museums and Galleries

Page references are given at the end of each entry. Numbers in italics refer to the captions. Letters in brackets are the grid references for the map.

Apsley House
see **Wellington Museum.**

Artillery Museum
The Rotunda, Woolwich Common, S.E.18. Monday-Friday 10–12.45; 2–5; Saturdays 10–12; Sundays, 2–5 (4 in winter).
Collection of guns, muskets etc. in a building developed from a Regency tent designed by John Nash for victory celebrations in St James's Park, 1814.

Arts Council Gallery (Hayward Gallery)
Belvedere Road, S.E.1. South Bank (by Waterloo Station).
Loan exhibitions, often of major importance. 185. [DH]

Banqueting House
Whitehall, S.W.1. 10–5; Sundays 2–5. Closed Mondays.
Inigo Jones's masterpiece, 1619–25; painted ceiling by Rubens. Almost the only surviving part of the former Royal Palace of Whitehall. 32, 69, 69, 74, 80, 116. [CH]

Battersea House
or Old Battersea House, 30 Vicarage Crescent, S.W.11. Monday-Friday 9.30–12; Saturdays 2–4.
Rich Victorian interior with Pre-Raphaelite decor.

Bethnal Green Museum
Cambridge Heath Road, E.2. 10–6; Sundays 2.30–6.
A branch of the Victoria and Albert Museum: Spitalfield silks, dolls houses, model theatres, local topography, loan exhibitions, etc.

British Museum
Great Russell Street, W.C.1. 10–5; Sundays 2.30–6.
Founded 1753: the main building (on the site of Montague House) by Sir Robert Smirke 1823–47: northern extension (King Edward VII Galleries) by Sir John Burnet, finished 1914. Comprises the National Library — books, mss., prints and drawings; the national collections of antiquities — Egyptian, Western Asiatic, Greek and Roman, British and Medieval, Oriental; of Coins and Medals; and of Ethnography (now rehoused in Burlington Gardens). A major expansion, between Great Russell Street and New Oxford Street, is scheduled for the 1970s. 9, 11, 14, 154, 178, 187, 188, 191-2, 199-201, *202, 203, 204,* 206, 208, *208,* 210, 212, 214, 218, 224. [CG]

British Theatre Museum
Leighton House, 12 Holland Park Road, W.14. Tuesdays, Thursdays, Saturdays, 11–5.
Temporarily housed here until it finds a permanent home. 231.

British Transport Museum
Clapham High Street, S.W.4. 10–5.30, closed Sundays.
History of public transport, including rolling stock, royal carriages, etc. 228.

Buckingham Palace
see **Queen's Gallery** and **Royal Mews.**

Burlington House
see **Royal Academy of Arts.**

Camden Arts Centre
Arkwright Road, Hampstead, N.W.3. Tuesday-Saturday 11–8; Sundays 2–7.
Loan exhibitions, usually contemporary art.

Carlyle's House
24 Cheyne Row, S.W.3. 10–1; 2–6 or dusk (not Tuesdays); Sundays 2–6 or dusk.
In a terrace row of small Georgian houses; Thomas Carlyle and his wife Jane lived and worked here for 47 years till his death in 1881. Original decor, and many associational items. A good statue of Carlyle, by Sir J.E. Boehm, 1882, is nearby in Cheyne Walk. 232. [AI]

Charlton House
Charlton Road, Greenwich, S.E.7. Interior by appointment only.
Spectacular Jacobean house, built for Sir Adam Newton, 1612, tutor and secretary to Henry, Prince of Wales. 66-7, *66.*

Charterhouse
Charterhouse Square, E.C.1. Usually parties only by previous arrangement.
A charitable foundation (Sutton's Hospital in Charterhouse) with a fine range of buildings, medieval to Renaissance; gatehouses remnants of cloisters, Great Hall and Chapel. Badly bombed, but restored. 58-9, 190. [DG]

Chelsea Royal Hospital
Chelsea Embankment, S.W.3. Generally 10–12; 2–5; Sundays 2–5. Tips are expected.

Founded by Charles II for army pensioners; built by Sir Christopher Wren, 1682–91. Still in use; pensioners have characteristic uniform. 112, 114, *114*, 227. [BI]

Chiswick House
Burlington Lane, W.4. April 10.30–5.30; May-September 10.30–7.00; October-March, Wednesday-Sunday 10.30–4.
Designed by Lord Burlington for himself, 1720–30, modelled on Palladio's Villa Rotonda. Magnificent gardens (now a public park) designed by William Kent. *117*, 120, 229.

Commonwealth Institute
230 Kensington High Street, W.8. 10–5.30; Sundays 2.30–6.
Permanent exhibition demonstrating the history, geography, artefacts, etc. of the Commonwealth countries. Building with remarkable hyperbolic paraboloid roof in green copper, by Sir R. Matthew, Johnson-Marshall and Partners, 1962. Cinema; temporary art exhibitions. 228.

Courtauld Institute of Art (Home House)
20 Portman Square, W.1. Can usually be visited in University vacation times, and on Saturday mornings 10–1, but best to ring first.
Beautifully preserved house by Robert Adam, built in the 1770s for the Countess of Home. 132, 228. [AG]

Courtauld Institute Galleries
Woburn Square, W.C.1. 10–5; Sundays 2–5.
Very important Impressionist and Post-Impressionist paintings (formerly collection of Samuel Courtauld); also the Roger Fry collection; and Old Masters (Lee of Fareham gift); objets d'art (Gambier-Parry Bequest); the Witt collection of drawings. 228. [CF]

Crosby Hall
Cheyne Walk S.W.3. 10.30–5.30; 2.30–5.30 Sundays 2.30–5.30.
Great hall, with fine timber roof, originally built in the 15th century in the City for the merchant Sir John Crosby. Reconstructed in Chelsea in 1910. 19, 27. [AI]

Cuming Museum
Walworth Road, S.E.17. 10–5.30 (Thursday 7, Saturday 5): closed Sundays.
Southwark local history and topography. [DI]

Cutty Sark *see* **Greenwich.**

Design Centre
28 Haymarket, S.W.1. 9.30–5.30 (Wednesdays and Thursdays to 9).
Changing showroom of best British contemporary design. [CG]

Dickens's House
48 Doughty Street, W.C.1. 10–5; 2–5. Closed Sundays.
Early 19th-century terrace house; Charles Dickens rented it 1837–39 and worked here on *Pickwick Papers, Oliver Twist*, etc. Collection of Dickensiana. 232. [CF]

H.M.S. Discovery
Victoria Embankment, W.C.2. Daily 1–4.45. [DG]
Ship used by Captain Scott for his Antarctic expedition, 1901–4.

Donaldson Museum *see* **Royal College of Music.**

Dulwich College Picture Gallery
College Road, S.E.21. May to August 10–6 (Sundays from 2); September to April, 10–4 (Sundays from 2); closed Mondays.
Building by Sir John Soane, 1811–12; destroyed by bombing, but rebuilt. A major collection of Old Master paintings. 151, 192.

Eltham Palace
off Court Yard, Eltham, S.E.9. Thursdays and Sundays 11–7 (November-April to 4). Free.
Former Royal Palace, with fine hammerbeam roof of the 1470s. 48.

Fenton House
The Grove, Hampstead, N.W.3. 11–5; Sundays 2–5 or dusk; closed Tuesdays.
Good late 17th-century house, with Binning collection of western and oriental ceramics; furniture; and the Benton-Fletcher collection of early key-board musical instruments.

Foundling Hospital *see* **Thomas Coram Foundation.**

Geffrye Museum
Kingsland Road, E.2. 10–5; Sundays 2–5; closed Mondays.
18th-century almshouses, with period rooms and furniture.

Geological Museum
Exhibition Road, S.W.7. 11–6, Sundays 2.30–6. [EF]
Collections relating to national and world geology, including a comprehensive display of precious stones. Developed from the Geological Survey (1835); now in a building by J. H. Markham, 1935. 208, 218–9 [AH]

Greenwich - The Cutty Sark
King William Walk, S.E.10. April-September 11–6; Sundays 2.30–6; October-March 11–5; Sundays 2.30–5.
A classic specimen of the great sailing tea clippers, built 1869, preserved in dry dock.

— The National Maritime Museum
Romney Road, S.E.10. 10–6; Sundays 2.30–6.

Collections of paintings, drawings, prints and books; instruments, barges, ship-models; charts, globes; uniforms and weapons; Nelsoniana relating to the nation's maritime history. Housed in Inigo Jones's Queen's House, 1635, built for Henrietta Maria, and other, modern, buildings. 48, 64, 112, 227.

— The Queen's House
Part of the National Maritime Museum. 64, 64-5, 67, 86, 115, 116, 227.

— The Royal Hospital (Royal Naval College)
Greenwich, S.E.10. Usually 2.30–5; closed Thursdays.
Founded by William III, 1694, for seamen pensioners; latterly the Royal Naval College. By Webb, Wren, Hawksmoor and Vanbrugh. Chapel by James 'Athenian' Stuart 1789. 64, 114, 115–16, 125.

— Old Royal Observatory
Greenwich Park, S.E.10.
Now annexed to the National Maritime Museum. Includes Flamsteed House. By Wren; exhibition of chronological and astronomical instruments.
— *see also* Charlton House *and* Artillery Museum (Rotunda).

Guildhall
Gresham Street, E.C.2. 10–5; closed Sundays.
Administrative and ceremonial centre of the City of London. Crypt and entrance hall survive from a rebuilding of 1411; the Great Hall, restored after the Great Fire of 1666 and again after 1945, is still 15th-century in character. The present façade, Gothic with moorish or Indian and classical accents, is by George Dance the Younger, 1788/89. Library. Picture Gallery (permanent collection, mainly London topography and history), loan exhibitions, and statuary from demolished London buildings. 22-5, 84, 93, 105. [EG]

Guildhall Museum
Gillett House, 55 Basinghall Street, E.C.2. (temporary site).
Collection of antiquities of London, etc.; leathercraft museum. Eventually scheduled to be united with the London Museum in a new building. 9, 12, 14, 23, 187, 226, 232 [EG]

Gunnersbury Park Museum
Gunnersbury Park, W.3. October-March, Wednesday, Saturday and Sunday 2–4; April-September, Monday to Friday 2–5; Saturday and Sundays 2–6.
Fine Regency house, formerly a Rothschild home; local history and transport.

Ham House
Petersham, Richmond, Surrey. March-October, 2–6; November-February 12–4; closed Mondays.
(Administered by the Victoria and Albert Museum). Dates from 1610, but much rebuilt in the later 17th century as home for the Duke of Lauderdale; with its original furnishings and pictures, it preserves to a remarkable degree its post-Restoration atmosphere. 229.

Hampton Court Palace
Hampton Court, Middlesex. May-September, 9.30–6; Sundays from 11; November to February 9.30–4 (Sundays from 2); March to April, and October, 9.30–5 (Sundays from 2).
Originally Cardinal Wolsey's palace, appropriated by Henry VIII; magnificent 15th-century brick work and Tudor great hall; in part much altered and added to by Wren for William III. Houses an important part of the Royal Collection of paintings, most notably Mantegna's *Triumph of Caesar* cartoons (Orangery). Original Tudor kitchens; tennis court. Decorations by Kent, Verrio, etc. Fine formal garden. 32, 54–5, 57–58, 57, 58, 114 15, 122, 188.

Hayward Gallery *see* Arts Council Gallery.

Henry VIII's Wine Cellar
Whitehall, S.W.1. Saturday afternoons only by previous application to Sec. A/38, Ministry of Public Building and Works, Lambeth Bridge House, S.E.1.
Only Tudor survival from old Whitehall Palace. [CG]

Hogarth's House
Hogarth Lane, Great West Road, W.4. Summer 11–6; Sundays 2–6; Winter 11–5 (Sunday 2–5). Closed Tuesdays.
Modest brick house, once Hogarth's country villa, but now set in factory development. Prints and associative material. 231.

Holland House
Kensington High Street, W.8.
Fragment of spectacular Jacobean house (destroyed by bombing) in Holland Park. Begun 1605; later the residence of the Fox family (Lords Holland, and Earls of Ilchester), and in the 19th century a major focus of Whig political, social and intellectual fashion.

Horniman Museum
100 London Road, S.E.23. 10.30–6; Sundays 2–6.
Ethnographical, zoological (with aquarium); musical instruments. *Art*

nouveau building by C.H. Townsend, 1901.

House of St Barnabas
1 Greek Street, W.1. Mondays 10.30–12; Thursdays 2.30–4.15. Also Monday, Wednesday, Friday 1.15–3.30.
Early Georgian house on Soho Square with good plaster work. [CG]

Houses of Parliament
St Margaret Street, S.W.1. Saturdays, also Easter Monday and Tuesday; Spring Bank Holiday Monday and Tuesday; and Monday, Tuesday and Thursday in August, and Thursdays in September 10–5. Westminster Hall, weekdays from 10 till one hour before the Commons meet.
Seat of the national legislature, the House of Lords and the House of Commons. The former buildings, the Palace of St Stephen's, were all destroyed (except fragments of a cloister, the (now much-restored) crypt of St Stephen's Chapel and Westminster Hall) in the fire of 1834. Entirely re-designed and built by Sir Charles Barry and A. W. Pugin, 1840–60. *31, 30–2, 46, 62, 129, 155, 158, 159, 161, 161, 176,* 232. [CH]

Hunterian Museum *see* Royal College of Surgeons.

Imperial War Museum
Lambeth Road, S.E.1. 10–6; Sundays 2–6.
Founded 1917; housed from 1936 in the surviving portion of the former Bethlem Hospital, or Bedlam (by James Lewis, finished 1815; dome added by Sydney Smirke, 1846). Collections relating to the 1914/18 and subsequent wars: weapons, aircraft, models, uniforms and all kinds of equipment. Art collections mainly the work of official war artists (Paul Nash, Wyndham Lewis, Stanley Spencer, etc.; fine portrait bronzes by Epstein). 226–7. [DI]

Institute of Contemporary Art (I.C.A.)
Carlton House Gardens (entrance from the Mall), S.W.1.
Avant-garde art exhibitions. [CH]

Iveagh Bequest
Kenwood, Hampstead Lane, N.W.3. 10–7 or dusk; Sundays from 2.
House remodelled by Robert Adam, for Lord Mansfield, from 1764; spectacular Adam library: major collection of paintings, especially English 18th-century (Reynolds, Gainsborough, Romney), and Dutch (Rembrandt, Vermeer, Hals, Cuyp, etc.). Overlooking Hampstead Heath; concerts by the lake in Summer. *133, 133, 140,* 229–30.

Jewel Tower
Old Palace Yard, S.W.1. 10.30–6.30 (October-February to 4).
14th-century fragment of old Westminster Palace. 31. [CH]

Jewish Museum
Woburn House, Upper Woburn Place W.C.1. Monday to Thursday 2.30–5; Fridays and Sundays 10.30–12.45; closed Saturdays and Jewish Holy Days. [CG]

Dr Johnson's House
17 Gough Square, Fleet Street, E.C.4. 10.30–5 (4.30 in Winter). Closed Sundays.
Probably late 17th-century house, red brick; Samuel Johnson lived here 1748–59, when working on the Dictionary. Johnson relics. 232. [DG]

Keats's House
Wentworth Place, Keats's Grove, N.W.3. 10–6; closed Sundays.
John Keats lived here 1818–20. Keats relics. 232.

Kensington Palace
Kensington Gardens, W.8. State-rooms, 10–5; Sundays 2–5 (closing at 5 November to February).
Originally Nottingham House (built *c.* 1605 for Sir George Coppin); remodelled by Wren as royal palace for William and Mary from 1691. The beautiful Orangery (1704) is ascribed to Hawksmoor and Vanbrugh. Further alterations by Benson and W. Kent for George I from 1718. Kensington Gardens still reflect the lay-out designed by Charles Bridgeman from 1728. Interior decor in part by Kent especially grandiose Cupola Room. Royal portraits; sculpture by Roubiliac, Guelfi, etc.
See also London Museum. *51, 54, 55, 116, 117,* 129, 188, 226. [AH]

Kenwood House *see* Iveagh Bequest.

Kew Palace
In Kew Gardens, Kew, Surrey. April to September, 11–5.30; Sundays 2–6.
Known as the Dutch House, early 17th century, bought by George III, who lived there 1802–18.

Lambeth Palace
Lambeth Palace Road, S.E.1. Telephone for opening times.
London residence of the Archbishop of Canterbury. Crypt goes back to the 13th century; Tudor gatehouse, late 17th-century Hall still in the Gothic manner, and much later additions and alterations. Important library with collection of mss. Portraits (by Van Dyck, Hogarth, Reynolds etc.). *59–60, 61.* [DI]

Lancaster House
Stable Yard, St. James's, S.W.1. Usually open Easter to mid-December, Saturdays and Sundays 2–6.
Formerly called York House, then

Stafford House. By Benjamin Wyatt and Robert Smirke, from 1825. Spectacular interior (altered by Charles Barry, 1858) with copies after Veronese: ceiling of lantern, S. Crisogono, by Guercino, 1622; in an anteroom, ceiling by P. Veronese, *Cupid and three graces*. Once, in the Duke of Sutherland's time, a focus of Victorian society: now used for Government conferences. *142, 228.* [CH]

Leighton House Art Gallery and Museum
12 Holland Park Road, W.14. Weekdays 11–5.
Built by Aitchison, from 1865, for Lord Leighton, President of the Royal Academy. Remarkable period piece; collection of Leighton's work; temporary exhibitions. 176, 231.
See also British Theatre Museum.

London Museum
Kensington Palace W.8. 10–6, Sundays 2–6 (closing at 5 in Winter)
Founded 1910; in its present home since 1951, pending amalgamation with the Guildhall Museum (q.v.) in a new building on London Wall. Collections relating to the history of London from Stone Age periods to the 20th century. Antiquities, armour; rich theatrical and costume collections; the Cheapside hoard; historical paintings, drawings and prints. 9, 12, 117, 187, 226. [AH]

MCC Memorial Gallery
Lord's Cricket Ground, N.W.8. Usually Monday-Friday 9.30–4.30.
Illustrating the history of cricket. [AF]

Madame Tussaud's Waxworks
Baker Street Station, N.W.1. 10–6.
Founded by Mme Tussaud, fresh from Revolutionary France in the 1790s with wax models of heads decapitated in the Terror. Wax models of the famous and the infamous. Spectacular, with full sound and smell effect, of the Battle of Trafalgar. Chamber of Horrors. 222. [BG]

Mansion House
E.C.2. (by the Bank of England). Saturday afternoons by previous appointment only.
Residence of the Lord Mayor of London: built by George Dance the Elder, 1739–53. Palladian design: pediment sculpture (*Dignity and Opulence of the City*) by Sir Robert Taylor. Interior includes the grandiose Egyptian Hall; formidable array of Victorian statuary. 108, 129, *130, 151.* [EG]

Marble Hill House
Richmond Road, Twickenham, Middlesex. Tuesday to Saturday, 10–5 (or dusk); Sundays 2–5 (or dusk).
Fine example of English Palladian style: originally 'country villa' built 1728/29 by Roger Morris for the Countess of Suffolk (mistress of George II, friend of Alexander Pope); later home of Mrs Fitzherbert, secret wife of George IV. Fine interior. Temporary exhibitions in summer. 120.

Marlborough House
Pall Mall, S.W.1. Usually opens Easter to September on Saturdays and Sundays, 2–6.
Including Inigo Jones's Queen's Chapel. Designed by Wren for the Duchess of Marlborough, 1709–11; much altered by Sir W. Chambers, 1771, and Sir J. Pennethorne in the 1860s (for the then Prince of Wales). Murals of Marlborough's victories by Laguerre; O. Gentileschi's ceiling paintings (once in the Queen's House, Greenwich). Now used by Commonwealth delegations. 64, 86, 228. [CG]

Monument, The
Monument Street, E.C.3. 9–6 (4 in Winter); Sundays, May-September only, 2–6.
Designed by Wren and Robert Hooke as memorial to the Great Fire of 1666: 202 feet high, the fire having started in Pudding Lane, 202 feet away. Built 1671–77. Relief on plinth, of the resurrection of the City, by C. G. Cibber. 83, *83*, 94. [EH]

William Morris Gallery
Water House, Lloyd Park, Forest Road, Walthamstow, E.17. Weekdays 10–5 (Tuesdays and Thursdays from April to September till 8); first Sunday each month 10–12, 2–5.
Former home of Morris, with collection of his work. 231.

National Army Museum
In Chelsea Hospital grounds.
Formerly housed at the Royal Military College, Sandhurst, Camberley.
Collections of weapons, uniforms, etc., also portraits, and historical paintings, prints and drawings, relating to the history of the British armies till 1914. Cf. Imperial War Museum. [BI]

National Gallery
Trafalgar Square, W.C.2. 10–6; Sundays 2–6.
The national collection of Old Master painting, up to about 1900. Founded 1824 by the purchase of the John Julius Angerstein collection. Building (1834–37) by William Wilkins; extensions by E.M. Barry (1867) and others later. It has grown into one of the major collections of great paintings in the world, representing almost all the great figures in

European art at the peak of their quality. A large extension to the north is planned for the 1970s. *34, 39, 147, 155, 179, 188, 191, 191, 192-4, 193, 195, 198, 198-9, 200, 201, 220, 226, 230, 234.* [CH]

National Maritime Museum *see* **Greenwich.**

National Portrait Gallery
St Martin's Place, (off Trafalgar Square) W.C.2. 10–5; Saturdays 10–6; Sundays 2–6. Founded 1856, as 'gallery of the Portraits of the most eminent Persons in British History'. In its present building (Italian Renaissance *palazzo* style, by Ewart Christian) since 1895 (with later extensions). Eminence of the sitter, not that of the artist, is the qualification, but the collections include fine paintings, sculpture and drawings by Holbein, Hilliard, Lely, Kneller (the *Kitcat* portraits), Hogarth, Reynolds, Gainsborough and Romney: Rysbrack, Roubiliac, Nollekens, and many others. *31, 220-1, 221, 222, 224, 227.* [CH]

National Postal Museum
King Edward Buildings, King Edward Street, E.C.1. 10–4.30; Saturdays 10–4.; closed Sundays.
British postage stamps from 1840 on. [DG]

Natural History Museum
Cromwell Road, S.W.7. 10–6; Sundays 2.30–6.
The national collection of animals and plants, minerals and rocks. Originally part of the British Museum (founded 1753; q.v.), it has developed from the collection of Sir Hans Sloane. Transferred to the present building (in somewhat Byzantine mode, by Alfred Waterhouse) in 1880. A major extension to the east is planned for the 1970s. *201, 208, 218.* [AH]

Old Battersea House *see* **Battersea House.**

Old Royal Observatory *see* **Greenwich.**

Orangery *see* **Kensington Palace.**

Osterley Park House
Thunbury Road, Osterley, Middlesex. March to October, 2–6; November to February 12–4; closed Mondays.
(Administered by the Victoria and Albert Museum). Originally an Elizabethan house, built for Sir Thomas Gresham. Later belonged to the Childs, a banking family, till a Childs heiress brought it to the Earls of Jersey by marriage in 1804. Remodelled drastically by Robert Adam from 1761 to 1780. *133, 229.*

Percival David Foundation of Chinese Art
53 Gordon Square, W.C.1. Monday 2–5; Tuesday-Friday 10.30–5; Saturday 10.30–1; closed Sundays (and for two weeks in August).
Major collection of Chinese bronzes and ceramics. *228.* [CF]

Planetarium
By Baker Street Station, N.W.1. 11–6; Sundays 1–6.
see also Madame Tussauds. *222.* [BG]

Postal Museum *see* **National Postal Museum.**

Post Office Tower
Maple Street, W.1. Monday-Friday 9.30–9.30; Saturdays and Sundays 9–9.30.
580-foot telecommunication tower with restaurant. [BG]

Prince Henry's Room
17 Fleet Street, E.C.4. Weekdays 1.45–5 (Saturdays to 4.30).
Jacobean plaster and timber work of *c.* 1610, over a gateway to the Temple: named after King James I's son. Good plaster work in interior. *61, 91.* [DG]

Public Record Office
Chancery Lane, W.C.2. Museum, 1–4 Monday to Friday only.
Established 1838 for the National Archives: the present buildings, begun by Pennethorne, date from 1851 on. The Museum is housed in the remains of the medieval Rolls chapel (effigy of Dr Young, d. 1516, attrib. to Torrigiani: statue of George I, by L. Delvaux). Official and other documents from Domesday book on; holographs of Chaucer, Shakespeare, Milton, Wellington, Nelson, etc. *226.* [DG]

Queen's Chapel *see* **Marlborough House.**

Queen's Gallery
Buckingham Palace, Buckingham Palace Road, S.W.1. Tuesdays-Saturday. 11–5; Sunday 2–5, closed Mondays.
Exhibition gallery for changing selections from the Royal Collections of works of art. *188-9.* [BH]

Roman Bath
5 Strand Lane, W.C.2. 10–12.30; closed Sundays.
Dubiously Roman, perhaps Tudor. [CG].

Rotunda Museum *see* **Artillery Museum.**

Royal Academy of Arts
Burlington House, Piccadilly, W.1. 10–6; Sundays 2–6.
The Academy was founded by Royal Charter in 1768; moved from

Somerset House via the National Gallery in 1868, into a building remodelled by Sydney Smirke on Colen Campbell's former structure for Lord Burlington of 1715/16. Parts of this survive inside, decorations by S. Ricci, William Kent, B. West, A. Kauffmann. Summer exhibitions of work by current members and others; other important loan exhibitions. Its own permanent collection includes work by members (Reynolds, Gainsborough, Lawrence, Turner, Constable etc. etc.) also a great early marble tondo by Michelangelo. Its own collections can sometimes be visited. 120, 129, 131, 190-1. [BH]

Royal College of Art
Kensington Gore, S.W.7. By previous application only.
Fine building of 1962–64, by H.T. Cadbury-Brown, Sir Hugh Casson and R.Y. Goodden. Collection of good contemporary art. 208. [AH]

Royal College of Music
Prince Consort Road, S.W.7. Apply to the Registrar.
Building of 1883–84, by Sir A. Blomfield, in neo-French-Baronial manner. Stages warmly enthusiastic concerts by its students. Donaldson Museum of musical instruments: see also the portraits of musicians. 208, 219. [AH]

Royal College of Physicians
Albany Street, N.W.1. By previous arrangement only.
Rehoused in 1964 in a remarkable building by Denys Lasdun; panelled court room from Robert Hooke's 17th-century building in the City; collection of medical portraits (by Reynolds, Lawrence, Roubiliac, Edward Pierce, Epstein, etc.). Founded by Linacre (1460–1524); most recent premises (by Sir R. Smirke, 1824–27) form the west flank of Trafalgar Square, and are now incorporated in Canada House. 25, 147. [BF]

Royal College of Surgeons
Lincoln's Inn Fields, W.C.2. By previous arrangement only.
Building by Sir Charles Barry, 1835–36, much blown out by extensions and additions since. Houses the Hunterian Museum, based on the anatomical collections of John Hunter (d. 1793) but including paintings by Stubbs, etc., of exotic fauna. Good busts and medical portraits, and Holbein's cartoon of the Barber-Surgeons Company. 202. [CG]

Royal Geographical Society
1 Kensington Gore, S.W.7. Usually Monday to Friday 9.30–5.30, Saturday 9.30–1, but telephone to check.
Building (formerly Lowther Lodge)

by Norman Shaw, 1873. Geographical collections; maps, charts, relics of explorers. 206. [AH]

Royal Hospital, Chelsea *see* **Chelsea.**

Royal Mews
Buckingham Palace Road, S.W.1. Usually Wednesday and Thursdays, 2–4 (closed in Ascot week).
The Queen's horses, carriages and Coronation Coach. Dates from 1764; design modified by John Nash; sculpture in pediment, *Hercules and the Thracian Horses*, by W. Theed the Elder. [BH]

Royal Naval College *see* **Greenwich, Royal Naval Hospital.**

Royal Observatory *see* **Greenwich.**

Royal Society of Arts
6–8 John Adam Street, W.C.2. By prior appointment only. [CG]
Premises of the former Society for the Encouragement of Arts, Manufacturers and Commerce (founded 1754), built 1772–74, by Adam. Series of epic history paintings by James Barry (Lecture Room). 132.

St Bride's Church
Fleet Street, E.C.4. 9–4.30; closed Saturdays and Sundays.
Crypt museum, incorporating archaeological remains from Roman times on. [DG]

St John's Gate
St John's Square, E.C.1. By written application.
Gatehouse of 1504, surviving from the former Priory of St John of Jerusalem. Memorials of the Knights Hospitallers of St John of Jerusalem.

St Thomas's Operating Theatre
St Thomas Street, S.E.1. Monday, Wednesday, Friday, 12.30–2.30.
Unique survivor of 1821, in the former chapel of the Hospital which moved to Lambeth in 1868. [DH]

Science Museum
Exhibition Road, S.W.7. 10–6; Sundays 2.30–6.
Formerly part of the old South Kensington Museum, which split into the Victoria and Albert Museum and the Science Museum in 1909. The national collection of material illustrating the history and principles of science and technology in countless aspects, from the earliest times up to space exploration. 208, 217-18. [AH]

Sir John Soane's Museum
13 Lincoln's Inn Fields, W.C.2. 10–5; closed Sundays, Mondays, and all August.
Founded by Soane, the great architect, being the house he built for himself and the extraordinary collections

he brought together, and arranged, before his death in 1837. Architectural models, plans and drawings; sculpture (especially Flaxman), and remarkable paintings — Watteau, Canaletto, Turner, Hogarth (*The Rake's Progress*; *The Election*) and others. *155*, 201-2. [CG]

South London Art Gallery
Peckham Road, S.E.5. 10–6; Sundays 3–6.
Paintings, prints, and loan exhibitions.

Stock Exchange
Throgmorton Street, E.C.2. Monday to Friday, 10–3.15 (but check before going during re-building).
Public viewing gallery. 91, 170. [EG]

Syon House
Park Road, Isleworth, Middlesex. Check before going for opening times.
Originally a 15th-century convent (see the exterior), the interior entirely re-created by Robert Adam, 1762–69, a superlative example of his elegance. A family house of the Dukes of Northumberland; good furniture, fine portraits by Van Dyck, Lely, Reynolds, Gainsborough, etc. Gardens by 'Capability' Brown; celebrated glass conservatory by Charles Fowler. Modern horticultural centre. 133, *136*, 170, 229.

Tate Gallery
Millbank, S.W.1. 10–6; Sundays 2–6.
The national collections of: 1. British Painting; 2. British Sculpture from the 19th century on; 3. 20th-century art of all schools. Built (from a gift by Sir Henry Tate) by Sidney R.J. Smith, 1897. A major extension on the Westminster-side is planned for the 1970s. 170, 199, 208, 223-6, *223*, *227*, 229, *230*, *231*, *232*, *234*, *236*, *237*. [CI]

Thomas Coram Foundation for Children (Foundling Hospital Art Treasures)
40 Brunswick Square, W.C.1. Mondays and Fridays, 10–12, 2–4.
Collection of paintings (Hogarth, R. Wilson, Gainsborough etc.) started by Hogarth in aid of the now demolished Foundling Hospital; shown in the original panelled court-room transferred from the former building. 151, 190. [CF]

Tower of London
Tower Hill, E.C.3. Mid-March - October 9.30–5; Sundays 2–5; November-February 9.30–4; closed Sundays.
Keep, palace, prison and fortress. Building began by William the Conqueror 1067 (?); the White. Tower completed by 1097, including the fine Norman chapel of St John. The other towers, curtain walls, domestic housing, a slow agglomeration through the centuries. Besides the Tower itself, the National Museum of Armour: the Crown Jewels. 12, 15-18, *17*, *18*, *19*, *22*, *23*, 25, 62, 173, 222. [EH]

University College
Gower Street, W.C.1. By previous application.
Corinthian portico and dome, by William Wilkins, 1827–29; now one of the colleges of London University. Museum of Egyptian Archaeology; also collection of sculpture and drawings by John Flaxman, and works by past students of the Slade School. 179. [CF].

Victoria and Albert Museum
Cromwell Road, S.W.7. 10–6; Sundays 2.30–6.
Originally part of the old South Kensington Museum, 1851. Present building by Sir Aston Webb, 1899–1909; intended originally to improve, by example, the standard of design in applied arts, its collections have become immensely rich and world-famous; houses the national collections of Post-Classical Sculpture (excluding 20th century); of British miniatures, water-colours and English silversmith's work, also the National Art Library, but its range extends far beyond those: arms and armour, textiles, costume, furniture, glass, prints and drawings, music, ceramics from all over the world, oriental collections, etc. Paintings include a great representation of Constable; the Raphael cartoons, and a richly various selection of European masters and of the English 19th-century school. 32, 62, 133, 134, 138, 150, 188, 203, 206, 208, 214-15, *215*, *217*, 217, *219*, 220, 224, 229. [AH]

Wallace Collection
Hertford House, Manchester Square, W.1. 10–5; Sundays 2–5.
Formed as a private collection by the 3rd and 4th Marquesses of Hertford, and the latter's natural son, Sir Richard Wallace whose widow (d. 1897) bequeathed the collection and the house (built originally by the 4th Duke of Manchester, 1776–78) to the nation. Especially rich in French 18th-century art — Boucher, Fragonard, Watteau; furniture, Sèvres porcelain — but holds also major masterpieces from other schools (Titian, Canaletto; Rembrandt, Hals, de Hooch; Velasquez; Van Dyck and Rubens; Reynolds, Gainsborough, Bonington). Fine *objets*

d'art — bronzes, enamels, etc.; and a major collection of armour. 193, 222-3. [BG]

Wellcome Historical Medical Museum and Library
The Wellcome Building, 183 Euston Road, N.W.1. Weekdays 10–5; closed Sundays.
History of medicine from the earliest times. [BF]

Wellington Museum
Apsley House, Hyde Park Corner, W.1. 10–6; Sundays 2.30–6.
Branch of the Victoria and Albert Museum. Built 1771–8 by Robert Adam; altered by B. D. Wyatt. The home of the 1st Duke of Wellington, and known as No 1. London. Contains his collections, especially Spanish paintings (Velasquez, Goya); also works by Correggio, Rubens, de Hooch, and Canova. Wellington relics. 133, *138, 139,* 228-9, 231, 237. [BH]

Wesley's House and Chapel
47 City Road, E.C.1. 10–1; 2–4; closed Sundays.
Home (*c.* 1770) of John Wesley, founder of Methodism. Wesley relics. 231. [DF]

Westminster Hall *see* **Houses of Parliament.**

Whitechapel Art Gallery
80 Whitechapel High Street, E.1. 11–6; Sundays 2–6; closed Mondays.
Loan exhibitions, sometimes major, usually of contemporary art.

Whitehall *see* **Banqueting House**

Windsor Castle
Windsor, Berks. Very varying opening hours, and closed when the Queen is in residence.
The oldest royal palace still used as residence by the reigning monarch: much altered by Wyattville in the 19th century. St George's Chapel is one of the finest late Gothic buildings in England. The state-rooms include some of the cream of the Royal collection of paintings, especially Van Dycks. The Library holds a famous series of Old Master drawings (especially Holbein, Leonardo da Vinci) and of portrait miniatures. 41, *52, 54, 57, 59,* 188.

Zoo
Regent's Park, N.W.1. 9–7 or dusk; Winter, 10–dusk. 17, 54, 145, 218. [BF]

Historic Buildings and Churches

Adam Street, *Strand, W.C.2.* - *see* **The Adelphi.**

Adelphi, The, *W.C.2.* (Greek *adelphoi* - brothers) Speculative building programme by the Adam brothers, 1768–82. Terrace of houses on waterfront (demolished 1936) whose inhabitants included David Garrick, Thomas Hardy and Bernard Shaw. Little survives — hints of the original in 7-10 Adam Street. 131-2, *131,* 215. [CG]

Admiralty, Whitehall, *S.W.1.* Original building by Thomas Ripley, 1722–26, behind fine screen by Robert Adam, 1760. Where Nelson lay in state after Trafalgar (1805). Main building with cupolas built 1895–1907. 129. [CH]

Albany, *W.1.,* between · Sackville Street, Piccadilly and Burlington Gardens. Built by Sir William Chambers in 1770. Converted into suite of rooms for bachelor gentlemen; alterations by Henry Holland. Politicians and literary figures have resided there: George Canning, Edward Heath; Lord Byron, Lord Macaulay; Harold Nicolson and Graham Greene. Not open to the public. 129. [BF]

Albert Bridge, *S.W.3.* Links Chelsea with Battersea. By R. W. Ordish, opened 1873. One of the few remaining examples of the suspension bridge. 172, *172.* [BJ]

Albert Memorial, *Off Kensington Gore, S.W.7.* Colossal statue of Prince Albert (d. 1856) in rich'y elaborate shrine designed by Sir G. Gilbert Scott, finished 1872.

Aldwych, *W.C.2.* Crescent at eastern end of Strand, with the Aldwych and Strand theatres, separated by the Waldorf Hotel, on the north side. Part of the Kingsway development scheme, 1889–1906, connected with slum clearance. South side has pompously grand institutional buildings — Bush House (B.B.C. foreign services), India House, Australia House etc. A good statue of

Gladstone in the roadway at the east end. 118, 169, 174. [cg]

All Hallows Barking, *Great Tower Street, E.C.3.* Founded probably late 7th century (from Barking Abbey in Essex, hence its name). Includes Roman remains (undercroft), also Saxon and Norman ones: much rebuilt in the 14/15th centuries: the tower added 1658/59. Blitzed, and restored. Famous carved font cover of 1689, and good brasses. 10, *13,* 14, 26, *102,* 150, *154.* [eg]

All Saints Church, *Margaret Street, W.1.,* between Little Titchfield Street and Wells Street. Red brick building by William Butterfield, 1849–59, with harshly but brilliantly spectacular interior: reredos by William Dyce. 164. [cg]

All Souls, *Langham Place, W.1.,* northern limit of Regent Street. By John Nash, built 1822–24. Basilica plan with elegant classical features, originally a pivotal point in Nash's Regent Street plan. A victim of the Blitz, restored in 1951. 142, 145, *146.* [bg]

Apsley House - *see* list of Museums, (Wellington Museum).

Baker Street, Regent's Park, *W.1.,* (north) to Portman Square (south). A main traffic artery from the north. Originally laid out about 1790; mostly rebuilt, the few surviving houses (south of Marylebone Road) disguised by shop fronts. Attractive side streets. Arthur Conan Doyle's *Sherlock Holmes* had rooms here. 135. [bg]

Bank of England, *Threadneedle Street, E.C.2.* Occupies a 4 acre site bounded by Lothbury (north), Threadneedle Street (south) Bartholomew Lane (east) and Princes Street (west); a huge building seven storeys high with three more below ground level. Founded 1694, it gradually became the Government's Banker and was nationalized in 1946 when the capital stock was transferred to the Treasury. Largely reconstructed (1924–39) by Sir Herbert Baker; the only visible survivor of Sir John Soane's building of 1788–1833 is the massive external wall with its mock Corinthian columns. Sculptures include the *Old Lady of Threadneedle Street* (nickname for the Bank) in the pediment above the main entrance. The entrance hall with its colourfully attired attendants is accessible to visitors. A detachment of the Brigade of Guards have protected the building at night since 1780. Additional buildings, erected 1963, are located in Cheapside. [eg]

Bankside, *Southwark, S.E.I.* Runs close to the river by Hopton Street, with several 18th-century buildings (No. 61 of *c.* 1700 and the Almshouses of 1752) and Park Street, with the plaque marking the site of the Globe Theatre (q.v.). Dominated by the Bankside power station and lined with warehouses but a few 17th- and 18th-century houses and the rejuvenated Anchor Inn survive. Rose Alley and Bear Garden, two tributary streets, are reminders that amusement gardens and theatres (the Rose and the Hope) were here. 81. [dh]

Banqueting House, *Whitehall* - *see* list of Museums.

Barbican, *E.C.2.* An ambitious twin development scheme in the worst-bombed area of the City with commercial premises situated along London Wall and a residential section (by Chamberlin, Powell & Son) in the Barbican, just north of St Paul's. Imaginative piazzas and elevated pedestrian ways are some of the features: to be completed early 1970s. 185, *186.* [dg]

Battersea House - *see* list of Museums.

Bedford Row, *W.C.1.,* between Theobalds Road (north) and Sandland Street (south). An exceptionally wide street containing examples (Nos 36-43) of Dr Nicholas Barbon's speculative building activity but with early 18th-century modifications and restoration following bomb damage. Now mainly occupied by accountancy and law. 86. [dg]

Bedford Square, *Bloomsbury, W.C.1.,* north of Great Russell Street. Laid out *c.* 1775 by Thomas Leverton on land belonging to the Duke of Bedford; with all its original houses. Famous inhabitants have included Asquith, the Liberal Prime Minister, and Forbes Robertson, the actor. 135, [cg]

Belgrave Square, *Belgravia, S.W.1.* Principal square of the district of Belgravia, by Basevi (1825) with fine houses — Seaford House designed by Philip Hardwick. Former domicile of dukes, it is now given over to embassies and the headquarters of professional bodies: private citizens have mostly withdrawn to the old stable cottages (mews) behind the mansions. 152. [bh]

Belgravia, *S.W.1.* The district west of Grosvenor Place and Sloane Street, consisting of Belgrave Square, Eaton Square etc. Laid out from 1825 onwards by Thomas Cubitt with George Basevi. 152, 154, 175. [bh/bg]

Berkeley Square, *Mayfair, W.1.* Laid out 1739–47: almost entirely rebuilt except for Nos 44-46, west side (44, by W. Kent, with a spectacular interior: Lord Clive, great administrator in India, committed suicide at No. 45, 1774). Magnificent plane trees dating from about 1790: fountain (nymph with pitcher) by Alexander Munro, associated with the Pre-Raphaelite group. 120, *121.* [BH/BG]

Bermondsey, *S o u t h w a r k , S.E.1.* Bounded by the Thames from London Bridge to Rotherhithe and on the south by the Old Kent Road. Long association with leatherworking (Leather Market, opened 1833, and the National Leathersellers College); riverside largely made up of wharves. Two interesting churches: St Mary Magdalen, off Tower Bridge Road — good 17th-century woodwork and fragments from the Abbey established by the Cluniacs on this site in 1082; St James's, Spa Road/Jamaica Road junction — built 1827–29 by James Savage. 25. [DH]

Billingsgate, *Lower Thames Street, E.C.3.* Central fish marketing building of 1876.

Bishopsgate, *E.C.2.* Norton Folgate (north) to Cornhill (south). Since Roman times, the main road north out of London. The gate itself (demolished 1760) stood at the Camomile/Wormwood Street junction. The city end is largely composed of banks including the building of 1865 by John Gibson for the National Provincial; further north, the churches of St Ethelburga and St Botolph Bishopsgate, and the Bishopsgate Institute (music, lectures, and a reference library). 12, 19, 26, 218, *219.* [EG]

Blackfriars Bridge, *S.E.1.* It links Southwark with the City. First built 1760–69; the present structure, by Joseph Cubitt, 1865–9, was widened in 1908. 172. [DG/DH]

Bloomsbury, *W.C.1.* District east of Tottenham Court Road and north of New Oxford Street. Late 17th-century — mid-19th-century development of Russell estates (Dukes of Bedford). Several famous squares (Bloomsbury, Bedford, Tavistock, Russell, Gordon, Woburn), and terrace streets. Now dominated by the British Museum and the University of London. Associated in the first half of the 20th century with a group of writers and artists centred on Leonard and Virginia Woolf (Roger Fry, Duncan Grant, Lytton Strachey, E. M. Forster, etc.). 86, 135, 136, 152, 179, 201, 228. [CG]

Bond Street, *W.1.,* Oxford Street (north) to Piccadilly (south). The narrow, congested 'High Street of Mayfair' made up of two unequal halves, New and Old, meeting at the junction with Burlington Gardens (q.v.). Never distinguished for its architecture but renowned for its highly fashionable shops, art dealers and Sotheby's, the book and fine art auction house. Two modern buildings, Time and Life and the Westbury Hotel, both by Michael Rosenauer — on opposite corners of the Bruton Street/Conduit Street junction. 90, 237. [BG/BH]

Brompton Oratory, *S.W.3.* London Oratory of St Philip Neri, Brompton Road. Very fashionable Roman Catholic Church in the Italian baroque style by Herbert Gribble, 1884, thirty years after the Order, founded in the 16th century, had been introduced to England by Cardinal Newman. Dome added 1896. Extensive use of marble, much of it imported in the form of statuary — the apostles by Mazzuoli, once in Siena Cathedral. 165. [AI]

Buckingham Palace, *S.W.1.,* west end of The Mall. Originally built as the home of the Duke of Buckingham, it has been the property of the Crown since 1762. Remodelled by John Nash for George IV in 1824, with later additions; façade reconstructed by Sir Aston Webb 1913. Became permanent London residence of the Sovereign with Queen Victoria in 1837. Queen's Gallery and Royal Mews — *see* list of Museums. 48, 146-7, 152, 188. [BH]

Buckingham Palace Gardens, *S.W.1.,* between Constitution Hill (north), Grosvenor Place (west) and the Royal Mews etc. (south). A triangular demesne of 40 acres, the private gardens of the monarch, where Royal garden parties are held in the summer — for invited guests only. 50, *50.* [CH]

Buckingham Street, *W.C.2.,* off John Adam Street, Strand. With its neighbour Villiers Street, named after George Villiers, Duke of Buckingham who rebuilt York House on this site. A few pleasing old houses with door hoods, Nos 17 and 18; Pepys lived 1679–85 at No. 12 (somewhat altered since his residency) and subsequently for fifteen years in a house on the site of No. 14. Other residents have included Charles Dickens and the painters William Etty and Clarkson Stanfield. 85. [CH]

Bucklersbury House, *Queen Victoria Street, E.C.4.* - *see* **Temple of Mithras.**

Burlington Arcade, *W.1.,* between Burlington Gardens and Piccadilly. A privately owned arcade of 72 exclusive shops built by Samuel Ware in 1819. The first of its kind in England. It is policed by two beadles — ex-soldiers of the 10th Hussars. 138, *145.* [BH]

Burlington Gardens, *W.1.,* between Bond Street (west) and Savile Row (east). On the south side are the north entrance to Albany (q.v.); the building in ornate Italian style built by Sir James Pennethorne in 1869 as the first headquarters of London University now housing British Museum Ethnological Display and north entrance Burlington Arcade (q.v.). North, at the corner with Savile Row, is a building by Giacomo Leoni of 1721, formerly Queensbury House, subsequently altered and now a bank. 120, 138, 201. [BG]

Burlington House, - *see* list of Museums, (Royal Academy of Arts).

Carlton House Terrace, *S.W.1.,* parallel to Pall Mall. Built by Nash in 1827–32, once housing the aristocracy, now mainly government departments, the Royal Society, etc. Near the site of Carlton House — now marked by the Duke of York's column at the head of a wide flight of steps which sweep on to The Mall. 143, 145, 146, *149,* 150, 199. [CH]

Carlyle's House - *see* list of Museums.

Cavendish Square, *W.1.,* between Henrietta Place and Wigmore Street. Laid out *c.* 1720 by John Prince. Few houses still survive, four of which, on the north side, now form the Convent of the Holy Child — an Epstein *Madonna and Child* above the archway. Noted residents have included Lord Nelson (No. 5) and Lord Asquith (No. 20). A statue of Lord George Cavendish Bentinck, the politician, stands among the trees in the Square. 121, 237. [BG]

Cenotaph, The, *Whitehall, S.W.1.* Monument designed, 1919–20, by Sir Edwin Lutyens in memory of those who fell in the 1914–18 war. An inscription 'To the Glorious Dead' was added after the Second World War. Annual Remembrance service in November attended by the Sovereign. A simple but very subtly designed stele (it has neither vertical nor horizontal lines). 176. [CH]

Chancery Lane, *W.C.2.,* between Holborn and Fleet Street. Thoroughfare with law stationers, patent agents etc. Its principal buildings are the Public Record Office and opposite, the Law Society, founded 1827, built by Lewis Vulliamy in 1831, which controls the training of

articled clerks and the admission of solicitors: a Tudor gateway gives on to Lincoln's Inn. 92. [DG]

Charing Cross, *S.W.1.,* junction of Whitehall and Trafalgar Square. The site of the cross, erected in 1291 by Edward I' marking the last stage of the funeral procession of his wife, Queen Eleanor, to Westminster Abbey; removed in 1647. Site occupied since 1675 by equestrian statue of Charles I by Le Sueur. The official centre of London for mileage measurements. 148, 214. [CH]

Charing Cross Road, *W.C.2.* St Giles Circus (north) to St Martin's Place (south). Unprepossessing thoroughfare, part of the slum clearance scheme of the 19th century, opened 1887. Largely bookshops and theatres. 148, 152, 170, 220. [CG]

Charing Cross Station, *S t r a n d , W.C.2.,* south side. One of the termini of the Southern Region, British Railways, built in 1864 on the site of Hungerford Market, by Sir John Hawkshaw. Hotel above the station designed by E. M. Barry (the top storey is a recent addition) who also designed the version of the Eleanor Cross in the forecourt (1865) [CH].

Charlton House - *see* list of Museums.

Charterhouse - *see* list of Museums.

Chelsea, *S.W.3.,* district lying between Kensington (north) and the river Thames. A fashionable out-of-town residential area in the 17th and 18th centuries, it has retained many of its interesting streets, old houses and small town atmosphere. Long association with artists and authors, particularly since the 18th century — Turner and Whistler; Thomas Carlyle, Tobias Smollett and Oscar Wilde all resided there. An attractive riverside promenade — Chelsea Embankment (q.v.) passing Chelsea Hospital (*see* list of Museums). 3, 150, 152, 175, *175,* 179, 191, 232.

Chelsea Embankment, *S.W.3.,* between Battersea Bridge and Chelsea Bridge. Laid out in 1874 by Sir Joseph Bazalgette. This tree-lined thoroughfare is bordered on the north side by a series of gardens; the Physic Garden (private) — a herb garden since 1673 — and those belonging to the Royal Hospital, in which is held the annual Chelsea Flower Show. 19, 172. [AI/BI]

Chelsea Old Church, *Chelsea Embankment, S.W.3.* Its origins date back to the 12th century though it has seen much rebuilding. Almost destroyed by a land mine in 1941, the south chapel, rebuilt in 1528 by

Sir Thomas More, survived, as did two Renaissance capitals. Restoration followed — the nave and tower in their former 17th-century style — and the church was reconsecrated in 1958. Many interesting monuments and tombs, including that of Sir Thomas More's first wife. 63. [BI]

Chelsea Royal Hospital - *see* list of Museums.

Chiswick House - *see* list of Museums.

Christchurch, *Spitalfields. Commercial Street, E.1.* By Hawksmoor, 1723–29. Spectacular tower and spire; under restoration. *118,* 119. [EG]

Christie's, *King Street, St James's, S.W.1.* Famous auction rooms, opened in 1766, specializing in works of art — books, furniture and pictures. Premises reconstructed after destruction by bombing. 190. [BH]

Church Row, *Hampstead, N.W.3.* Near Hampstead Underground Station, from Heath Row to St John's Church (1743; Constable is buried here). Fine red brick 18th-century houses. 136.

City Companies - *see* **Livery Companies, City.**

City Guilds - *see* **Livery Companies, City.**

City of London, *E.C.4.* The original 'Square Mile' of London as defined by the Roman wall, north of the Thames from the Tower of London but west beyond Ludgate to Temple Bar. London's financial and commercial centre, with the Bank of England, Stock Exchange, Lloyds, etc. Burnt out in 1666, rebuilt especially by Sir Christopher Wren (churches and St Paul's Cathedral); includes notably the halls of the old livery companies (Guilds), the Guildhall, and the Lord Mayor's Mansion House. 15, 19, 22-9, 60-1, 62-3, 72, 81-5, 90-112, *98,* 114, 117, 129, 135, 148, 151, 152, 164, 169, 170, 178, 179, 185, 188, 232.

Cleopatra's Needle, *Victoria Embankment, S.W.1.,* east of Charing Cross Underground Station. Pink inscribed Egyptian granite obelisk. From Heliopolis, *c.* 1500 B.C. Presented by Egypt, and set up in 1878. (No real connection with Cleopatra; its pair is in Central Park, New York.) [CH]

Cloth Fair, *E.C.1.,* off Smithfield, north of St Bartholomew the Great. Name derived from the former activity of the area; contains one interesting building (Nos 41-2), a possible survivor of the Great Fire. 84. [DG]

College of Arms, *Queen Victoria Street, E.C.4.* Handsome late 17th-century red brick building, headquarters of the English Heralds. Important genealogical and heraldic archive and library; establishes coats of arms and undertakes genealogical research (for a fee). 93. [DG]

Commonwealth Institute - *see* list of Museums.

Cooper's Row, *E.C.3.,* north of Trinity Square. Interesting Roman and medieval remains of the Old City Wall to be seen behind Midland House. 12. [EG]

Corn Exchange, *Mark Lane, E.C.3.* Founded 1750, rebuilt 1880; a victim of the Blitz, it was re-opened in 1953. 129. [EG]

Courtauld Institute Galleries, *Woburn Square* - *see* list of Museums.

Courtauld Institute (Home House), *Portman Square,* - *see* list of Museums.

Covent Garden, *W.C.2.,* originally Convent Garden, when the land belonged to Westminster Abbey. Laid out by Inigo Jones for the fourth Earl of Bedford in 1631–35 as a residential quarter — a square enclosed on the north and east by terraced houses with arcades (only a hint of which remains) and St Paul's church (q.v.) on the west side. 70-2, 90-1, 92, 135, 148. [CG]

Covent Garden Market, *W.C.2.* The market, established by the Duke of Bedford in 1661 under royal charter, grew into the principal market in London for flowers, fruit and vegetables. Most activity is in the morning — from about 6 a.m. Buildings in the centre by Charles Fowler, 1831–33. Scheduled to move to Nine Elms in 1973 when the area will be redeveloped. 71, 174. [GC]

Covent Garden Theatre, *W.C.2.* Correct name Royal Opera House; designed by Edward M. Barry in 1856–58, together with the glass-domed Floral Hall of the Market. World-famous for its opera and ballet companies. Its two predecessors were destroyed by fire, 1808 and 1856. The present building was planned especially for Italian opera. 174. [CG]

Crosby Hall - *see* list of Museums.

Crystal Palace. A revolutionary building in glass and iron designed by Sir Joseph Paxton for the Great Exhibition in Hyde Park, 1851. Later transferred to Sydenham, and there destroyed by fire in 1936. *169,* 170, 202.

Cutty Sark, *Greenwich* - *see* list of Museums (Greenwich).

Dean's Yard and **Little Dean's Yard,** *S.W.1.,* precinct of Westminster Abbey, off Broad Sanctuary. Dean's Yard has buildings of Westminster School (q.v.) including Ashburnham House, fine 17th century (*c.* 1662); also Church House (1935–39, by Sir H. Baker) at the far end. 46. [CH]

Design Centre, *Haymarket* - *see* list of Museums.

Dickens's House - *see* list of Museums.

H.M.S. Discovery - *see* list of Museums.

Dover House, *Whitehall, S.W.1.* Built by James Paine in 1755, portico by Henry Holland added in 1787. Now the Scottish Office. 122. [CH]

Downing Street, *Whitehall, S.W.1.* Named after its 17th-century builder, Sir George Downing. No. 10, residence of the Prime Minister since 1732, front rebuilt 1766–74; interiors of 10 and 11 (official residence of the Chancellor of the Exchequer) remodelled by Sir John Soane 1825 and Raymond Erith 1960–64 when No. 12, another Government office, was rebuilt. Demolition work revealed remains of the Palace of Whitehall, as well as an earlier, Saxon, structure and pottery of Roman and Tudor times. 129. [CH]

Drury Lane Theatre (Theatre Royal, Drury Lane), *Catherine Street, W.C.2., off Aldwych.* The fourth theatre on this site, the first in 1663 being rebuilt in 1674 by Wren, after a fire. The present building, 1809–12, by Benjamin Wyatt, with colonnade in Russell Street added by Samuel Beazley in 1831/2. Auditorium reconstructed in 1922, but some of Wyatt's interior survives — the only example of Georgian theatre interior in London. 71, 92, 96, 174. [CG]

Eltham Palace - *see* list of Museums.

Eton College. The most famous of English 'public' schools, near Windsor Castle. Fine chapel with important English late 15th century grisaille decorations. 57.

Fenton House - *see* list of Museums.

Fitzroy Square, *W.1.* Between the north end of Charlotte Street/Fitzroy Street and Euston Road. East and south sides by R. Adam 1790–94 (war-damaged and restored): the rest of 1825–29. 133. [BG]

Fleet Street, *E.C.4.,* busy thoroughfare running from Temple Bar to Ludgate Circus; name derives from the Fleet, one of London's hidden rivers — covered over in 1765. Associated with printing since the early 16th century and the traditional home of the English press — the offices of several newspapers remain,

Daily Telegraph and Daily Express. Access to two of the Inns of Court, the Inner and Middle Temple on the south side which also has the oldest bank in London, Child's (established 1671) — royalty (Charles II) and writers (Samuel Pepys) have been among its customers; also St Bride's, the parish church of the Press. As well as newspaper offices, the north side has the church of St Dunstan-in-the-West. 61, 90, 91, *91,* 92, 148, 149, 174, 232. [DG]

Foreign Office, *Parliament Street, Whitehall, S.W.1.* Occupies the western section of a large block of buildings designed by Sir Gilbert Scott in 1873. A branch of it is in a modern building of 1966 by Farmer and Dark near Vauxhall Bridge approach. 154, 161. [CH]

Foundling Hospital - *see* list of Museums (Thomas Coram Foundation).

Globe Theatre, *Bankside, Southwark, S.E.1.* Erected by Richard and Cuthbert Burbage in the late 1590s — destroyed by fire in 1613. Shakespeare appeared there as actor and playwright. The site is buried in the foundations of Messrs Courage and Barclay's brewery in Park Street, where a plaque on the wall records its existence. 62. [DH]

Globe Theatre, *Shaftesbury Avenue, W.1.* Built 1906. Good Edwardian interior. 175. [CG]

Goodwood House, *Chichester.* Home of the Dukes of Richmond.

Gray's Inn, *W.C.1.,* between High Holborn and Theobald's Road, west of Gray's Inn Road. One of the Inns of Court (q.v.). Much bomb-damaged, but restored. Famous gardens and 16th-century Great Hall (first performance there of Shakespeare's *Comedy of Errors,* 1594). Famous former members ('benchers') include Sir Francis Bacon (modern statue by F. W. Pomeroy); Thomas Cromwell; Archbishop Laud; Macaulay; etc. *88,* 92. [DG]

Great Queen Street, *W.C.2.* between Long Acre and Lincoln's Inn Fields. Built about 1640 in honour of Queen Henrietta Maria, wife of King Charles I; hints of its former status are given by the upper storeys of some houses; now dominated by the Freemasons' Hall, rebuilt 1927–33 as a war memorial to masons. [CG]

Green Park, *S.W.1.,* between Piccadilly (north east), Queen's Walk (east) and Constitution Hill (south). Added by Charles II to the Royal Parks, including a long-vanished 'ice-house'. 36 acres. 50, 122. [BH]

Greenwich - *see* list of Museums.

Grosvenor Square, *Mayfair W.1.,* (north west). Originally laid out *c.* 1720–25: now dominated by the new American Embassy (by E. Saarinen, 1958–61; west side). The whole area is sometimes referred to as 'Little America', the connection starting with John Adams, who was at No. 9 (one of the few old houses remaining) in 1785. Statue of Franklin D. Roosevelt (by Reid Dick, 1948) in the gardens. 120-1. [BG]

Guildhall - *see* list of Museums.

Gunnersbury Park - *see* list of Museums.

Guy's Hospital, *St Thomas Street, Southwark, S.E.1.* Founded 1721 by Thomas Guy (statues in the forecourt, by Scheemakers, and the chapel, by Bacon); Keats was at the Medical School 1814–16. 151. [EH]

Gwydyr House, *Whitehall, S.W.1.* Built by John Marquand in 1772, adjoins the Banqueting Hall. A survivor of the 18th-century mansions built on the site of the burned-out Palace of Whitehall. 122. [CH]

Ham House - *see* list of Museums.

Hampstead, *N.W.3.* Village on the hills, by Hampstead Heath, north of London; popular from the 18th century on as retreat for many writers and artists (Keats, Constable, Romney, Du Maurier, Burne-Jones, etc.). Some fine and grand old houses (Kenwood, Fenton House, etc.), and picturesque roads (Church Row, Flask Walk, Well Walk, the Mount, etc.). To the north Hampstead Garden Suburb is an early and influential example of suburban planning, laid out by Sir Raymond Unwin from 1907. 11, 133, 176, 178, 229, 232.

Hampton Court Palace - *see* list of Museums.

Hanover Square, *Mayfair, W.1.* (north east). Laid out *c.* 1717: largely rebuilt but the four-storeyed No. 24 in grey and red brick survives as an example of the original scheme. Garden with plane trees and a large bronze statue of William Pitt the younger by Sir Francis Chantrey erected 1831. The church — St George's (q.v.) — is off the south side in St George's Street. 120. [BG]

Harley Street, *W.1.,* between Marylebone Road (north) and Cavendish Square (south). One of the two famous streets housing prosperous medical specialists (the other being Wimpole Street,). J. M. W. Turner, the artist, lived at No. 64 (1803–12); Queen's College founded 1848, the oldest women's college in England, further down the street now encompasses No. 47, once the home of Florence Nightingale. 121. [BG]

Haymarket, *S.W.1.* From Piccadilly to Pall Mall. Originally the name was literal. Includes (east side) the Design Centre, and Nash's Haymarket Theatre (1820, on the site of a theatre founded 1720) with columned portico; west side, Pall Mall Corner, New Zealand House. 138, 145. [CH]

Highgate, *N. 6, N. 19.* North London. Suburb on the twin hill to Hampstead, similarly offering fine views over London and likewise retaining many attractive houses of the 18th century and earlier, especially on Highgate Hill (Cromwell House, *c.* 1637), and in the The Grove. It also has an open space — Waterlow Park and there is easy access to Kenwood House (*see* list of Museums). The cemetery (Swain's Lane) has the grave of Karl Marx; in St Michael's Church (by Lewis Vulliamy, 1832), the remains of Samuel Taylor Coleridge. 11, 170, 176.

Hogarth's House - *see* list of Museums.

Holborn, *W.C.1. & E.C.1.* Area north of Oxford Street to Euston and King's Cross Road, including Bloomsbury. High Holborn is a main east/west traffic artery from the City. 57, 62, *62,* 86, 92, 138, 168, 237.

Holland House - *see* list of Museums.

House of St Barnabas - *see* list of Museums.

Houses of Parliament - *see* list of Museums.

Hyde Park and **Kensington Gardens,** 636 acres, between Bayswater Road (north), Park Lane (east) Knightsbridge Road and Kensington Gore (south) and Kensington Palace (west). Hyde Park was originally part of Henry VIII's hunting reserve, and later the great fashionable venue for riding (Rotten Row). Speaker's Corner, the famous forum for London free speech is at the north-east corner (by Marble Arch). A fine bridge (by Rennie, 1826–28) over the large lake, the Serpentine (boating and swimming in summer) marks the transition into Kensington Gardens (once the grounds of Kensington Palace, q.v.), slightly more formal in character. Statuary includes a gigantic *Achilles* by Sir R. Westmacott, commemorating Wellington's victories, 1822, and *Byron,* by R. C. Belt (both near Hyde Park Corner); *Rima,* by Epstein, 1925, (memorial to W. H. Hudson) in a bird sanctuary north of the Serpentine; *Peter Pan,* by Sir G. Frampton; *Physical Energy* by G. F. Watts (both in Kensington Gardens); and the *Albert Memorial* (q.v.). A small gallery near the lake

(Serpentine Gallery) opened in 1970, offering facilities for art exhibitions by students and experimental artists. 51, 117, 147, 203, 220, 235, 237. [AH]

Imperial College of Science and Technology, *S.W.7.*, between Prince Consort Road and Imperial Institute Road, Queen's Gate. Now part of the University of London; laid out by Sir Aston Webb from 1909, but largely rebuilt since 1945, though retaining a fine campanile-like tower by T. E. Colcutt. 208, 217. [AH]

Inner Temple - *see* **Inns of Court,** and **Temple.**

Inns of Court, *W.C.2.* The medieval colleges of lawyers, through which all had to pass who wished to qualify for the legal profession; developed into a sequence of courts, gardens, and alleys running north from the Victoria Embankment (by Temple Station) to Theobalds Road. All badly blitzed but well-restored. The survivors are the Temple (Inner and Middle); Lincoln's Inn; Gray's Inn, q.q.v. 61, 91-2. [CG]

Iveagh Bequest, *Kenwood* - *see* list of Museums.

Jewel Tower - *see* list of Museums.

John Adam Street - *see* list of Museums (Royal Society of Arts).

Dr Johnson's House - *see* list of Museums.

Keats's House - *see* list of Museums.

Kensington, Royal borough bounded by Notting Hill (north), Chelsea (south) and Belgravia (east). Founded as a residential district: some fine squares (Kensington and Edwardes) south of the High Street and some charming streets (Bedford) north, off Church Street. The High Street, well known for its departmental stores also embraces, further west, the Commonwealth Institute (*see* list of Museums). 176, 231.

Kensington Gardens - *see* **Hyde Park.**

Kensington Palace - *see* list of Museums.

Kenwood House - *see* list of Museums (Iveagh Bequest).

Kew Gardens (Royal Botanical Gardens). On the south Thames bank, by Kew Bridge. 300 acres of magnificent botanical gardens, founded by Princess Augusta, 1759. Orangery and Pagoda by Sir William Chambers, 1760; important iron and glass Palm House by Decimus Burton, 1860. Includes Kew Palace (*see* list of Museums). 134, *134,* 170.

King Street, *E.C.2.* With Queen Street the only new roads in the City built after the Great Fire. 84. [EG]

King's College, *W.C.2.* The eastern range of Somerset House (q.v.), Strand; founded 1828, built by Sir Robert Smirke, 1829–35. A large modern extension added in the 1960s. Incorporated in the University of London q.v. 131. [EG]

King's Cross Station, *N.W.1.* By junction of Euston Road and Gray's Inn Road. Main line terminus for the north-east. Designed by Lewis Cubitt, 1852; fine functional façade. 161. [CF]

Knightsbridge, *S.W.1.* South of Hyde Park, between Hyde Park Corner and Kensington. Fashionable residential area, developed from a village in the early 19th century. Some pretty streets and squares (Montpellier, etc.), and celebrated department stores (Harrods, with famous *art nouveau* Meat Hall; Harvey Nichols, etc.). 174, 220. [AH/BH]

Lambeth Palace - *see* list of Museums.

Lancaster House - *see* list of Museums.

Law Courts (Royal Courts of Justice), *W.C.2.,* Strand. Built 1874–82 to the designs of G. E. Street. [DG]

Leadenhall Market. *Leadenhall Place, E.C.3.,* off Lime Street, City. Established in the 14th century as a poultry market. The present structure of wood and glass dates from 1881 when Roman remains including a basilica (about 500 feet long) were discovered. 12, 169. [EG]

Leadenhall Street, *E.C.3.* Cornhill to Fenchurch Street. Largely made up of banks, shipping company offices, and Lloyds (occupying the 20th-century buildings linked by a bridge across Lime Street). [EG]

Leicester Square, *W.C.2.,* joined to Piccadilly Circus by Coventry Street. Laid out in the 17th century, with Leicester House (Sidney family) on the north side. No old houses remain, and it is a centre for cinemas and inexpensive eating, though Hogarth and Reynolds both once lived here. In the centre, a copy of Scheemaker's statue (Westminster Abbey) of Shakespeare. 175. [CG]

Leighton House - *see* list of Museums.

Lincoln's Inn, *W.C.2.,* b e t w e e n Strand and High Holborn, west of Chancery Lane. One of the Inns of Court (q.v.). 15th-19th century courts, gateways and gardens. Gatehouse, 1518; Hall, 1490–92 (with Hogarth's *St Paul before Felix*). Associated with Sir Thomas More, Donne, and many other celebrities. Dickensian atmosphere. *80, 92,* 92, 176. [CG]

Lincoln's Inn Fields, *W.C.2.,* between Kingsway and Lincoln's Inn. Laid out in the 17th century, a very large square, rather than 'fields'. South side: Royal College of Surgeons, west side, Nos 59–60, Lindsey House, by Inigo Jones; north side, No. 13, Sir John Soane's Museum (*see* list of Museums). 70, 72, 92, 151, 155, 201, 202. [CG]

Lindsey House, - *see* **Lincoln's Inn Fields.**

Livery Companies, City. The survivors of the old medieval guilds, now mainly devoted to charitable purposes. There are over ninety, and their members, the liverymen, elect the Lord Mayor. Their central hall is the Guildhall (*see* list of Museums); many of their own halls were burned in 1666 or destroyed in 1940/44. Of the survivors, the Apothecaries Hall (Blackfriars Lane; 17th century and later; Watermen's Hall (16 St Mary-at-Hill; Adamish, from *c.* 1790); Skinner's Hall (Dowgate Hill; by W. Jupp, 1790); Goldsmiths' Hall (Foster Lane; by P. Hardwick, 1829–35), are particularly rewarding, but the Halls are very rarely opened to the public (enquire at City of London Information Centre, St Paul's Churchyard, E.C.4). 19, 22, 73, *77,* 93–4, *95,* 188.

Lloyds. *Leadenhall Street and Lime Street, E.C.3.* Most famous of insurance underwriters, developed from a 17th-century coffee-house run by Edward Lloyd (originally in Lombard Street). Main 'Room' with the Lutine bell; Nelson relics. (Entry only through introduction by a member.)

London Bridge, connects the City with Southwark over the Thames. Believed to be close to the site of the original Roman bridge, which was presumably wooden: the first stone bridge was built 1176–1209 slightly downstream from the present bridge: its roadway lined with houses (demolished about 1760) was a famous sight and it was the only bridge over London Thames till 1749: pulled down in 1832, replaced by a bridge by Rennie, which was in turn demolished in 1968/70 (sold to the U.S.A.) and replaced by a bridge by King and Brown, finished in 1971. 10, 26, 30, 90, 105, 170, 171–2, 230. [EH]

London University, *W.C.1.* Properly University of London. Received its royal charter only in 1836, but incorporates earlier colleges (University, Kings, q.q.v.) and has since become the largest university in Great Britain. Its original central buildings

are in Burlington Gardens, W.1 (by Sir W. Pennethorne, 1869), but it now centres on the Senate House (by Charles Holden, 1933, including the Library), north of the British Museum, and has absorbed a great deal of northern Bloomsbury. Its colleges are scattered all over London from Queen Mary College in the East End to Royal Holloway College (q.v.) at Egham in the west. *See also* Courtauld Institute of Fine Art; Percival David Foundation (*see* list of Museums); Warburg Institute. 131, 133, 169, 179, 201, 208, 228. [CG]

London Wall, *E.C.2.* Now specifically the very modern road (Route 11) between Aldersgate, Moorgate and Old Broad Street, in part the southern (commercial) development of the post-war Barbican (q.v.) scheme. Originally the Roman wall, built in the 2nd century AD, that first defined London; constantly patched and rebuilt through to the 15th century. The old gates (all long demolished) are recorded in street names (Aldgate, Moorgate, Aldersgate, Ludgate, etc.). Surviving fragments of the wall can be seen in the Tower of London; at Tower Hill, Cooper's Row, St Alphage Churchyard, etc. *9,* 12, 23, 26, *185,* 185, 226. [OH/EH]

Lord North Street, *S.W.1.* - *see* **Smith Square.**

Lowndes Square, *S.W.1.,* off Knightsbridge. Early Victorian square (1836–49), showing Georgian style veering (Jacobean motifs) to the Victorian. 152. [BH]

Mall, The, *S.W.1.* From Trafalgar Square to Buckingham Palace through St James's Park. Laid out anew (by Sir Aston Webb, 1910), including Admiralty Arch and the Queen Victoria Memorial. Flanked on the north by Carlton House Terrace, St James's Palace and Clarence House (residence of the Queen Mother). 143, 146. [BH/CH]

Manchester Square. In the angle of the junction of Baker Street and Wigmore Street. Built 1776–78. The Wallace Collection, Hertford House, is on the west side. 135, 223. [BG]

Mansion House - *see* list of Museums.

Marble Arch, *W.1.* At western end of Oxford Street. Designed by Decimus Burton (not Nash) in 1828 as the main gate to Buckingham Palace but erected on its present site in 1851. Splendid wrought iron gates; sculpture reliefs by E. H. Baily and R. Westmacott. 147. [BG]

Marble Hill House - *see* list of Museums.

Marlborough House - *see* list of Museums.

Mayfair. The area bounded by Piccadilly, Park Lane, Oxford Street, and Regent Street. Original May Fair (Shepherd Market, southwest part towards Hyde Park Corner), was suppressed in George III's reign. Mayfair was developed through the 18th century by various landowners, about some of London's most famous squares (Berkeley, Hanover, Grosvenor), and its name has become synonymous with high fashion and quality shopping. Bond Street (q.v.) is its main north/south axis. 90, 120–1, 170, 201. [BG]

Middle Temple - *see* **Inns of Court** and **Temple.**

Monument - *see* list of Museums.

National Film Theatre, *South Bank, S.E.I.* First opened in 1951 but rebuilt on present site in 1957. Designed by architects of the L.C.C.: Holds 500; members only. 185. [DH]

National Theatre, *South Bank, S.E.I.* Designed by Denys Lasdun, this new theatre, replacing the Old Vic, will have two auditoria and is expected to open in 1973.

Nelson's Column, *Trafalgar Square, S.W.1.* Designed by William Railton, 1843. Fluted Corinthian column, supporting E. H. Baily's statue of Nelson. Height of column 167ft 6½ ins; statue 17ft 4½ ins. Round the pedestal are four bronze reliefs. At the base 4 bronze lions by Sir Edwin Landseer were added later. 148, 189. [CH]

New Scotland Yard. *Victoria Embankment, S.W.1.,* by Westminster Bridge. Former headquarters of the London Police (now in Victoria Street); baronial style building by Norman Shaw, begun 1888. Threatened with demolition. 175. [CH]

Nine Elms. South of the river at Vauxhall, original site of terminus of the London and S. W. Railway (moved to Waterloo, 1848); the Covent Garden Market is scheduled to move here in 1973. 71.

Nonsuch Palace, *Surrey.* One of Henry VIII's palaces, built on the ruins of Cuddington village, 1538–47. It later fell into disrepair and its demolition began in 1682. 63.

Old Bailey (Central Criminal Court), *E.C.4.,* corner of Newgate Street and Old Bailey, built 1902–07, by E. W. Mountford on the site of old Newgate Prison. [DG]

Osterley Park House - *see* list of Museums.

Oxford Circus, *W.1.* At the crossing of Regent Street and Oxford Street. Originally by John Nash, in his Regent Street (q.v.) development but entirely rebuilt. 145. [BG]

Oxford Street, *W.1.,* between Marble Arch and St Giles Circus, thence continued east by New Oxford Street. A main route from the City westward (also once to Tyburn, where famous gallows long stood at the north-east corner of Hyde Park); by the early 19th century had replaced Cheapside as main shopping street; now the home of great department stores (Selfridge's etc.) and centres for mass shopping. A fine survivor, Derby House (by R. Edwin, 1773; Adam-style interiors) in Stratford Place (near Selfridge's). 121, 135, 139, 168, *168,* 170, 174, 201. [BG/CG]

Paddington (Little Venice). Developed from a country village from 1820, about the Paddington Canal (1795–1801) and Paddington Station, main line terminus from the west (begun 1850; by P. C. Hardwick, 1850–52). Southern areas contain good examples of square-and-crescent planning, in rivalry with Belgravia and once known as 'Tyburnia'. 'Little Venice' (round Blomfield Road and Warwick Avenue) is a charming canalside area of stucco houses much loved by artists and writers. 176.

Palace of Westminster - *see* list of Museums (Houses of Parliament).

Palace of Whitehall, *S.W.1.* Cardinal Wolsey's palace (York House) on the Thames was taken over by Henry VIII, and transformed into Whitehall Palace. This was the main London residence for Tudor and Stuart Kings till destroyed by fire in 1698. The site was then let out, and developed gradually into the modern Whitehall (q.v.). The only surviving parts are Inigo Jones's Banqueting House, and Henry VIII's Wine Cellar (*see* list of Museums). 31–2, 48, 54, *55,* 57, 58, 69, 114, 116, 122, 129, 188. [CH]

Pall Mall, *S.W.1.,* between Trafalgar Square and St James's Street. The name derives from a French ball game, pronounced 'pell mell', played here in the early part of the 17th century. The most fashionable of St James's streets in the 17th and 18th centuries; Thomas Gainsborough, Nell Gwynn and the Duchess of Marlborough lived here. Now noted for its gentlemen's clubs, including the Athenaeum, by Decimus Burton, 1830, the Reform and the Travellers', both by Sir Charles Barry modelled on Italian *palazzi,* and the United Services, by John Nash 1827, altered by Decimus Burton in 1858. 86, 148, 150, *150,* 152. [CH]

Percival David Foundation of Chinese Art - see list of Museums.

Piccadilly, *W.1.* Developed in the late 17th century as a fashionable residential area, it is now one of the most famous shopping areas of London. On the north side the Royal Academy of Arts (Burlington House — *see* list of Museums), Albany and the Piccadilly Hotel; the south side includes St James's Church (q.v.) and the Royal Institute of Painters in Water Colours. Piccadilly Circus, at the top of the Haymarket, is one of London's busiest thoroughfares, in the centre of which stands the statue known as 'Eros', 1893, actually a memorial to the seventh Earl of Shaftesbury. 90, 120, 138, 145, 169, 179, 228, 237. [CH]

Piccadilly Arcade, *W.1.,* between Piccadilly and Jermyn Street with black and white marble floor and charming bow-fronted windows; it is, in fact, a copy of Regency style. 138. [CH]

Port of London Authority. *Trinity Square, Tower Hill.* Headquarters of the controlling body of London's port and the Thames estuary, in a flamboyant building by Sir Edwin Cooper, 1912–20. 169.

Portland Place, *W.1.,* between Langham Place and Regent's Park. Layout and houses by the Adam brothers, *c.* 1775; incorporated by Nash in his grand Regent Street route. Much interrupted by bomb damage and later insertions. 132, 145, 168. [BG]

Portman Square, *W.1.* South end of Baker Street. Laid out after 1761, but almost entirely re-developed. No. 20 (Home House, by R. Adam, 1773–77) houses the Courtauld Institute (*see* list of Museums). 132, 135, 136. [BG]

Post Office Tower - *see* list of Museums.

Prince Henry's Room - *see* list of Museums.

Public Record Office - *see* list of Museums.

Pudding Lane, *E.C.3.,* between Lower Thames Street and Eastcheap. The Great Fire of London started here 2 September 1666, and thence burned for five days, consuming 436 acres, 13,000 houses and 89 churches. 81, 83. [EG/EH]

Queen Anne's Gate, *off Broadway, S.W.1.* Well preserved enclave of early 18th-century dark-brick domestic architecture, with weathered statue of Queen Anne (?by F. Bird;

said to have come from the portico of St Mary-le-Strand) near No. 13. 122, 123, *135,* 136. [BH]

Queen Street, *E.C.4.,* from Cheapside to Upper Thames Street. A 'new' street created after 1666. Good 18th-century houses at Nos 27-28, 84. [EG]

Queen Victoria Street, *E.C.4,* from Blackfriars Bridge to Cannon Street. Built from 1867, but badly blitzed. On the north side, from Blackfriars: The Black Friar, *art nouveau* pub; the new *Times* building with sundial by Henry Moore: Wren's St Andrew-by-the Wardrobe; the College of Arms (q.v.); Wren's St Nicholas. South side: Wren's St Benet's. 12, 93, 105, 237. [DG/EG]

Queen's Chapel - *see* list of Museums, (Marlborough House).

Regent Street, *W.1.,* including Lower Regent Street. From St James's Park and Waterloo Place to Langham Place. Originally a grand processional route planned by Nash, built from 1817, from the Prince Regent's palace (Carlton House) to Regent's Park, pivoting at Piccadilly Circus and Langham Place, and dividing Mayfair from Soho. The Nash-style buildings have almost all gone (for exception, see All Souls, Langham Place; Suffolk Place; Haymarket Theatre), and the street is now a main shopping thoroughfare. 145–6, 150, 168, 175. [BG]

Regent's Park, *St Marylebone, N.W.1.* Originally part of the royal hunting demesne; laid out by Nash from 1812, with grand villas in gardens, lake, and the famous terraces on its fringe. The Zoo borders the northern edge. 54, 132, 143, 145–6, *147,* 154. [BF]

Richmond Great Park. Originally the royal hunting demesne of (long-demolished) Richmond Palace. 2½ miles across (2,358 acres). South of the Thames from Roehampton almost to Kingston. Fine trees, fish ponds, deer, etc. 54.

Ritz Hotel, *W.1.,* Arcaded hotel in Piccadilly designed by Mewes and Davis, 1906, was the first steel-framed building in London. Faced in Portland stone — the arcade in Norwegian granite — it stands next to Green Park. 169. [CH]

Roehampton Estate (Alton West), *S.W.15.,* off Roehampton Lane. Celebrated municipal housing venture, by the L.C.C. Housing Division 1956–61, with tall blocks in a mature landscaping.

Roman Bath - *see* list of Museums.
Roman Wall - *see* **London Wall**; and **Coopers Row.**

Royal Academy - *see* list of Museums.

Royal Albert Hall, *Kensington Gore, S.W.7.* Circular brick auditorium, by Captain Fowke, 1867–71; terracotta frieze (by Armitage, Pickersgill, Marks and Poynter) of the Triumph of Art and Letters. Seats 8,000; used for concerts (including the Promenade Concerts), other entertainments and mass meetings. *179, 206, 208, 219.* [AH]

Royal Artillery Memorial, *Hyde Park Corner, S.W.1.* By C. S. Jagger, 1925: in the same area, the Machine Gun Corps Memorial by Derwent Wood, 1925; equestrian Wellington, by Boehm, 1888. *176.* [BH]

Royal College of Art - *see* list of Museums.

Royal College of Music - *see* list of Museums.

Royal College of Organists, *Kensington Gore, S.W.7.,* immediately west of the Albert Hall. Building by H. H. Cole, 1875 with sgraffito decoration by F. W. Moody [AH]

Royal College of Physicians - *see* list of Museums.

Royal College of Surgeons - *see* list of Museums.

Royal Exchange, *E.C.2.* In the junction of Threadneedle Street and Cornhill. The first Exchange was set up, 1565, by Sir Thomas Gresham; burned 1666 and its successor also burned in 1838. Present building by Sir William Tite 1842–44. The gilt grasshopper above is Gresham's emblem. In the pediment, sculpture by Westmacott the Younger. Long the centre of London's commerce, literally for 'exchange', it has not been so used since 1939. *25, 28, 28, 64, 91, 93, 129, 155.* [EG]

Royal Festival Hall, *South Bank, S.E.1.* The first part (1951) to be built (by Sir R. H. Matthew and Sir L. Martin) of the post-war cultural centre on the South Bank (q.v.). For concerts, now supplemented by Queen Elizabeth Hall and the Purcell Room. *185.* [CH]

Royal Geographical Society - *see* list of Museums.

Royal Holloway College, *Egham.* Fantastic late Victorian Chateau, now part of London University. Has a good collection of Victorian academic paintings. *169.*

Royal Mews - *see* list of Museums.

Royal Naval College - *see* list of Museums (Greenwich).

Royal Observatory - *see* list of Museums (Greenwich).

Royal Opera Arcade, *Pall Mall, S.W.1.* A handsome arcade, survivor of the theatre on this site by Nash and Repton 1816–18. Now incorporated into New Zealand House. *138.* [CH]

Royal Opera House, *Covent Garden, W.C.2.* First built 1731; rebuilt after fire in 1808, and again after 1856; by E. M. Barry. Home of the national opera and ballet companies. *71.*

Royal Society of Arts - *see* list of Museums.

Russell Square, *Bloomsbury, W.C.1.* Laid out by James Burton after 1800, the gardens by Humphry Repton. Once an upper middle class residential area but now mostly rebuilt — with hotels on the east, and offices of professional bodies and departments of London University elsewhere, including Nos 25–29 (west side) survivors of Burton's scheme. Gardens redesigned since 1945 with tree lighting — statue by Westmacott of Francis, 5th Duke of Bedford. *135.* [CG]

St Alphage Churchyard, *E.C.2.* Just north of London Wall; fragments of the medieval church are preserved, and good sections of the Roman and medieval wall are visible. *12.* [DH]

St Alphege, *Greenwich High Road, S.E.10.* By Hawksmoor and James, 1711–30; much bomb damaged.

St Andrew-by-the-Wardrobe, *Queen Victoria Street, E.C.4.* Rebuilt by Wren in 1685–95, it suffered severe bomb damage but was restored in 1961. It utilizes furnishings from other bombed churches. Its name is believed to have indicated its proximity to the King's Great Wardrobe or storehouse, established by Edward III. *102, 119.* [EG]

St Andrew Undershaft, *Leadenhall Street, E.C.3.* Medieval church, rebuilt 1532 (the 'shaft-under-which' was a local maypole). Altar rails by Tijou; font by N. Stone. Monument to John Stow (London's first historian), by N. Johnson, 1605, and plaque to Holbein. [EG]

St Anne, *Limehouse.* By Hawksmoor, 1712–30. Spectacular tower. *119.*

St Anne, *Soho, Dean Street, W.1.* Wren church destroyed by bombing, but idiosyncratic tower by Cockerell, 1802–6, survives. Hazlitt was buried here. [CG]

St Augustine Kilburn, *Kilburn Park Road, Kilburn, N.W.6.* Best Victorian Gothic, by J. L. Pearson, 1870–80. Paintings (given by Lord Northcliffe) by or attributed to Crivelli, Filippino Lippi, Marco Palmezzano and Titian. *165, 165.*

St Augustine, *Watling Street, E.C.4.* Destroyed by bombs, but Wren's tower is incorporated in the new Choir School, opposite the east end of St. Paul's. [DG]

St Bartholomew the Great, *Smithfield, E.C.1.*, east side. Originally church of the Augustinian priory, founded by Rahere (tomb with effigy, retrospective, of *c.* 1500) in 1123. Only the Norman chancel and crossings (restored) survive; Lady chapel of *c.* 1330. Pretty Elizabethan timber work at entrance gate. Hogarth was baptized here. *25, 26, 60, 61, 84.* [DG]

St Bartholomew's Hospital, *West Smithfield, E.C.1.* Oldest teaching hospital in London, rebuilt by James Gibbs, 1730–59. Fine Great Hall, with Hogarth's *Pool of Bethesda* and *Good Samaritan* on the staircase. Octagonal church (St Bartholomew-the-Less) by T. Hardwick, 1823. The Gateway is of 1702, with statue of *Henry VIII* by F. Bird. *25, 150, 155.* [DG]

St Benet, *Paul's Wharf,* rebuilt by Wren 1677–85, rather Dutch in character, this brick church has a tower with a lantern and cupola. Used by Welsh Episcopalians since 1879; the interior contains excellent wood-carving. Henry Fielding was married here to his second wife in 1747 and Inigo Jones was buried in the earlier church on this site. *102.*

St Bride, *E.C.4.* Off Fleet Street, south side. By Wren, 1670–84, with famous tiered spire (1701–3; 226 feet high). Gutted in the Blitz and restored. The 'parish church' of the national press in Fleet Street. Crypt with museum (*see* list of Museums). *104, 105, 110.* [DG]

St Clement Danes, *Strand, W.C.2.* Medieval church, rebuilt by Wren 1680–82; spire mainly by Gibbs. Burnt out in 1941, and restored as the official church of the R.A.F. Dr Johnson's parish church (his statue, by P. Fitzgerald, 1910, is outside, east end). Opposite the west end, the Gladstone memorial by Sir H. Thornycroft, 1905. *114, 118, 119.* [CG]

St Cyprian, *Clarence Gate, N.W.1.* Fine modern church by Sir Ninian Comper, 1903. [BG]

St Dunstan-in-the-East, *St Dunstan's Hill, E.C.3.* Only the tower with delicate open spire, by Wren, survives after bombing.

St Dunstan-in-the-West, *Fleet Street, E.C.4.* Gothic church of 1829–33, by John Shaw; fine clock by T. Harris 1671, with elaborate strike. Statue

of Elizabeth I (1586, but restored) formerly on Ludgate. *90.* [DG]

St Ethelburga, *Bishopsgate, E.C.2.* Minute medieval church with features ranging from the 15th to the 17th or 18th centuries. *25, 26.* [EG]

St George, *Bloomsbury Way, W.C.1.* By Hawksmoor, 1731. Tiered obelisk spire with statue of George I; columned portico. *119.*

St George, *Hanover Square* (*St George's Street*), *W.1.* By John James, 1721–24; its columned portico set a London fashion. Reredos, painting of *The Last Supper* by W. Kent. At the front door, two popular cast-iron dogs said to be by Landseer. Fashionable church for weddings. *119.* [CG]

St George-in-the-East, *Cannon Street Road, E.1.* Splendid exterior by Hawksmoor, 1715–23; bombed, rebuilt within.

St Giles, *Cripplegate, Fore Street, E.C.2* (in the Barbican development). 14th-century church, restored after bomb damage. Milton was buried here. Fragment of medieval London wall. [DG]

St Giles-in-the-Fields, *St Giles's High Street, W.C.2.* Rebuilt by Henry Flitcroft (signed on the doorway) 1731–3; interior influenced by Gibbs's St Martin-in-the-Fields. Memorials to Lord Herbert of Cherbury; Andrew Marvell, George Chapman (this said to be an Inigo Jones' design), etc. *119–20, 152.* [CG]

St Helen's, *Bishopsgate* ('Great St Helen's'), off Bishopsgate, E.C.3. Large medieval church, 13th century onward, with two naves (one originally belonging to a nunnery). Interesting 17th-century doors; many fine tombs, including Sir Thomas Gresham's. *26–9, 62, 72, 188.* [EG]

St James's. District bounded by Mayfair (north) St James's Park (south) Haymarket/Lower Regent Street (east) and Green Park (west). Favoured by the artistocracy and men of fashion in the 17th and 18th centuries, the court acting as the magnet. Has since gradually yielded to gentlemen's clubs, commerce, and a section of the London art market. *86, 90, 174.*

St James Garlickhythe, *Garlick Hill, E.C.4.* Fine Wren church of 1687, well restored after bomb damage. *104.* [DG]

St James, *Piccadilly, S.W.1.* By Wren, 1684, for the St James's Square development. Blitzed, but well restored, with font and reredos by Grinling Gibbons. *110, 119.* [BH]

St James's Palace, *S.W.1.* The Tudor

gate tower faces up St James's Street, the back is on St James's Park. Originally a leper hospital; the palace built by Henry VIII after 1532, in red brick. Later alterations by Wren, Hawksmoor, and others. Interior has important work by Kent, William Morris, Grinling Gibbons and a fine ceiling of Holbein's time but is very rarely open. The main inner London residence of the Monarch in the 18th and early 19th centuries; now houses private apartments, the Lord Chamberlain's offices, etc. *48*, 48, 58, 69–70, 86, 96, 129. [BH]

St James's Park. Between the Mall (north), Whitehall (east), Birdcage Walk (south) and Buckingham Palace. The oldest of London's parks, expropriated by Henry VIII, 1532, from a hospital run by the Sisters of St James in the Fields; St James's' Palace (q.v.) was then built on its north side. Remodelled into its present 'picturesque' informal manner early in the 19th century in connection with Nash's Regent Street schemes. The view from the lake (the island in which is a bird sanctuary) to the east over Whitehall is famous. Green Park (q.v.) continues from it over the Mall by Buckingham Palace. 48, 50, 54, 70, 123, 132, 136, 143, 146. [CH]

St James's Square, *S.W.1.* Laid out after 1660 by Henry Jermyn, 1st Earl of St Albans, as a fashionable residential area. Several old houses survive; No. 4, probably by Edward Shepherd; No. 10 (Chatham House) built by Henry Flitcroft, 1736; and No. 15 (the residence of three Prime Ministers) by 'Athenian' Stuart, 1763. No. 14 in the north west corner houses the London Library — for subscribing members only. In the garden a bronze equestrian statue of William III by John Bacon (1808). 86, *86*, 133, 145, 214, 235. [CH]

St James's Street, *S.W.1.,* from St James's Palace (south) to Piccadilly (north).

St James-the-Less, *Thorndike Street, S.W.1,* off Vauxhall Bridge Road. Important Victorian Gothic church, by G.E. Street, 1860–61. Fresco by G.F. Watts. 165. [CH]

St John's, *Smith Square, Westminster, S.W.1.* Baroque church by T. Archer, 1721–28. Gutted in the Blitz, but restored as an arts centre (concerts especially). 119, 122. [CI]

St John's Chapel. In the White Tower (first floor), Tower of London. Superb early Norman architecture. For long, the official chapel of the Order of the Bath. Henry VI

and also Elizabeth of York lay in state here, and Mary I married, by proxy, Philip of Spain. 16, 19. [EH]

St John's Gate - *see* list of Museums.

St John's Wood, *N.W.8.* District, Marylebone north-west. Built up in the early to mid-19th century and retaining some of its original character. Brick terraces, stuccoed villas, with classical or Gothic style features, among the 20th-century flat developments. 154.

St John's Wood Church, *St John's Wood High Street, N.W.8.* Very elegant white and gold church by T. Hardwick, 1813. [AF]

St Katharine Creechurch, *Leadenhall Street, E.C.3.* Name derived from Christchurch, an Augustinian priory of that name in 1108. The tower dates from 1504, the body of the church rebuilt 1628–31; consecrated by Archbishop Laud. Gothic Perpendicular tradition. The 17th-century stained glass east window is in the form of a Catherine wheel. Since 1962, the headquarters of the Industrial Christian Fellowship. 81, 96. [EG]

St Katharine Docks. Immediately east of Tower Bridge, north Bank. Built 1825–28 (magnificent warehouses by Telford), leading into London Docks (by A. Alexander, 1800–05). Now disused, to be redeveloped in the 1970s. 170, 173. [EH]

St Lawrence Jewry, *Gresham Street, E.C.2.* Magnificent Wren church, 1670–86, next to the Guildhall and 'parish church' of the City Corporation. Gutted in the war and restored. [DG]

St Luke's Church, *Sydney Street, Chelsea, S.W.3.* Built in 1820–24 by James Savage, it is the parish church of Chelsea. Gothic Perpendicular structure. Charles Dickens married here in 1836. *164*, *164*. [AI]

St Magnus the Martyr, *Lower Thames Street, E.C.3.* By Wren, 1671–85; steeple finished 1706. Fine clock of 1709. 104, *104*, 105, 105. [EH]

St Margaret, *Lothbury, E.C.2.* Wren 1686–93; a rich church ('parish church' of the Bank of England opposite) with sumptuous fittings, many from other now demolished churches. Font, wooden screen, pulpit, etc; fine busts — *Ann Simpson*, by Nollekens; *Alderman Boydell*, by Banks and a rare early 17th-century one (*Sir P. Le Maire*, 1631). 105. [EG]

St Margaret Pattens, *Eastcheap, E.C.3.* By Wren, 1684–9. Unusual medieval-type spire; fine woodwork; altar-piece by Carlo Maratta. 102.

St Margaret Westminster, *S.W.1.* Alongside Westminster Abbey, and the parish church of the Houses of Parliament; very fashionable for weddings. Founded *c.* 1100, building mainly early 16th century, restored in the 18th century. Font by Nicholas Stone. Important east window, Netherlandish, intended for Henry VII's Chapel, showing Prince Arthur and Katharine of Aragon. Many interesting monuments. 46. [CH]

St Martin-in-the-Fields, *Trafalgar Square, W.C.2.* Rebuilt by James Gibbs, 1722–26. Interior with galleries; bust of Gibbs by Rysbrack, 1726. Crypt (used as shelter by homeless) has many relics. 118, 119, *123, 148.* [CH]

St Martin Ludgate, *Ludgate Hill, E.C.4.* By Wren, 1677–87, with elegant dark spire enhancing St Paul's dome as seen from Fleet Street. Good woodwork. [DG]

St Mary Abchurch, *Abchurch Yard, E.C.4.* (north of Cannon Street). By Wren, 1680–87; altarpiece by Grinling Gibbons, ceiling painting by William Snow. 105. [DG]

St Mary Aldermanbury. By Wren, 1670–86, but gutted in the Blitz, and now re-erected as memorial to Sir Winston Churchill in Westminster, Fulton, Missouri. A bust of Shakespeare (his editors, Condell and Heminge, were buried here) remains in a garden. 95.

St Mary Aldermary, *Watling Street, E.C.4.* By Wren, 1682, copying earlier Gothic with plaster fan tracery; claimed as earliest 'Gothic Revival' church. 105, *108.* [DG]

St Mary-at-Hill, *Lovat Lane, E.C.3.* By Wren, 1676. Rich in furnishings and perhaps gives the best surviving impression of what Wren's interiors looked like, though in fact much of it is brilliant Victorian pastiche. 105 [EG]

St Mary-le-Bow, *Cheapside, E.C.2.* By Wren, 1680, with one of his most complex steeples. The church of Bow Bells. Restored after heavy bomb damage. *96, 104,* 105. [EG]

St Mary-le-Strand, *Surrey Street, W.C.2.* The first of the fifty new churches ordered by an act of Parliament, this beautifully proportioned church was built by James Gibbs (1714–17). A fine coffered ceiling with cherubs' heads and flowers. 118, *119.* [CH]

St Mary Magdalene, *Woodchester Street, Paddington, W.2.* Fine Victorian Gothic church, by G. E. Street, 1868–78; crypt by Sir Ninian Comper, 1895. 105.

St Mary Overy - *see* Southwark Cathedral.

St Mary Somerset, *Upper Thames Street, E.C.4.* Built by Wren *c.* 1694, demolished 1871; only the tower, with its cluster of pinnacles, remains. 102. [DG]

St Mary Woolnoth, *E.C.3.* In the angle of Lombard Street and King William Street. By Hawksmoor, 1716–27; famous exterior, with remarkable window-cases, and tower. *119.* [EG]

St Michael Paternoster Royal, *College Hill, E.C.4.* By Wren, 1694, with very pretty tower and steeple of 1713. Restored after bomb damage. This was Dick Whittington's parish church originally. 104. [EG]

St Michael-upon-Cornhill, *E.C.3.* By Wren, 1677 but drastically restored in the 19th century. Tower of 1722 (from Gothic design by Hawksmoor). [EG]

St Nicholas Cole Abbey, *Queen Victoria Street, E.C.4.* Wren church of 1671–81, gutted in the war. [DG]

St Olave, *Hart Street, E.C.3.* Just missed by the Great Fire, but damaged in 1940–45. Basically of *c.* 1450: Pepys's parish church, with Bushnell's bust of his wife Elizabeth and other good monuments. [EG]

St Olave, Old Jewry. *Ironmonger Lane, E.C.2.* Wren's tower (1679) only survives, incorporated into a house. [EG]

St Pancras New Church, *Upper Woburn Place, W.C.1.* By W. and H. Inwood, 1822. Tribunes with massive caryatids (by Rossi) copied from the Erectheum. 150. [CF]

St Pancras Old Church, *Pancras Road, N.W.1.* 13th-century church 'normanized' in 1848; Saxon altar stone of *c.* 600 A.D. Claims to be the third oldest Christian site in Europe. Good monuments, including that by Sir John Soane for his wife, 1815, (in the churchyard). [CF]

St Pancras Station, *Euston Road, N.W.1.* Rail terminus for the north and north-east. Famous pinnacled façade by Sir G. G. Scott, 1868–74, contrasted with strictly functional glass and iron vault over the tracks by W. H. Barlow. 161, *162,* 169. [CF]

St Paul's Cathedral, *E.C.4.* Wren's noblest work, built by him, 1675–1711, on the site of the old cathedral (founded 604) which had been one of the great Gothic churches of Europe. The most famous surviving fragment from the old church is N. Stone's shrouded effigy of the poet Donne. External sculpture, west front, mainly by F. Bird. Interior very rich in woodwork (by Grinling Gibbons and others), stone carving, iron work (by Tijou). Paintings by Thornhill. Monuments to National heroes in neo-classic style, Nelson and other Napoleonic warriors: Alfred Stevens' monument to Wellington, and many others. In the Crypt, tombs of Nelson and Wellington, and many other monuments and memorials of famous men, including Wren's own. The Library has Wren's model for an early design, and other relics. Ascent to the top of the dome is available. 14, 29, *29,* 61, 70, 81, 96, *99,* 102, 110–2, *111, 112,* 117, 185, 232, 234. [DG]

St Paul's Church, *Covent Garden, W.C.2.* Originally by Inigo Jones, 1631–38; largely rebuilt to the original design, after a fire, by T. Hardwick, 1795. Monuments by Flaxman and others; many literary and dramatic personalities were buried here. 70–1, *71,* 96 [CG]

St Peter, *Vere Street, W.1.* Built by James Gibbs in 1721–24, described by Sir John Summerson as a 'miniature forecast' of St Martin-in-the-Fields, also by Gibbs. 121. [BG]

St Peter-ad-Vincula, *Tower of London.* Late Perpendicular church, *c.* 1512, with many monuments and historic associatioins. 18. [EG]

St Stephen Walbrook, *Walbrook, E.C.4.* By Wren, 1672–79; steeple 1714–17. The masterpiece of his parish churches, in the complexity of its interior anticipating St Paul's Cathedral. Well restored after bomb damage. With some good original furnishings. 104, 108, *108.* [DG]

St Thomas's Operating Theatre (Hospital) - *see* list of Museums.

St Vedast, *Foster Lane, E.C.2.* By Wren, 1695–1701; exceptionally complex though simple-seeming spire of 1709–12. Gutted, and restored. 104. [DG]

Savile Row, *W.1.* between Conduit Street (north) and Burlington Gardens (south). Street famous for its tailors. Some interesting houses: Nos 3–17 an 18th-century terrace, the remainder becoming increasingly modern. Noted residents have included R. B. Sheridan, the playwright, who died at No. 17, later occupied by George Basevi the architect of Belgravia. 120, 175. [BG]

Serpentine. An artificial lake of approximately 40 acres, shared by Hyde Park and Kensington Gardens where it is known as the Long Water; was created at the wish of Queen Caroline, wife of George III in 1730. It attracts numerous waterfowl—and all-the-year-round bathers. 51. [AH]

Shaftesbury Avenue, between Piccadilly Circus, Cambridge Circus and St Giles Circus. Constructed (west part) 1877–87, part of a slum clearance operation; now the centre of West End theatres. Named after the famous philanthropist-statesman, the Earl of Shaftesbury. 152, 174–5. [CG]

Smithfield, *E.C.1.* at the north end of Giltspur Street. Originally 'Smooth Fields', an open space from time immemorial, where citizens disported, Richard II faced Wat Tyler in 1381, and cloth-fairs were held. Also execution place in the 16th century for heretics. On the east side, St Bartholomew's Hospital and St Bartholomew the Great. North side, the meat market (1886). Beyond the church, Cloth Fair, with a rare 17th-century façade at Nos 41-42. 64, 169. [DG]

Smith Square, *Westminster, S.W.1.,* off Millbank (opposite Victoria Tower Gardens). Centre of a charming early Georgian development by Sir James Smith, *c.* 1725, with Archer's St John's Church (q.v.), the square itself somewhat disrupted by the Conservative and Unionist Central Office, and its antagonist, Transport House, offices of the Labour party. Some streets off the square very well preserved—Lord North Street, Cowley Street, Barton Street. 123. [CI]

Soho Square, *W.1.,* north-east corner of Soho, in the angle of Oxford Street and Charing Cross Road. Originally King Square, after Gregory King who developed it on the site of Monmouth House in the 1680s. Statue of Charles II, by Cibber. Now mostly 19th-century building, but see the House of St Barnabas (*see* list of Museums) on the corner of Greek Street. Some old houses survive in the streets going south (Greek and Frith) behind the restaurant and stripclub frontages. 90. [CH]

Somerset House, *Strand, W.C.2.,* south side, opposite the Aldwych. Protector Somerset built an important house here *c.* 1550, subsequently used as Henrietta Maria's palace. Present building by Sir William Chambers from 1776 to house governmental offices and also the first home of the Royal Academy. Spectacular river frontage. Ambitious sculptural groups in the courtyard by John Bacon the Elder. Later extended, to the east by King's College (q.v.), to the west by Sir J. Pennethorne, 1856, in matching style. Now houses notably the national archive of wills, and register of births, marriages and deaths. 64, 69, 81, 112, 130-2. [CG]

South Bank. Now used specifically to denote the area south of the river between Waterloo Bridge and Hungerford Bridge, developed since the war as a cultural centre, with the Royal Festival Hall, Queen Elizabeth Hall and Purcell Room (all for music); the Hayward Gallery (Arts Council); the National Film Theatre, and (to be built in the 1970s, architect, Denys Lasdun) the National Theatre. 62, 185, *186*. [CH]

South Kensington. Area south of Hyde Park from Kensington Gore. Site of the great concentration of museums (Victoria and Albert, Science, Natural History, Geology, etc) started out of the profits of the 1851 exhibition, with educational institutions (Royal College of Music, of Organists, of Art; the Imperial Institute); the Royal Albert Hall and the Albert Memorial. 170, 201, 203, 208, 214-15, 217-20.

Southwark. The suburb formed originally about the southern approaches to the Roman London Bridge. In the Middle Ages, free of the City's jurisdiction, it became the site of prisons, brothels and then the Elizabethan theatres, such as Shakespeare's Globe. Has it own cathedral (q.v.); is mainly an area of warehouses and railways, but has a good Thames-side walk (Bankside). 11, 30, 62, 90, 151, *170,* 175.

Southwark Cathedral, *Borough High Street, S.E.1.* Founded as church of the Augustinian Priory of St Mary Overie ('over the water'?) 1106; Southwark Cathedral since 1905. Excellent Early English chancel and retrochoir; nave by Sir Arthur Blomfield 1890-97. Harvard Chapel (1907) commemorates John Harvard, founder of Harvard, baptized here 1608. Monuments to the poet John Gower; to Henslowe, Fletcher and Massinger; Lancelot Andrewes; a strange baroque celebration of Lyonell Lockyer, maker of pills. Modern (1912) memorial to Shakespeare, whose brother Edmund is buried here. Fine set of wooden bosses. 26, 188. [EH]

Spanish and Portuguese Synagogue, *Heneage Lane (off Bevis Marks), E.C.3.* Built 1700-01 by Avis, a Quaker. Contemporary furnishings; unique in Britain for date and fine preservation. [EG]

Spencer House, *No. 27 St James's Place, S.W.1.,* with a fine Palladian façade on to Green Park. 1752-54, by J. Vardy; interiors by J. Stuart, Sir R. Taylor and H. Holland; formerly town house of the Earls of Spencer. An interesting contrast with the good, very 20th-century flats alongside (by D. Lasdun, 1959/60). 122. [BH]

Spitalfields. Once a distinct hamlet within Stepney, and site of the silk-weaving industry established by Huguenot refugees in the 18th century (their products represented in Bethnal Green Museum). Some houses of the period survive (Falgate Street, Spital Square, etc), and a famous fine 18th-century shop façade is in Artillery Lane. 152.

Staple Inn, *Holborn, E.C.4.,* southside. Former Inn of Chancery, with unmistakeable black-and-white timber façade (restored, but essentially from *c.* 1586). Courts behind blitzed, and rebuilt (First Court, No. 2, where Dr Johnson wrote *Rasselas*). 62, *62,* 92. [DG]

Stepney. Innermost borough to the City on the river to the east, and developed by monastic houses; then, in the 17th and 18th centuries, becoming badly overcrowded following the building of the inner docks in the 19th century. A strange mixture of docks, slums, decaying old houses modern municipal housing and great churches by Hawksmoor. See also Spitalfields. 119, 175.

Stock Exchange - *see* list of Museums.

Strand, *W.C.2.* Main east/west throughfare, between City and Westminster, from the City limit at Temple Bar end of Fleet Street, to Trafalgar Square. Estates of great medieval mansions here were developed in the 17th century. Churches of St Mary-le-Strand, and Clement Danes; Somerset House; Savoy Hotel. 31, 57, 64, 85, 86, 90, 118, 130, 161, *162,* 170, 174. [CG]

Strawberry Hill. On the Thames, Waldegrave Road, Twickenham. Horace Walpole's 'little plaything house' 1749-76, which set the style for the Gothick fashion of domestic architecture. Now houses St Mary's Roman Catholic Training College, who generally agree written applications from students to visit. 134.

Suffolk Street, *S.W.1.* North of Pall Mall East, well preserved houses of Nash's Regent Street development style. 145. [CH]

Syon House - *see* list of Museums.

Tavistock Square, *Bloomsbury (north east), W.C.1.* Laid out by Thomas Cubitt in 1826; survivors from the original scheme on the west side— Nos 30-45 now house departments of London University. Woburn House (north side) occupies the site of Tavistock House, the home of Charles Dickens, 1851–60. The British Medical Association building, on the east side, is by Sir Edwin Lutyens, 1925. 135. [CG]

Temple, *E.C.4.* Between the Thames (Victoria Embankment, east of Temple Station) to Fleet Street (several entrances, including Prince Henry's Room—*see* list of Museums). Comprises (east) Inner and (west) Middle Temple, Inns of Court (q.v.), with famous lawns, Great Halls, courts and the Temple Church. Blitzed, but well restored; King's Bench Walk has good late 17th–century houses. Many historical associations. *Twelfth Night* was staged in Middle Temple Hall, 1602; Oliver Goldsmith lived at No. 2 Brick Court. *77, 91, 92, 93.* [DG]

Temple Church, *E.C.4.* In the Inner Temple, but serving both Inner and Middle Temple. Round nave, built by the Templars, a military knighthood, *c.* 1160–85; chancel *c.* 1220–40. Blitzed, but well restored. Crusader effigies: bust by Scheemakers of Dr Mead; tomb of John Selden. 25, 27, 59, 92. [DG]

Temple of Mithras, *Queen Victoria Street, E.C.4.* (forecourt of Bucklersbury House). Roman, excavated 1954, 18 feet deep, and remains reassembled here. *9, 10,* 12-13. [DG]

Thames. London's river; rises in the Cotswold hills, near Cirencester. Tidal through London as far west as Teddington, but not navigable to big ships west of London Bridge. The main dock systems extend east of Tower Bridge for some twenty miles. River-buses run east as far as Greenwich, and west as far as Hampton Court, from piers by Tower Bridge and Westminster Bridge. 9, 10, 11, 12, 25, 30, 57, 60, 90, 132, 152, 169, 185.

Thomas Coram Foundation for Children - *see* list of Museums.

Tower Bridge, *E.1.* Spans the Thames immediately east of the Tower of London. By Jones and Wolfe Barry, 1894. Combination of High Victorian Gothic styling with High Victorian precision engineering in suspension and bascule machinery. 170, 173-4, *173, 181.* [EH]

Tower Hill, *E.C.3.* Immediately above the Tower of London. Dominated by the Port of London Authority building, Trinity Square. All Hallows Barking church; fragments of Roman wall (Cooper's Row); elegant 18th-century headquarters of the Brethren of the Trinity (Trinity

House, by S. Wyatt, 1792–94). Open air forum, equivalent of Speaker's Corner at Hyde Park. 10, 12, 17, 169. [EG]

Tower of London - *see* list of Museums.

Trafalgar Square. At the junction of Whitehall, the Mall, Cockspur Street, Pall Mall, Charing Cross Road, Strand and Northumberland Avenue. Conceived by Nash in the 1820s, but laid out by Sir Charles Barry, 1840, centred on Nelson's Column (1839–42; 145 feet high). Le Sueur's equestrian statue of Charles I (1633) looks down Whitehall. South-west corner, Admiralty Arch (by Sir Aston Webb, 1911); west, Canada House (former Royal College of Physicians); north, National Gallery; east, St Martin-in-the-Fields, S. Africa House. Victorian statuary, and modern fountains (1939, by Lutyens). A great national forum for mass-meeting. 118, 147-8, 199, 235, 189. [CH]

University College - *see* list of Museums.

Victoria Embankment. The consolidation of the north bank of the Thames, from Blackfriars Bridge, to Westminster Bridge, carried out mainly by Sir J. Bazalgette, 1864–70. 83, 235. [CH]

Victoria Street, *S.W.1.,* between Westminster Abbey and Victoria Station, originally cut through slums from 1852, largely rebuilt after 1945. 152, 165. [CH]

Walbrook, *E.C.4.,* from Mansion House south to Cannon Street, on the course of the tributary stream, of this name (now buried deep beneath) that ran between the two hills of the City to the Thames. 11, 13. [DG]

Warburg Institute, *Woburn Square, W.C.1.* Founded in Hamburg by Aby Warburg for the study of mediterranean iconography; transferred to London in the 1930s and has been immensely influential in the study of art history. Unique library. Part of London University. [CG]

War Office, *Whitehall (south side), S.W.1.* Late Victorian baroque, by W. Young, 1898–1907; sculpture by A. Drury. 169. [CH]

Waterloo Bridge, *Strand (north) to South Bank (south).* Five arch, steel and concrete structure, designed by Sir G. G. Scott, completed 1945—a worthy successor to its famous predecessor, the first Waterloo Bridge, designed by John Rennie, 1811–17. 172. [DH]

Wesley's House and Chapel - *see* list of Museums.

Westminster. The western area of medieval London, from Charing Cross to Westminster Abbey, it developed as the centre of royal and national administration, concentrated on the Palace of Westminster (now Houses of Parliament, q.v.), St James's and Buckingham Palace, and then Whitehall (Civil Service Ministries and Cabinet Office). North of this, the St James's area was developed as highly fashionable residential area after 1666, and has, including Mayfair, always remained so. The Parks are a great amenity of the area. 15, 25, 57, 63, 85, 90, 123, 129, 151, 152, *158,* 161, 170.

Westminster Abbey, *Broad Sanctuary, S.W.1.,* opposite the Houses of Parliament. The Collegiate Church of St Peter in Westminster. Rebuilt, from the church started (1065) by Edward the Confessor, by Henry III from 1245 in a French-influenced Gothic style; nave mainly by Henry Yevele, started 1375; the spectacular addition of Henry VII's Chapel in late Gothic (probably by Robert and William Vertue) 1503–12; the west towers finally by Hawksmoor, 1735–40. Monarchs are crowned here, and it is the last resting place of the famous, packed with tombs and memorials. Cloisters and Chapter House (early 13th century), survive, and a museum (Chapel of the Pyx) shows wax funeral effigies from Henry III to Nelson, and other relics. 14, 27, 30, 31, 32-48, *32, 36, 38, 41, 43, 44, 46,* 57, 62, 64, 112, 123, *129,* 148, 159, 176, 187, 188, 232. [CH]

Westminster Bridge, between the Houses of Parliament, north bank and County Hall, south bank. First bridge here completed 1750; present one, in cast iron, by T. Page, 1862. The view east to the City is famous (see Wordsworth's Sonnet). 10, 11, 30, 123, 171. [CH]

Westminster Hall - *see* list of Museums, (Houses of Parliament).

Westminster Roman Catholic Cathedral, *Francis Street, S.W.1.,* (south of Victoria Street). By J. F. Bentley, finished 1903; brick in Byzantine mode with spectacular campanile. Marbling of the interior still under way. The major Catholic church of England. 165, *165,* 168. [BI]

Westminster School, *S.W.1.,* off Dean's Yard, in the precincts of Westminster Abbey. Originally a medieval monastic school, refounded by Elizabeth I in 1560; long one of the great 'public' schools of England. Alumni include Ben Jonson, Locke, Wren, Gibbon, etc. 46. [CI]

Whitehall, *S.W.1.* Trafalgar Square to Parliament Square (including Parliament Street). Centre of national administration, and grand ceremonial route to Parliament and Westminster Abbey; on the site of the Palace of Whitehall (q.v.) (burnt 1698). South side (from Trafalgar Square): War Office; Banqueting House (Inigo Jones, 1619); Richmond Terrace. North side: former Admiralty (screen by Adam); Horseguards (by Kent); Dover House (Scottish Office); old Treasury (façade by Sir Charles Barry, from 1844); Downing Street (No. 10, the Prime Minister's House and Cabinet Office); Foreign Office (by Sir G. G. Scott). Monuments include statues to the Duke of Cambridge; Earl Haig; and the Cenotaph. 80, 123, 129, 148, 154, 174, 176, 192, 234. [CH]

Wigmore Street, *W.1.,* links Cavendish Square to Portman Square, parallel with Oxford Street. Wigmore Hall is famous for chamber music concerts. 121. [BG]

Wimpole Street, *W.1.,* links Wigmore Street (east end) with Marylebone Road, parallel with Harley Street, and also much used by medical consultants. The Barretts of Wimpole Street (Elizabeth Barrett Browning) lived at No. 50 (plaque). 121. [BG]

Windsor. Pleasant country town on the Thames west of London, dominated by Windsor Castle with Eton College below. 57.

Windsor Castle - *see* list of Museums.

Woburn Square, *Bloomsbury, W.C.1.* A narrow square, laid out about 1828. Bordered on the west by London University buildings; in the north-west corner, the Courtauld Institute Galleries (*see* list of Museums) and Warburg Institute share a modern building—by Charles Holden, 1958. The south-east has Christ Church by Lewis Vulliamy 1833, with an altarpiece incorporating paintings by Burne-Jones. 135, 228. [CF]

York Water Gate, *Victoria Embankment Gardens. S.W.1.* Tripartite arch, erected 1626; long ascribed to Inigo Jones but probably by Balthasar Gerbier with sculptures by Nicholas Stone. The only surviving part of York House, the Duke of Buckingham's mansion, built 1625, demolished 1676. Now isolated by the Embankment, it originally gave access to the river from the house. 85, *85.* [CH]

Zoo, *Regent's Park* - *see* list of Museums.

Painters, Sculptors and Architects

This Appendix lists those artists — painters, sculptors, architects and crafts-men — whose names are particularly associated with London, especially as embellishers of its fabric or illustrators of its life and its townscape. Not all are necessarily mentioned in the text.

The major masters of the *European schools of painting and sculpture* are generally only listed when they have some specific London connection. Their work is to be found in the great public collections: the National Gallery for masterpieces of all European schools of painting up to about 1900, also the Wallace Collection; the Dulwich College Picture Gallery; the Courtauld Institute Galleries; the Iveagh Bequest, Kenwood; Sir John Soane's Museum; the Victoria and Albert Museum; also in the Royal Collection (Hampton Court and Windsor Castle, and the changing selections shown in the Queen's Gallery, Buckingham Palace). For *British art,* especially, the national collections are in the Tate Gallery (paintings); Victoria and Albert Museum (water-colours, and sculpture up to the 19th century); and the British Museum (drawings and watercolours); rich representation in specialized subject matter in British painting and sculpture is in the National Portrait Gallery, the London Museum, the National Maritime Museum, the Imperial War Museum, the Army Museum and the Royal Academy. For *20th-century painting and sculpture* of all schools, the Tate Gallery; for *Old Master drawings,* most importantly, the British Museum, but also the Victoria and Albert Museum; the Courtauld Institute Galleries (Witt Collection); Sir John Soane's Museum and the Royal Institute of British Architects (Portland Place), both for architectural drawings; the National Maritime Museum (especially Van de Velde drawings); and the fabulous collections in the Library at Windsor Castle. For *illuminated manuscripts,* the British Museum, and also the Victoria and Albert Museum.

For details of opening hours etc. see the list of Museums, for general accounts of the collections see Chapter 7.

Abbreviations: N.P.G.: National Portrait Gallery
                 V.& A.: Victoria and Albert Museum

Adam, Robert (1728–92). Architect. Screen-wall to the Admiralty (White-hall); The Royal Society of Arts (John Street); Apsley House (Piccadilly); Lansdowne House (Berkeley Square); Chandos House (Chandos Street, Cavendish Square). No. 20 Portman Square, now the Courtauld Institute of Fine Art. Some of his houses at Portland Place and Fitzroy Square survive, also in the almost entirely redeveloped Adelphi, south of the Strand (he lived at No. 1-3 Robert Street, Adelphi). Kenwood House, Syon House, and Osterley Park. David Garrick's Drawing Room from the Adelphi (V. & A.); large collection of his drawings is at the Soane Museum. Often worked with his brothers, James and John. 129, *131, 133,* 132-3, 136, *136, 138, 139, 139,* 140, 145, 201, 204, 229.

Adams, Holden and Pearson - *see* **Holden, Charles**

Anrep, Boris (b. 1883). Russian artist in mosaic, working in England from 1918. Mosaic floors in National Gallery and Tate Gallery; work in

Westminster Cathedral, Bank of England, etc.

Archer, Thomas (1668?–1743). Architect. St John the Evangelist, (Smith Square, Westminster, gutted 1941, and restored as arts centre); St Paul's (Deptford); Roehampton House (facing Roehampton Lane; now part of Queen Mary's Hospital). 119, 122.

Avis, Joseph (fl. 1675–1702). Quaker Architect, Carpenter and Joiner. Spanish and Portuguese Synagogue (Heneage Lane, off Bevis Marks, City) 1699–1702.

Bacon, Francis (b. 1910). English figurative painter, represented in the Tate Gallery. 225, 236.

Bacon, John (1740–99). Sculptor; worked for Mrs Coade (q.v.) benefit-ed from the influence of King George III. Fountain group *George III and the River Thames* in bronze (Somerset House); equestrian statue of *William III,* completed by his sons (St James's Square); figures and reliefs on the façade and a marble statue of *Thomas Guy,* the founder (Guy's Hospital); *Lord Chatham* (Guildhall and Westminster Abbey); other important examples of his work can be seen in St Paul's and Westminster Abbey. 25.

Bacon, John, the Younger (1777–1859). Sculptor, second son of John Bacon. Restored *Madness* and *Melancholy* by C.G. Cibber (q.v.) and completed the equestrian statue of *William III* (St James's Square) begun by his father. Examples of original work can be seen at the British Museum, *Pitt*; the National Portrait Gallery, *Duke of Wellington;* in St Paul's, *Sir John Moore* and Westminster Abbey, *Warren Hastings*. 235.

Baily, Edward Hodges (1788–1867). Sculptor. Pupil of John Flaxman (q.v.) His best known work is the statue of *Nelson*, surmounting the column (Trafalgar Square); he was responsible for the sculpture reliefs on the south side of the Marble Arch and the statuary on the façade of the National Gallery. *Eve listening to the voice* (Bethnal Green Museum), *Morning Star* (Mansion House); monuments in St Paul's and Westminster Abbey; busts of *Flaxman* and other artists (Burlington House). 148.

Baker, Sir Herbert (1862–1946). Architect. Responsible for the much abused remodelling of Soane's Bank of England (Threadneedle Street) 1921-37; also India House (Aldwych) 1928–30; Ninth Church of Christ Scientist (Marsham Street, Westminster) 1929; South Africa House (Trafalgar Square) 1931-33; Church House (Dean's Yard, Westminster) 1937-40, etc. 151, 169.

Banks, Thomas (1735–1805). Sculptor, Group of *Thetis and her nymphs* (V. & A.); monuments to *Giuseppe Baretti* (Marylebone Chapel); two soldiers of the Napoleonic wars *Captain Burgess* and *Captain Westmacott* (St Paul's Cathedral); *Sir Eyre Coote* and the hymn writer *Isaac Watts* (Westminster Abbey); examples of his work can also be seen in the N.P.G., *Warren Hastings*, the Soane Museum, *George Soane*, and the Royal Academy. 105, 232.

Barbon, Nicholas (c. 1640–98). Notorious speculative building developer, active all over London, and initiator of Fire Insurance. Schemes included development of the Essex estate, south of the Strand; Red Lion Square; Buckingham and Villiers Streets (site of York House), etc. His type of house best seen in Bedford Row (Nos. 36-43, though somewhat altered). 85-6.

Barlow, William Henry (1812–1902). Architect/engineer. Glass and ironwork (St Pancras Station) 1863–65. 161.

Barry, Sir Charles (1795–1860). Architect. Initiated the Italian palazzo style for London clubs with The Reform Club, 1837–41 and The Travellers' Club, 1829–31 (Pall Mall). Palace of Westminster and Houses of Parliament, 1840–60. (completed by his son E.M. Barry) but Pugin was responsible for the detail. Bridgewater House (Cleveland Place, St James's) and parts of Lancaster, formerly Stafford, House (Cleveland Row, St James's). He designed the layout for Trafalgar Square, 1840. *142, 150, 152, 155, 158.*

Barry, Edward Middleton (1830–80). Architect; son of Sir Charles Barry (q.v.). Covent Garden Theatre, 1857, and Floral Hall, 1858. Charing Cross Station Hotel and the Eleanor Cross 1865; Cannon Street Station, main block, 1866. Extensions in the National Gallery. 174, 199.

Barry, James (1741–1806). Painter, principally of history, and writer on the arts. Professor of Painting at the Royal Academy. Series of six large paintings depicting the progress of *Human Culture* (Library, Society of Arts) ranging in subject from the story of Orpheus to the Distribution of Premiums in the Society of Arts; *King Lear weeping over the Dead Body of Cordelia* (Tate Gallery; *Self portrait* (N.P.G.). 132.

Basevi, George (1794–1845). Architect; pupil of Sir John Soane (q.v.). Houses in Belgrave Square and Thurloe Square, 1843; The Conservative Club House (St James's Street) in association with S. Smirke; St Jude's Church (Chelsea); etc.

Bazalgette, Sir Joseph (1819–91). Civil engineer; mainly responsible for embankments of the Thames, in connection with a fundamental re-organization of the London sewage and drainage systems in the 1860s; also Hammersmith Bridge, 1887, Battersea Bridge, 1887–90; etc. A bust of him is in the Embankment wall (north side) by Charing Cross Bridge.

Beazley, Samuel (1786–1851). Architect and writer of fiction. Specialized in the design of theatres — The Royal Lyceum, The Drury Lane Theatre. He was also responsible for part of London Bridge Station.

Bedford, Francis (1784–1858). Architect. St John's Church (Waterloo Road) 1823-25; Holy Trinity (Little Queen Street, Holborn) 1829–31; Holy Trinity (Trinity Square) 1823–24.

Behnes, William (1794/5–1864). Sculptor. His statue of *Sir Henry Havelock* (Trafalgar Square) is the earliest example, 1861, of a photograph being employed as source material by a sculptor; among other statues are those of *Dr Babbington* (St Paul's Cathedral) and *Sir Thomas Gresham* (face of the campanile, Royal Exchange) and monuments include that to *Joseph Nollekens* (q.v.) in Paddington Parish Church. Examples of his work are also in the N.P.G. (*Thomas Arnold, etc.*).

Belcher, Sir John (1841–1913). Architect. Institute of Chartered Accountants (Great Swan Alley, Moorgate), 1893. Holy Trinity (Kingsway) 1910 — with J. J. Joass; Royal Society of Medicine (Hamilton Place) 1912.

Bell, John (1812–95). Sculptor. His best known work in London is the *Guards' Crimean War Memorial* (junction of Pall Mall and Waterloo Place). *Eagle and Slayer* (Bethnal Green Museum) was in the Great Exhibition of 1851; other examples of his work are on the Albert Memorial (*America*) and in the Guildhall.

Bell, Robert Anning (1863–1933). Painter and designer. Designed *SS Andrew and Patrick* mosaics (Central Lobby, Houses of Parliament) executed by Gertrude Martin; mosaics illustrating the history of St Stephen's Hall (St Stephen's Hall, Houses of Parliament); mosaic of *Virgin and Child* (Westminster Cathedral — above the altar); works in the Tate Gallery — *Mary in the House of Elizabeth*, etc.

Bentley, John Francis (1839–1902). Architect. Westminster Cathedral, 1895–1903. 165, *165*.

Bird, Francis (1667–1731). Sculptor, who worked under Grinling Gibbons (q.v.) and C. G. Cibber (q.v.). He is best known for his work at St Paul's Cathedral — statues of apostles and evangelists and in particular the *Conversion of St Paul* for the great pediment (west front), 64 feet long and 17 feet high. His statue of *Queen Anne*, intended to stand in front of the Cathedral has been replaced by a poor Victorian copy but his *Henry VIII* (Gateway of St Bartholomew's Hospital, Smithfield) can still be seen. Monuments include that to the *Earl of Huntingdon* (St James's Piccadilly) and the *Duke of Newcastle* (Westminster Abbey).

Blake, William (1757–1827). Engraver, painter and poet. A large and representative assembly of his work is on view at the Tate Gallery, including the illustrations to Dante's *Divine Comedy* — *Beatrice Addressing Dante from the Car* and his interpretation of biblical texts — *God creating Adam*, among his most powerful works. His grave is in Bunhill Fields Cemetery; Epstein's evocation of Blake's life mask (N.P.G.) is in Poets' Corner, Westminster Abbey. He lived some time at 74 Broadwick Street, W.1 (marked with an inscription). 225, 226.

Blomfield, Sir Arthur (1824–99). Architect. St Peter's (Eaton Square) rebuilt in a classical style, 1857; St Mark's (North Audley Street) 1878 rebuilt in a Victorian Renaissance style. Royal College of Music (Prince Consort Road) 1894; etc. 169.

Blomfield, Sir Reginald (1856–1942). Architect, nephew of Sir Arthur Blomfield. Recast some of the façades of John Nash's Regent Street 1923; designed Lambeth Bridge 1929–32 with G. T. Forrest.

Boehm, Sir Joseph Edgar, Bt. (1834–90). Sculptor. Equestrian statues of the *Duke of Wellington* (opposite Apsley House, Hyde Park Corner) and *Lord Napier of Magdala* (junction of Kensington Road and Queen's Gate); statues of *Thomas Carlyle* (Cheyne Walk, Chelsea) and *William Tyndale* (Victoria Embankment Gardens). Statues of *Victoria* and *Edward VII* on Temple Bar Memorial (Strand near Chancery Lane), denoting the boundary between the cities of London and Westminster. Monuments in Westminster Abbey include that of *Lord Beaconsfield*. Copious busts by him are in the N.P.G.

Bonington, Richard Parkes (1802–28). English painter of landscape etc., spent most of his adult life abroad, principally in France. Superbly represented at the Wallace Collection; also works at the Tate Gallery; V. & A.; British Museum. 222.

Brangwyn, Sir Frank (1867–1956). Painter and designer. Mural decorations, 1902, in Skinners Company Hall; others in the Royal Exchange. *The Poulterer's Shop* (Tate Gallery).

Bridgeman, Charles (d. 1738). Landscape gardener. With Henry Wise he laid out Kensington Gardens, 1728 onwards. 117.

Brock, Sir Thomas (1847–1922). Sculptor. His most conspicuous work is the *Queen Victoria Memorial* (The Mall facing Buckingham Palace) with the bronze figure of Victory, the Queen herself, seated, in marble and symbolic groups, also in marble.

Bronze statue of *Captain Cook* (The Mall, Admiralty Arch end), the monument to *Lord Leighton* (St Paul's Cathedral) and the statues of *W. E. Gladstone* (Westminster Abbey, north transept), *Sir John Millais* (Tate Gallery by the entrance), *Irving* (bottom of Charing Cross Road), and busts in the N.P.G.

Broker, Nicholas (active in the 1390s). Sculptor and coppersmith. Bronze effigy of *Richard II* and *Anne of Bohemia* (Westminster Abbey) with Godfrey Prest, begun 1394. 39.

Burbage, Richard (1567?–1619). Actor and painter; friend of William Shakespeare. The only two reasonably certain paintings by him are both in Dulwich Picture Gallery, including a *Self-Portrait.* 192.

Burlington, Richard Boyle, 3rd Earl of, (1694–1753). Architect and patron of the arts; leading inspiration of the Palladian movement in England. Designed his own villa (Chiswick Park); his London house was Burlington House (in part designed by himself, also by Colen Campbell and Gibbs) which now houses the Royal Academy, etc. but parts of the original interior survive. He built the Dormitory at Westminster School. *117,* 120, 190.

Burne-Jones, Sir Edward Coley Bt (1833–98). Painter and designer. Examples of his stained glass (Holy Trinity Church, Sloane Street); altarpiece paintings (Christ Church, Woburn Square) *King Cophetua and the Beggar Maid* with a large number of works, some unfinished, together with studies for paintings and stained glass (Tate Gallery); collaborated with William Morris and Philip Webb on the Green Dining Room (V. & A.).

Burnet, Sir John J. (1857–1938). Architect. King Edward VII building (North entrance, British Museum) 1907–14; Adelaide House, 1924; Lloyd's Bank (Lombard Street) 1930; Unilever House (Blackfriars) 1932; etc.

Burnham, Daniel H.E. (1846–1912). Chicago architect, consultant in the building of Selfridge's store (Oxford Street) 1908. 169.

Burton, Decimus (1800–81). Architect. Ionic screen entrance (now rearranged) to Hyde Park and Constitution Arch (Hyde Park Corner) and several buildings in the Pall Mall, Carlton House Terrace, St James's area — notably the Athenaeum Club (Pall Mall); Charing Cross Hospital. Work in Regent's Park includes some buildings and gardens for the Zoo and Botanical Gardens. 145, 147, 150, *150.*

Bushnell, John (d. 1701). Sculptor who worked abroad for over twenty years, Italy especially. Statues of *Charles I, Charles II* and *Sir Thomas Gresham* (Old Bailey) were originally intended for the Royal Exchange. Magnificent standing figure of *Lord Mordaunt* (Fulham Parish Church); monuments to *Sir Palmer Fairborne* and *Abraham Cowley* (Westminster Abbey); bust of Samuel Pepys's wife, Elizabeth (St Olave's Church).

Butterfield, William (1814–1900). Architect of several churches, etc. the most noteworthy being All Saints (Margaret Street) 1859. 164-5.

Canaletto (Canal) Giovanni Antonio (1697–1768). Venetian view painter, largely producing work for the English market from *c.* 1726 onwards; worked in England 1746–1755/6. Represented by Venetian and/or English views in the National Gallery (*Eton College* etc.); Wallace Collection; National Maritime Museum; and elsewhere but especially in the Royal Collection (Windsor: more than 50 paintings and over 140 drawings, bought for George III from Canaletto's English patron in Venice, Consul Smith). His house (41 Beak Street) is marked with a plaque. *98,* 102, 149, 188, 192, 201, 222.

Casson, Sir Hugh Maxwell (In practice 1970). Architect; coordinating designer of the Festival of Britain, 1951. Health Exhibition Centre (Royal Society of Health, Buckingham Palace Road) 1957; King George VI Memorial Youth Hostel (Holland Park) 1959 — with N. Condor; Royal College of Art (Kensington Gore) 1962 — with others.

Chambers, Sir William (1723–96). Architect; member of several societies abroad. Surveyor-General and Comptroller. Somerset House (Strand) 1776–86; Albany, originally Melbourne House (Piccadilly). Designed the Royal State Coach (Buckingham Palace Mews), and designed the gardens, orangery, temples and Chinese pagoda at Kew for the Princess Dowager of Wales, 1757-62. 64, 129-32, 134, *134,* 201.

Chantrey, Sir Francis Legatt (1781–1841). Sculptor. Equestrian statues of *George IV* (Trafalgar Square, north east) originally intended for Marble Arch, and the *Duke of Wellington* (Royal Exchange) completed by Weekes; statues of *William Pitt the Younger* (Hanover Square gardens) and *James Watt* (Westminster). Abbey, where other examples of his work are found e.g. *Richard Brinsley Sheridan*) and many busts in institutions and museums — *Sir Walter Scott, Canning* and *Castlereagh* (N.P.G.); *J. R. Smith* (V. & A.); *B. West* (Royal Academy); *Sir J. Banks* (Royal Society). His preparatory work included drawings via a *camera lucida* (large collection in the N.P.G.). 147, 232.

Chippendale, Thomas (Active c. 1760). Famous furniture maker, well represented in the V. & A. His workshop was near 61 St Martin's Lane, W.C.2.

Cibber, Caius Gabriel (1630–1700). Sculptor in ordinary to William III; father of Colley Cibber, the actor. He was responsible for the allegorical relief — *London destroyed and London restored* (The Monument), the statue of *Charles II* (Soho Square), *Madness* and *Melancholy* (Guildhall Museum) formerly at the Bethlehem Hospital and the *Boy playing bag-pipes* (V. & A.); the wooden figures *Moses* and *St John the Baptist* (St Katharine's Chapel, Regent's Park); the pediment on the east front of Hampton Court. 83, *83,* 115.

Cipriani, Giovanni Battista (1727–85/90?). Italian painter and designer, working in London. Painted decoration on the state carriage (Royal Mews) 1762 and the Lord Mayor's coach. *126.*

Clarke, Geoffrey (b. 1924). Sculptor, stained glass artist, designer. Abstract sculpture in bronze (Thorn House, St Martin's Lane); Metal screen (Royal Military Chapel, Bird cage Walk).

Coade, Mrs Eleanor (Firm flourished 1769–1820). Artificial stone manufacturer in Lambeth who capitalized on an early 18th-century recipe (now lost); employed prominent sculptors including Bacon, Banks, Flaxman and Rossi, and found ready markets in England and abroad. The product, a kind of terracotta, practically impervious to the weather, was used extensively on the decoration of London buildings. Examples are at St Pancras Church (caryatids, etc. designed by Rossi); Soane Museum (façade); Greenwich Hospital (capitals and medallions; the figures of *Hope, Meekness, Charity* and *Faith* in the ante-chapel but most notably, the tympanum of the west pediment, designed by Benjamin West); also monuments in Lambeth Parish Church and churchyard (*Admiral Bligh*, etc.), Westminster Abbey (*Edward Wortley Montagu*) and the monumental lion, at the foot of Westminster Bridge, by County Hall.

Cockerell, Samuel Pepys (c. 1754–1827). Architect of St Anne's (Wardour Street, Soho), the tower of which remains; etc.

Cocteau, Jean (1889–1963). French wit, writer and artist. Decorations in Notre Dame de France, 1960 (off Leicester Square).

Colcutt, T. E. (1840–1924). Architect. Tower of Imperial College of Science and Technology (Exhibition Road, South Kensington) 1893, all that remains of the original Commonwealth Institute buildings, erected in 1893; Lloyd's Register of Shipping (Fenchurch Street) 1901. 208.

Colt, Maximilian (Working c. 1595–c. 1645). Sculptor, came from Arras to England in the mid-1590s. Best known for his tomb of *Elizabeth I,* and the effigy, in her cradle, of the infant *Princess Sophia,* (both in Westminster Abbey). 38.

Constable, John (1776–1837). Landscape painter; along with J. M. W. Turner, the major English landscape painter of the 19th century. Superbly represented in London collections: *The Cornfield* and *The Hay Wain,* etc. (National Gallery); *Chain Pier, Brighton* and *Sketch for Hadleigh Castle,* etc. (Tate Gallery); *The Leaping Horse* and *The Lock* (Royal Academy). A large body of work, bequeathed by his daughter, is in the V. & A.; drawings and watercolours also in the British Museum. He lived at 76 Charlotte Street, W.1 and 40 Well Walk, Hampstead (both marked with plaques). 176, 191, 199, 208, 224, 225.

Cooper, Sir Edwin (d. 1942). Architect. St Marylebone Town Hall (Marylebone Road) 1914–20; Port of London Authority Building (Trinity Square) 1922; National Provincial Bank (Poultry) 1931.

Cooper, Samuel (1609–72). Painter of miniatures. An important group of works, *Edward Montagu, 1st Earl of Sandwich*; *Henrietta, Duchess of Orleans,* etc at the V. & A.; *Charles II* and *A Lady* (Wallace Collection); *Duke of Lauderdale,* etc (N.P.G.); National Maritime Museum; and a rich representation in the Royal Collection (Windsor). 217, 220.

Cope, Charles West (1811-90). Painter. Frescoes, including a series of eight depicting episodes from the Stuart and Commonwealth periods of English history (Central lobby, Houses of Parliament).

Copnall, Edward Bainbridge (b. 1903). Sculptor. Reliefs on the façade of the R.I.B.A. (corner of

Weymouth Street/Portland Place); War memorial sculpture (Trade Union Congress H.Q., Gt Russell Street, Bloomsbury) and the bronze *Stag* (Stag Place, Westminster).

Corfiato, H.O. (In practice 1970). Architect. Notre Dame de France (Leicester Place) 1955; new buildings for University College (Gower Street) 1960.

Cosmati. Dynastic name of Roman mosaic workers, 12th–14th centuries. Work by them, including Odericus and Petrus Romanus, in Westminster Abbey, *c.* 1270, including Henry III's tomb. 39.

Crunden, John (1740–c. 1828). Architect. Boodles Club (St James's Street) 1765. 149.

Cubitt, Lewis (1799–?). Architect. Designed houses in Belgravia and Bloomsbury built by his brother Thomas (q.v.); Kings Cross Station is his masterpiece, 1851 (in collaboration with his brother, Thomas). 152, 161.

Cubitt, Thomas (1788–1855). Architect and speculative builder. Responsible for the overall planning of the districts of Belgravia and Pimlico; the terrace of shops in Woburn Walk (St Pancras Church east end), and many other developments in Bloomsbury, Islington, etc. 175.

Cundy, Thomas junior (1790–1867). Architect, eldest son of Thomas Cundy senior, whom he succeeded as surveyor to Lord Grosvenor's estates. St Paul's (Wilton Place, Knightsbridge) 1840–43.

Cure, Cornelius (d. 1608). Sculptor, member of an immigrant family of Dutch sculptors. Made the monument to *Mary, Queen of Scots*, in Westminster Abbey, and that to *Sir Roger Aston* at Cranford.

Dalou, Jules (1838–1902). French sculptor, working in England 1871–80. Group in bronze, *Maternity* (behind the Royal Exchange) 1878; a group of works at the Tate Gallery.

Dance, George, the Elder (?–1768). Architect; Clerk of the City works. The Mansion House 1739–52; St Botolph's Church, Aldgate 1741–44. *129, 130.*

Dance, George, the Younger (1741–1825). Architect; yougest son of George Dance senior, whom he succeeded as Clerk of the City Works. All Hallows Church (London Wall) 1765–67; St Bartholomew the Less (Smithfield), rebuilt by T. Hardwick to Dance's design which had been executed in wood; and some work at the Mansion House and the

façade of the Guildhall. The portico of the Royal College of Surgeons (Lincoln's Inn Fields) remains after the rebuild by C. Barry. His masterpiece, the famous Newgate Prison (on the site of the present Old Bailey) was demolished in 1902. 22, 150, 151, *154,* 201.

De Jongh, Claude (d. 1663). Dutch painter. A view of *Old London Bridge* (Iveagh Bequest, Kenwood), 1630. 230.

Delvaux, Laurent (1698–1778). Flemish sculptor, worked in London 1717–28 mainly with Scheemakers (joint tombs by them in Westminster Abbey). Statue of *George I* (Public Record Office Museum); works in the V. & A. and Royal Academy.

Dobson, William (1610–46). English painter of portraits; works include *Inigo Jones*, the architect (Chiswick House); *Endymion Porter* (Tate Gallery); *Unknown Man* (National Maritime Museum); also represented in the N.P.G. and the Royal Collection (Windsor).

Drury, Alfred (1856–1944). Sculptor; works include statues of *Sir Joshua Reynolds* (Burlington House forecourt) and *Elizabeth Fry* (Old Bailey, main hall); *War Memorial* (Royal Exchange); decorative sculpture on the façade of the V. & A. and the War Office (Whitehall); *Griselda*, in bronze (Tate Gallery).

Dyce, William (1806–64). English painter; works include the reredos in All Saints Church (Margaret Street); frescoes, episodes from the *Legends of King Arthur* and events in British history (Houses of Parliament); *Pegwell Bay* etc. (Tate Gallery).

Edwin, Richard (fl. 1764–77). Architect, pupil of Matthew Brettingham; Stratford Place (Oxford Street) 1774 in the style of Robert Adam; Stratford House survives.

Epstein, Sir Jacob (1880–1959). Sculptor, born in New York, lived in England from 1905. Works include *Pan*, group in bronze (Bowater House entrance to Hyde Park), the sculptor's last work; the panel, *Rima*, Spirit of Nature (Kensington Gardens, near Queen Anne's Alcove); *Madonna and Child* (above the arch, Convent of the Holy Child, Cavendish Square); *Night and Day* on London Transport building (Broadway, Westminster); statue of *General Smuts* (Parliament Square); several important works, *The Visitation* etc. (Tate Gallery); busts, *Joseph Conrad*, etc. (N.P.G.), the Imperial War Museum and elsewhere. 51, 226, 235, 237.

Eworth, Hans (fl. 1540–73). Portrait painter of Flemish birth; *Sir John Luttrell* (Courtauld Institute Gallery) and *Unknown Lady* (Tate Gallery); *Nicholas Heath*, etc. (N.P.G.).

Fanelli, Francesco (Worked 1608–65). Italian sculptor, active in England in the 1630s. *The Diana Fountain* (Bushey Park) was made for Hampton Court; several bronzes in the V. & A.

Flaxman, John (1755–1826). Neo-classical designer, sculptor and theoretician; member of the Academies of Carrara, Florence and Rome; Professor of Sculpture, Royal Academy. Works include the statue of *Comedy*, and a relief (Covent Garden Theatre façade); *Sir Joshua Reynolds* and several monuments, *Lord Nelson* etc. (St Paul's Cathedral); monuments in St Paul's (Covent Garden) and Westminster Abbey. Works in the museums include a *Self-Portrait* in terra-cotta (V. & A.). The Flaxman Gallery (University College) contains a large collection of drawings and models; also the Soane Museum. 201, 232.

Flitcroft, Henry (1697–1769). Architect; protégé of Lord Burlington. *St Giles-in-the-Fields*, 1731–4, where his original wooden model for the building can be seen; *Chatham House* (No. 10, St James's Square) 1734. 120.

Foley, John Henry (1818–74). Sculptor; works include the group *Asia* and the seated figure of the *Prince Consort* (Albert Memorial, Kensington Gardens); figures of *Egeria* and *Caractacus* (Mansion House); statues of *Sir Charles Barry* (Palace of Westminster) and *Lord Herbert of Lea* (Waterloo Place); monument to *James Ward* (Kensal Green Cemetery) and busts (N.P.G.).

Fowke, Captain Francis (Royal Engineers) (1828–65). Architect and Engineer of the Science Department, South Kensington; designed the Royal Albert Hall, 1867–71. 179, 206.

Fowler, Charles (1791–1867). Architect; Covent Garden Market buildings, 1828–30 (considerably altered since then); Conservatory (Syon House).

Frampton, Sir George James (1860–1928). Sculptor; works include statues of *Peter Pan*, the celebrated evocation of the character in Sir James Barrie's play of the same name (west side of the Long Water, Kensington Gardens); *Edith Cavell*, the nurse heroine of the Great War, 1914–18 (in front of the N.P.G.)

and *Quintin Hogg* founder of the Regent Street Polytechnic (South end, Portland Place). 51, 235.

Frith, William Powell (1819–1909). English painter of genre subjects. His best known work *The Derby Day* is in the Tate Gallery and a group of subjects taken from English Literature — Dickens and Goldsmith — are at the V. & A.

Gainsborough, Thomas (1727–88). English landscape and portrait painter; important works include *Lady Howe*, etc. (Kenwood), *The Watering Place, Mrs Siddons, Mr and Mrs Andrews* (National Gallery), *The Market Cart*, etc. (Tate Gallery); also represented in the Diploma Gallery (Royal Academy), the National Maritime Museum, N.P.G., Wallace Collection, and elsewhere. His residence in Schomberg House (No. 80 Pall Mall) 1774-88 is marked by a plaque. 86, 149, 190, 191, 198, 220, 223, 225, 229, 230, 234.

Gandy (later **Deering**), **John Peter** (1787–1850). Architect, whose buildings include University College (Gower Street) with William Wilkins (q.v.) who was principally responsible for the design; St Mark's (North Audley Street), the interior since reconstructed by Blomfield (q.v.).

Gentileschi, Orazio (1562–1647). Italian Caravaggesque painter, working in England from 1626 for Charles I. Ceiling paintings representing the Arts and Sciences (Marlborough House, Pall Mall) originally in the Queen's House at Greenwich. 64, 86.

George, Sir Ernest (1839–1922). Architect, responsible for the Royal Academy of Music (Marylebone Place) 1911; Southwark Bridge, 1913–21; etc.

Gerbier, Sir Balthasar (1593–1667). Artist, political agent, and architect. Protegé of the Duke of Buckingham; friend of Rubens. *Buckingham House Watergate* (Victoria Embankment) 1626, is attributed to him. 85, 85.

Gheeraedts, Marcus, the Younger (1561–1635). Portrait painter; of immigrant Flemish family. Works include *Lady Scudamore* (N.P.G., on loan to the Tate Gallery); Royal Collection (Hampton Court). 224.

Gibbons, Grinling (1648–1720). Dutch-born sculptor, renowned for his carving of festoons of flowers, fruit, etc., many examples of which, in city churches, are credited to him. Fine examples of his work are the reredos (St Mary Abchurch); choir stalls, organ case, festoons on the exterior, relief on the north pediment (St Paul's Cathedral). Statues of *Charles II* (main courtyard, Chelsea Hospital) and *James II*, in bronze (outside the National Gallery); works also in the V. & A. *102, 105,* 110, 112, *112,* 114, 217, 232, 234.

Gibbs, James (1682–1754). Architect; one of the most successful of his time. St Mary-le-Strand (Strand) 1714–1717; St Peter's Vere Street (Henrietta Place, off Cavendish Square) 1721–24; St Martin-in-the-Fields (Trafalgar Square 1721–26), where the original model for the building is preserved; the spire of St Clement Danes (Strand). He also did some work at Burlington House and the Great Hall and other buildings in the quadrangle of St Bartholomew's Hospital (Smithfield) of which he was a governor. 118, 119, *119,* 121, *123, 155.*

Gibson, John (1790–1866). Neoclassical sculptor. Examples include statues of *William Huskisson* in marble (Pimlico Gardens), *Sir Robert Peel* (Westminster Abbey) and *Queen Victoria,* between the figures of Justice and Mercy (Royal Gallery, Houses of Parliament); *Hylas and the Naiads* group (Tate Gallery); *Venus and Cupid* relief (Burlington House); several busts, *Sir Charles Eastlake,* etc. (N.P.G.).

Gilbert, Sir Alfred (1854–1934). Sculptor. Best known for the Shaftesbury Memorial, *Eros* (Piccadilly Circus); bronze bust of *John Hunter* (over the entrance, St George's Hospital, Hyde Park Corner); *Queen Alexandra memorial* (opposite St James's Palace), and work at Windsor. 237.

Gill, Eric (1882–1940). Designer and sculptor. *Prospero and Ariel* relief (over main entrance, Broadcasting House, Portland Place); some of the sculptured decoration on the London Transport Board offices (Broadway); the *Stations of the Cross;* etc. (Westminster Cathedral); *Mankind,* etc. (Tate Gallery).

Gillray, James (1757–1815). Caricaturist. *Self portrait,* etc. (N.P.G.); a very full representation of his satirical prints is in the British Museum. Buried at St James's Church, Piccadilly.

Grant, Sir Francis (1803–78). Portrait painter; President of the Royal Academy. A group of his portraits is in the N.P.G. including a *Self-portrait* and several of his fellow artists (*Sir Edwin Landseer,* etc.); also represented in the Royal Collection, etc.

Gribble, Herbert (1847–94). Architect.

Brompton Oratory (Brompton Road, South Kensington) 1884. 165.

Hardwick, Philip (1792–1870). Architect; son of Thomas Hardwick (q.v.) Christ Church (Lisson Grove, Marylebone); Warehouses, etc (St Katharine's Docks); Goldsmiths' Hall (Foster Lane) 1729-35; Seaford House (Belgrave Square, south east corner). 77.

Hardwick, Thomas (1752–1829). Architect. Rebuilt St Paul's (Covent Garden) to the original design following the fire of 1795; St Marylebone New Church; St John's Chapel (St John's Wood). 77.

Hawksmoor, Nicholas (1661–1736). Architect, worked with Wren and Vanbrugh. Clerk of Works, then Assistant Surveyor at the building of Greenwich Hospital; he worked with Wren on St Paul's and added the towers to Westminster Abbey. His own designs include St George-in-the-East (Wapping), Christchurch (Spitalfields), St Anne (Limehouse), St George (Bloomsbury), and St Mary Woolnoth. His work at St Alphege (Greenwich) and on the towers of Westminster Abbey was continued by John James. 34, *114,* 116, 117, 118, *118,* 119, 123, 125, *129.*

Haydon, Benjamin Robert (1786–1846). Painter, principally of historical subjects. *The Raising of Lazarus* and *Chairing of the Member* (Tate Gallery); several portraits including three of poets — *Leigh Hunt, John Keats* and *William Wordsworth* (N.P.G.).

Hennequin de Liège (d. 1369). Flemish sculptor. Tomb of *Queen Philippa of Hainault* (Westminster Abbey), paid for, 1367, finished by John Orchard. 39.

Hepworth, Dame Barbara (b. 1903). Sculptor. *Winged Figure* (external wall of John Lewis's, Oxford Street) and *Meridian* (courtyard of State House, High Holborn). Examples of her work are in the Tate Gallery (*Bicentric Form* etc.). *229, 237.*

Herland, Hugh (c. 1330–c. 1405). Carpenter. Hammerbeam roof (Westminster Hall), 1395–1400. 31, *31.*

Highmore, Joseph (1692–1780). English portrait and genre painter; represented in the Tate Gallery (*Mr Oldham and Friends;* illustrations to *Pamela,* etc.); N.P.G.; Thomas Coram Foundation (Foundling Hospital); etc. 220.

Hilliard, Nicholas (fl. 1547–d. 1619). Painter, mainly of miniatures. Brilliantly represented in the V. & A. (*Young Man amongst Roses* etc.); N.P.G. (*Elizabeth I, Raleigh,* etc.);

National Maritime Museum (*Earl of Cumberland*); Royal Collection (Windsor Castle). The Tate Gallery has a life-scale painting of Elizabeth I (on loan from the N.P.G.): he probably did the original colouring on Elizabeth's effigy by Colt (Westminster Abbey. 217, 220, 224.

Hitchens, Ivon (b. 1893). Painter. Represented in the Tate Gallery; also large mural decorations in Cecil Sharpe House, Regent's Park Road, N.W.1.

Hogarth, William (1697–1764). Painter and engraver. *The Election* series and *The Rake's Progress* series (Soane Museum); *Marriage à la Mode* series, *The Shrimp Girl*, etc. (National Gallery); portrait of *Captain Coram* (Thomas Coram Foundation) and other works; *Paul before Felix* (Lincoln's Inn Old Hall), *The Pool of Bethesda* and *The Good Samaritan* (St Bartholomew's Hospital). Works at Dulwich, Lambeth Palace, N.P.G. and a representative group at the Tate Gallery (*Calais Gate*; and *Hogarth's Servants*, etc.). *See* also Hogarth's House (list of Museums). 25, *80*, 135, 149, 151, *155*, 190, 192, 198, *201*, *202*, 220, 224, 225, 227, 231.

Holbein, Hans, the Younger (1497/8 –1543). German painter, working in England 1526/28 and 1531–43. *The Ambassadors* and *Duchess of Milan* (National Gallery); cartoons: *Henry VIII and Henry VII* (N.P.G.); *Henry VIII and the Barber Surgeons* (Royal College of Surgeons, Lincoln's Inn Fields); also represented in the V. & A. A great series of portrait drawings in the Royal Collection (Windsor Castle). A fine painted ceiling in the Chapel Royal (St James's Palace) is wrongly attributed to him; a copy of the lost painting *Sir Thomas More and his family* is in the Dining Hall, Crosby Hall (Chelsea). Commemorated by a plaque in his parish church, St Andrew Undershaft. 31, 39, 48, 57, 63, 116, 188, 202, 217, 220, 224.

Holden, Charles (1875–1960). Architect; senior partner of Adams, Holden and Pearson. Designed Piccadilly Circus Underground Station, 1928; Head Offices, London Transport (Broadway, Westminster); Senate House, University of London (Malet Street), and other University buildings including the Warburg Institute (Woburn Square) 1958. 179.

Holland, Henry (1745–1806). Architect. Erected, 1771 onwards, the estate known as Hans Town (Chelsea) including Sloane Street, Cadogan Place, etc. (many of the buildings

have since been altered or destroyed); converted the Albany (Piccadilly) into residential chambers; Brooks's Club (No. 60, St James's Street) 1776–78; added the portico etc. to what is now the Scottish Office (Whitehall) 1787. 143, 149.

Hollar, Wenceslaus (1607–77). Engraver. Born in Prague, working in England (at first for the Earl of Arundel) from 1636. His great series of architectural and topographical views form a unique and invaluable record of London before the Great Fire of 1666 (British Museum; London Museum). 29, *29*.

Honthorst, Gerard van (1590–1656). Dutch painter; worked in England for a short time in 1628. Large allegorical painting of *Charles I and Henrietta Maria* (Hampton Court); also represented in Kensington Palace, State Apartments; N.P.G., and National Gallery.

Hooke, Robert (1635–1703). Architect and mathematician; designed the Monument with Sir Christopher Wren, 1671–77. 83, *83*.

Hopper, Thomas (1776–1856). Architect; designed Nos 69-70 St James's Street, now the Carlton Club, 1826.

Hunt, William Holman (1827–1910). English Pre-Raphaelite painter, represented in the Tate Gallery; the V. & A.; St Paul's Cathedral (*Light of the World*); N.P.G.; Guildhall Art Gallery (*Eve of St Agnes*). 225.

Inwood, Henry William (1794– 1843). Architect; son of William Inwood (q.v.). Assisted his father in the design and building of St Pancras Church and St Peter's Chapel (Regent Square), his contribution being his knowledge of Grecian antiquities. 150.

Inwood, William (c. 1771–1843). Architect; father of Henry William Inwood (q.v.). Designed St Pancras Church, 1819–22, Camden Town Chapel, 1822–24 (since 1948 used by the Greek Orthodox Church) and St Peter's Chapel (Regent Square) 1824–26. 150.

Jagger, Charles Sargeant (1885–1934). Sculptor. *Royal Artillery War Memorial* (Hyde Park Corner), 1925; stone groups at Imperial Chemical House, (Millbank) etc. 176.

James, John (c. 1672–1746). Architect, succeeded Hawksmoor as Clerk of the Works at Greenwich Hospital. Designed St George's (Hanover Square) 1713–24. 119.

Jones, Adrian (1845–1938). Sculptor (started as a veterinary surgeon); works include the four-horse chariot

Peace Quadriga, surmounting the Wellington Arch (Hyde Park Corner); *Cavalry War Memorial* (Stanhope Gate).

Jones, Sir Horace (1819–87). Architect and surveyor to the city of London; works include Billingsgate Market, 1874; Temple Bar Monument (Fleet Street), 1880; Smithfield Market, 1886. With Sir John Wolfe-Barry he designed Tower Bridge. *173,* 174, *181.*

Jones, Inigo (1573–1652). Architect and designer for court masques; Surveyor of the King's works 1615–42. Responsible for the first Palladian style buildings in England: the Queen's House (Greenwich) 1617 onwards; most notably the Banqueting House (Whitehall) 1619-22; also the Queen's Chapel (facing St James's Palace) 1626/7. Laid out Covent Garden with the piazza and the church (since rebuilt); Lindsey House (Nos. 59-60 Lincoln's Inn Fields) *c.* 1640. A portrait by Dobson and a statue of him by Rysbrack are at Chiswick House. 29, 32, 64, *64,* 66-7, *69,* 69-73, *71,* *74,* 80-1, 96, 110, *114,* 115, 116, 120, 135, 190.

Joseph, Samuel (1791–1850). Sculptor, whose masterpiece is the statue of *William Wilberforce* (Westminster Abbey). Other works include the statue of *Sir David Wilkie* (Tate Gallery); monument to *William Vassall* (Battersea Parish Church); busts at Apsley House and the N.P.G.

Joynes, Henry (1684–1754). Architect of Nos. 57-58 Lincoln's Inn Fields which illustrate the influence of Inigo Jones on the work of succeeding architects. 72.

Kauffmann, Angelica (1741–1807). Swiss decorative painter who worked in England 1766–81; wife of Antonio Zucchi. Four ovals, *Painting, Design, Genius* and *Composition* (Burlington House, entrance hall ceiling); other examples in 20, Portman Square and Kenwood House. Represented in the N.P.G. and the Tate Gallery. 132.

Kay, Joseph (1775–1847). Architect; pupil of S. P. Cockerell. Laid out Mecklenburgh Square and designed the block of houses on the east side, 1812–21.

Kent, William (1684–1748). Architect, painter and designer; protégé of Lord Burlington. Alterations to Kensington Palace include rooms designed and decorated by him; *Adventures of Ulysses* (King William's Gallery ceiling) etc.; also mural decorations at Hampton Court; altarpiece painting *The Last Supper* (St George's, Hanover Square). Built

the Horse Guards, 1742–52 with John Vardy; the Treasury building, now the Cabinet Office (Whitehall); No. 22 Arlington Street; No. 44 Berkeley Square. Designed the gardens at Chiswick House. He also designed monuments (e.g. *Shakespeare,* carved by Scheemakers, in Westminster Abbey). 116, *117,* 120, *121,* 122, 190.

Kneller, Sir Godfrey, Bt (1646–1723). German-born painter, working in England from 1674; portrait painter to King William III and the most prolific recorder of English society of his time. Copiously represented in the N.P.G. including 42 portraits of members of the Kit-Cat Club (*Vanbrugh, Sir Robert Walpole, Congreve,* etc); an equestrian *Duke of Marlborough,* a self-portrait, etc. There are works at Chelsea Hospital; in the Royal Collection; Lambeth Palace; the Mansion House; Tate Gallery; National Maritime Museum; and elsewhere. He lived at Kneller Hall, Twickenham; a monument to him by Rysbrack is in Westminster Abbey. 220, 224, 227.

Knott, Ralph (1878–1929). Architect; designed County Hall (Westminster Bridge, south side) with W. E. Riley.

Laguerre, Louis (1663–1721). French painter, working in England from 1683–84. Executed the wall paintings *Battle of Blenheim* and the staircase decorations *Battle of Ramilies, Battle of Malplaquet* (Marlborough House). 86.

Laing, David (1774–1856). Architect responsible for the central frontage of the Custom House (Lower Thames Street) 1814–17; rebuilt by Sir R. Smirke in 1825.

Lanchester, H. V. (1863–1953). Architect; collaborated with E. A. Rickards on the design of the Central Hall Westminster (Storey's Gate) 1905–11 and the Third Church of Christ Scientist (Curzon Street) 1910–12.

Landseer, Sir Edwin Henry (1802–73). Painter. The four lions couchant at the foot of Nelson's Column (Trafalgar Square) were cast from a single model by him, 1868. *Monarch of the Glen* is in the possession of Dewar's, the distillers (Haymarket). Represented in the Tate Gallery, N.P.G.; Wallace Collection, Royal Academy and elsewhere. 148, *189.*

Lasdun, Denys (In practice 1970). Architect of some distinctive modern buildings in London, including the block of flats, No. 26 St James's Place, 1959; Messrs Peter Robinson (Strand) 1959; Royal College of

Physicians (Regent's Park south east), 1964. He is also the designer of the National Theatre, being built on the South Bank, east of Waterloo Bridge. 185-6.

Latham, Jasper (d. 1693). Sculptor. Lead statue of *Captain Richard Maples* (Trinity House) *c.* 1680.

Lawrence, Sir Thomas (1769–1830). Painter; President of the Royal Academy. The prolific portrait painter of Regency society. Copiously represented in the N.P.G. and Royal Collection (especially the Waterloo Chamber, Windsor Castle); also National Gallery (*Queen Charlotte*), Tate Gallery, Wallace Collection, Soane Museum, and elsewhere. A monument to him is in St Paul's Cathedral. 149, 220, 228.

Ledward, Gilbert (1888–1960). Sculptor; examples include the figures of SS. *Nicholas and Christopher* (Hospital for Sick Children, Gt Ormond Street); fountain with sculpture (Sloane Square) 1953. Represented in the Tate Gallery.

Leighton, Frederic, Baron (1830–96). Painter, sculptor and designer; President of the Royal Academy. Well represented in the Tate Gallery; also N.P.G. but particularly Leighton House (*see* list of Museums). A monument with effigy to him is in St Paul's Cathedral where he is buried. 176, 231.

Lely, Sir Peter (1618–80). Painter of Dutch extraction; worked in England from *c.* 1647 and succeeded Van Dyck as Principal Painter to Charles II in 1661. Represented in most public collections in London including Dulwich, N.P.G., and the Tate Gallery; double portrait *Charles I and the Duke of York*, 1647 (Syon House); *Charles II* (Chelsea Hospital). Well represented in the Royal Collection, notably at Hampton Court with the series of portraits of Court ladies, the *Windsor Beauties*; a contrasting series of Admirals, the *Flagmen* is in the National Maritime Museum. 57, 220, 224, 227, 229.

Le Nôtre, André (1613–1700). French landscape gardener; in England in 1662. Advised on original layout for St James's Park; also Greenwich Park for Charles II.

Leoni, Giacomo (*c.* 1686–1746). Architect; protégé of Lord Burlington and author of an influential volume, *Palladio* 1715–17. Works include Queensbury House, now the Royal Bank of Scotland, (Burlington Gardens) 1721, since reconstructed; Argyll House (King's Road, Chelsea) 1723; designed the monument to

Daniel Pultney (Westminster Abbey), executed by Rysbrack (q.v.). 120.

Le Sueur, Hubert (1596?–1650?). French sculptor, worked in England for James I and Charles I, *c.* 1626–43. Equestrian statue of *Charles I,* 1633 (Charing Cross, facing down Whitehall); *Bust of James I* (Banqueting House, Whitehall, above internal doorway); massive tombs in Henry VII's chapel at Westminster. 105, 148, 234.

Leverton, Thomas (1743–1824). Architect. Probably built most or all of Bedford Square; No. 65 Lincoln's Inn Fields, 1772.

Lutyens, Sir Edwin Landseer (1869–1944). Architect; President of the Royal Academy. Many works in London including British Medical Association (Tavistock Square) 1925; Y.W.C.A. (Great Russell Street) 1931; Midland Bank (Piccadilly). Designed the Cenotaph (Whitehall) 1919–20; the Merchant Seamen's War Memorial 1914–18 (Tower Hill), 1928, and the fountains in Trafalgar Square, 1928. 169, 176.

Maclise, Daniel (1806–70). Painter. Executed, 1858-65, the frescoes *Death of Nelson, Meeting of Wellington and Blücher after Waterloo* (Royal Gallery, Houses of Parliament); also represented by portraits, *Charles Dickens*, etc. (N.P.G. and the Tate). 161.

Maiano, Giovanni da. Italian sculptor, working in England from *c.* 1521. Terracotta roundel reliefs of Emperors, some of them formerly at Whitehall Palace and now set into the walls and gateway of Hampton Court. 32, 57, *58, 63.*

Malissard, Georges. Sculptor. Bronze equestrian statue of *Marshal Foch* (Grosvenor Gardens).

Mantegna, Andrea (*c.* 1431–1506). Italian painter. Besides the fine representation of his work in the National Gallery, the great *Triumph of Caesar* series is at Hampton Court. *57, 57.*

Marochetti, Baron Carlo (1805–67). Italian sculptor, working in England from 1848. Equestrian statue of *King Richard I, Cœur de Lion* (Old Palace Yard, Westminster); *Robert Stevenson,* the railway engineer (Euston Station approach); busts by him in the N.P.G.

Marshall, Edward (1598–1675). Sculptor and Master Mason to the Crown in 1660 and twice Master of the Masons' Company. Monuments to *Michael Drayton* (Westminster Abbey) and *Sir Robert and Lady Barkham* (Tottenham Parish Church).

Marshall, Joshua (1629–78). Eldest son of Edward Marshall (q.v.) whom he succeded as Master Mason to the Crown. Made the pedestal for the statue of Charles I by Le Sueur (q.v.) at Charing Cross; the monument to the Princes, Edward and Richard, murdered in the Tower (Westminster Abbey); stone coat of arms (Cleves Almshouse, Kingston).

Marshall, Joshua (In practice 1970). Architect; collaborated with Sir Robert Matthew on the design of New Zealand House (Pall Mall/Haymarket junction) 1957-63 and the Commonwealth Institute (Kensington High Street) 1962.

Marshall, William Calder (1813–94). Sculptor; works include the group *Agriculture* (Albert Memorial); statues of *Edward Jenner* (Kensington Gardens) and *Thomas Campbell* (Westminster Abbey).

Martin, Sir Leslie (b. 1908). Architect; collaborated with Sir Robert Matthew on the design of the Royal Festival Hall (South Bank) 1951; played a large part in the Roehampton developments.

Matthew, Sir Robert (In practice 1970). Architect; collaborated with Sir Leslie Martin on the design of the Royal Festival Hall (South Bank) 1951 and with Joshua Marshall : New Zealand House (Pall Mall/Haymarket junction) 1957-63 and the Commonwealth Institute (Kensington High Street) 1962.

Maufe, Sir Edward (b. 1883). Architect; works include St Columba's, Church of Scotland (Pont Street) 1950-55; the libraries of Gray's Inn (High Holborn) and the Middle Temple (Middle Temple Lane), both completed 1958. Also designed the Merchant Seamen's War Memorial 1939-45 (Tower Hill), 1955.

Mazzuoli, Giuseppe (1644–1725). Italian sculptor. Statues of the Apostles (*c.* 1680-85) formerly in Siena Cathedral, now in the Brompton oratory. 165.

Mewes and Davis. Firm of architects; their work includes the Ritz Hotel (Piccadilly), 1906, the first steel-framed building in London, and the Royal Automobile Club (Pall Mall), 1911. .

Millais, Sir John Everett, Bt (1829–96). Painter, original member of the Pre–Raphaelite Brotherhood; later President of the Royal Academy. Well represented in the Tate Gallery; also in the N.P.G. and the V. & A. A statue of him is outside the Tate Gallery. He lived and died at 2 Palace Gate, W.8. 225.

Monet, Claude (1840–1926). French Impressionist painter; made two famous series of London views, 1899–1904 and 1905. Represented in the National Gallery, Tate Gallery and Courtauld Institute Gallery. 228.

Moore, Henry (b. 1898). Sculptor. An early work, *West Wind*, 1929, on the façade of the London Transport building (Broadway, Westminster) is easier to see than the later frieze which decorates the Time/Life building (junction of Bruton Street and Bond Street) where one of his reclining figures, 1953, is sited on the terrace inside. The range of his work can best be studied at the Tate Gallery — *Family Group, King and Queen*, etc. (he has made a great gift of many works to the Tate, to be housed in the new extension). Also in the vicinity of the Tate, two recent sculptures; east, near the Jewel Tower, and west, near Vauxhall Bridge. 225, 226, *227*, 237, *240*.

Morris, William (1834–96). Architect, painter, poet, designer. Founded the firm of Morris Company in 1861. Well represented in the V. & A. (the Green Dining-Room; drawings, books, furniture, wallpapers, textiles, etc); also in the Tate Gallery. The William Morris Gallery (Water House, Lloyd Park, E.17 — *see* list of Museums, etc) is in a house where he lived, and is primarily for his work. He also lived at the famous Red House, Bexleyheath (by P. Webb, 1859), and at Kelmscott House, Upper Mall, Hammersmith. 152, 230-1.

Mottistone, Lord (d. 1966) and **Paget, Paul.** Architects, responsible for restoration of many important buildings which suffered damage during the Second World War; All Hallows Barking by the Tower; St Andrew's, Holborn; Charterhouse School etc.

Munro, Alexander (1825–71). Sculptor; works include the *Boy and Dolphin* fountain (by Grosvenor Gate, Hyde Park) and the fountain in Berkeley Square. His statue of *Queen Mary II* (Old Bailey) was originally intended for the Houses of Parliament when he was employed by Sir Charles Barry.

Myer, George Val (1884–1959). Architect; designed Broadcasting House (Langham Place) 1931 with F. J. Watson-Hart.

Mylne, Robert (1734–1811). Architect; rebuilt the east front of Stationers' Hall (Ludgate Hill), 1800.

Nash, John (1752–1835). Architect;

an intimate of the circle surrounding the Prince of Wales (later Prince Regent, then George IV). Succeeded James Wyatt as Surveyor General in 1813; personal architect to the Prince Regent and one of three architects who directed the Royal works. Responsible for the extensive use of stucco on buildings. Principally renowned for the Regent's Park scheme, a landscaped open space with private villas surrounded by terraces (Ulster Terrace, Marylebone Road) and the Royal route (Regent Street etc) originally intended to link the Park with Carlton House, the Prince's residence. Little of Nash's Regent Street scheme survives; exceptions are All Souls (Langham Place) north, and Carlton House Terrace, south. Other buildings, in the Pall Mall/St James's area include Clarence House, Haymarket Theatre, Royal Opera Arcade and the United Services Club. Remodelled St James's Park and reconstructed Buckingham House (subsequently the Palace). *48, 54, 132, 138, 142, 145-8, 146, 147, 149, 150, 152, 154, 168.*

Nemon, Oscar (b. 1906). Sculptor; seated bronze (Guildhall), and a colossal standing figure (Houses of Parliament) of *Sir Winston Churchill.*

Newton, William (d. 1643). Speculative developer, associated with area west of Lincoln's Inn Fields. *72.*

Nicholson, Ben (b. 1894). Painter. Representative group of works dating from 1928 onwards (Tate Gallery); a fine large painting in the Time/Life Building, New Bond Street. *225, 230.*

Noble, Matthew (1818–76). Sculptor. Examples include statues of *Sir John Franklin* (Waterloo Place) and *Peel* (Parliament Square); monuments to *Thomas Hood* (Kensal Green Cemetery) and others in St Paul's Cathedral and Westminster Abbey. Represented in the N.P.G., and Bethnal Green Museum (*Garibaldi*).

Nollekens, Joseph (1737–1823). Sculptor. Examples of his work include monuments to *Ann Simpson* (St Margaret Lothbury), *Elizabeth Grigg* (St Katharine's, Regent's Park), *Admiral Sayer* (St Paul's, Deptford) and *Dr Johnson* etc (Westminster Abbey); also numerous busts, *Duke of Wellington* (Apsley House), *Dr Charles Burney* (British Museum), *Lawrence Sterne* (N.P.G.); Windsor Castle; etc. He is fully represented in the V. & A. (*Castor and Pollux*; busts; etc). *105, 149, 220, 232.*

North, Roger (1653–1734). Architect, son of Dudley, 4th Lord North. Designed the Great Gateway leading from the Temple into Fleet Street, 1683–84.

Nost, John van (c. 1729). Sculptor. *George III* in Roman costume (Golden Square, Soho), executed for the Duke of Chandos' seat at Canons and erected on its present site in 1753. He produced a variety of work for the Royal Palaces, especially Hampton Court (some chimney pieces remain); represented in the V. & A.

Orchard, John (14th century). Sculptor. Effigy of *Philippa of Hainault* (Westminster Abbey). *15, 39.*

Ordish, Rowland Mason (1824–86). Engineer; designed the *Albert Bridge* (Chelsea), opened in 1873, employing the straight chain suspension system which he patented. *172.*

Page, Thomas (1803–77). Engineer; designed Westminster Bridge, 1854–62.

Paine, James (c. 1716–93). Architect of Dover House (now the Scottish Office, Whitehall) 1755.

Paxton, Sir Joseph (1801–65). Gardener and architect. Designed the Crystal Palace for the Great Exhibition, 1851, Hyde Park; re-erected at Sydenham 1853/4 but destroyed by fire 1936. *169, 170, 202.*

Pearce, Edward (d. 1695). Sculptor who worked with Wren on several city churches, St Andrew Holborn, St Clement Danes, etc, and at St Paul's Cathedral. Executed several statues for the City companies of which *Sir W. Walworth* (Fishmongers' Hall) survives. There is a bust of *Oliver Cromwell* by him at the London Museum, in bronze; of *Dr Hamey* (Royal College of Physicians), and a version of his masterpiece, the bust of *Christopher Wren* (Ashmolean Museum, Oxford) is in St Paul's Cathedral.

Pearson, John Loughborough (1817–97). Architect of St Augustine's (Kilburn). *165, 165.*

Pelle, H. (fl. 1684). Rare French baroque sculptor, best known for his bust of Charles II, 1684 (V.&.A.). *217.*

Pennethorne, Sir James (1801–71). Architect of the Public Record Office (Chancery Lane) begun 1851; the west wing of Somerset House, (Strand) 1856 and the north side of Burlington House (Burlington Gardens) 1869. *131.*

Philip, John Birnie (1824–75). Sculptor. Executed the statues in bronze-gilt of English monarchs from *King Alfred* to *Queen Anne* (Royal Gallery,

Houses of Parliament); also the friezes in marble depicting the great sculptors and architects of the world and the bronze statues symbolizing *Geometry, Geology, Physiology and Philosophy* (north and west sides, Albert Memorial).

Piero della Francesca (1410/20–92). Italian painter; well represented in the National Gallery (*Nativity; Baptism of Christ*). 193, *195.*

Piper, John (b. 1903). Painter and designer. Examples of his work include murals at Morley College and windows in St Margaret's Westminster. Represented at the Imperial War Museum and the Tate Gallery.

Pissarro, Camille (1830–1903). French Impressionist painter; in London after 1870 and for several visits thereafter. Represented in the National Gallery, Tate Gallery, Courtauld Institute Galleries. His son Lucien (1863–1944) settled in England, and became a well-known painter and book designer and illustrator (the Eragny Press). 228.

Pomeroy, Frederick William (1856–1924). Sculptor; works include bronze figure of *Justice* (surmounting the dome, Old Bailey, Holborn Viaduct) and the statue of *Francis Bacon* (Gray's Inn Library) 1912. Represented in the Tate Gallery.

Powell and Moya (In practice 1970). Architects responsible for the Churchill Gardens housing estate (Millbank) 1946.

Poynter, Ambrose (1796–1886). Architect of *St Katharine's Chapel* (Gloucester Gate) 1829, in the Gothic style; also Christ Church (Westminster Bridge Road) of which the spire only remains.

Poynter, Sir Edward (1836–1919). Painter. Designed the mosaics of *SS George and David* (Houses of Parliament, Central Lobby) 1870–98, executed by Salviati. Represented in the Tate Gallery.

Prest, Godfrey (Active in the 1390s). Sculptor and coppersmith. Bronze effigies of *Richard II* and *Anne of Bohemia* (Westminster Abbey), with Nicholas Broker, begun 1394. 39.

Pugin, Augustus Welby Northmore (1812–52). Architect and theoretician; son of the architect, Augustus Charles Pugin. Responsible for the detailed drawings for Barry's design of the Houses of Parliament; designed St George's R. C. Cathedral (Lambeth Road) 1840-8. There are pieces designed by him in the V. & A. 155, *158, 159, 161.*

Quellin, Arnold (1653–86). Sculptor, from Antwerp; settled in London in 1680; worked with Grinling

Gibbons and may have been responsible for much of the Gibbons statue of *James II* (outside the National Gallery, Trafalgar Square). He was employed by several City Companies to carve statues for presentation to the Royal Exchange. Works include statues of *Charles II* and *Sir John Cutler*, (Guildhall), originally executed for the Royal College of Physicians; monument to *Thomas Thynne* with a dramatic relief (Westminster Abbey). 25, 234.

Railton, William (c. 1801–77). Architect; designed Nelson's Column (Trafalgar Square) 1840-3—the statue itself is by Edward Hodges Baily and the lions, by Landseer, are a later addition. He also built or rebuilt several churches in East London including Holy Trinity (Hoxton) 1849.

Raphael (Raffaello Sanzio) (1483–1520). Italian painter. A group of masterpieces in the National Gallery (*Ansidei Madonna, St Catherine,* etc); also represented in the Dulwich Picture Gallery; drawings in the British Museum and Royal Collection (Windsor Castle). The great Cartoons are on permanent loan from the Royal Collection to the V. & A. 63, 192, 198, 208, 220.

Repton, George Stanley (?–1858). Architect, son of Humphry Repton. Remodelled the Royal Opera House (Haymarket) c. 1817, with John Nash, the only surviving part being the Arcade (Pall Mall). 138.

Repton, Humphry (1752–1818). Landscape gardener; laid out the gardens in Bloomsbury Square, 1800, which have been re-designed since the 1939-45 war.

Reynolds, Sir Joshua (1723–92). Painter; co-founder and first President of the Royal Academy. Richly represented in many collections: National Gallery (*The Montgomery Sisters; Lord Heathfield; Captain Orme,* etc); N.P.G. (*Dr Johnson, Boswell, Dr Burney, Warren Hastings,* etc); Tate Gallery (*Self-portrait,* etc); National Maritime Museum (especially early works, including *Keppel*); Iveagh Bequest, Kenwood; Dulwich Picture Gallery; Wallace Collection (*Nellie O'Brien,* etc); the Royal Collection; Royal Academy (*Self-portrait,* etc). Many of the institutions with collections of portraits of past members include examples (e.g. Royal Colleges of Physicians; of Surgeons; Lambeth Palace, etc). He lived in Leicester Square (No, 47, on the site of the present Fanum House); a bust is in the Square, a statue in the forecourt of the Royal Academy, and a memorial in St Paul's Cathedral. 112, 149, 190, 191, 198, 220, 223, 225, 227, 229, 230.

Reyns, Henry of (Active 1243–53). Master of the King's masons. In charge of early stages of the rebuilding of Westminster Abbey; probably English, though had equally probably worked at Rheims. 34.

Ricci, Sebastiano (1659–1734). Venetian painter; worked in England c. 1709-16, often in collaboration with his nephew Marco. *The Resurrection* (Chelsea Hospital Chapel); two large paintings *Diana and her Nymphs* and *The Triumph of Venus* (Burlington House, main staircase); there are also examples in the Royal Collection and ceiling paintings by Marco and Sebastiano in the private rooms of the Royal Academy. 114, 120, 190.

Richardson, Sir Albert. Architect. Responsible for the restoration of buildings damaged in the Blitz—St James's Church (Piccadilly) and for the design of buildings erected since the Second World War—Financial Times building (Cannon Street) 1959; etc.

Riley, W. E. (1852–1937). Architect and engineer; designed Vauxhall Bridge, 1906 with Sir Maurice Fitzmaurice; Central School of Arts and Crafts (Southampton Row) 1908.

Ripley, Thomas (c. 1683–1758). Architect of The Admiralty (Whitehall) 1723-6; the screen is by Robert Adam. 129.

Roberts, Henry (1803–76). Architect of Fishmongers' Hall (London Bridge approach) 1831-3.

Rodin, Auguste (1840–1917). French sculptor. Bronze cast of the *Burghers of Calais* (Victoria Tower Gardens, Millbank). A representative group of his works, especially bronzes, is in the Tate Gallery, including the marble *Le Baiser*. 226.

Rogers, William Gibbs (1792–1875). Woodcarver. Examples of his work survive in St Mary-at-Hill (Lovat Lane), 1849, the pulpit, gallery, etc; St Michael's (Cornhill), 1850, bench ends.

Romanus, Odericus and Petrus - *see* **Cosmati.**

Romney, George (1734–1802). Portrait painter. Well represented in the Tate Gallery, N.P.G., Wallace Collection, and Iveagh Bequest, Kenwood, etc. Lived in Hampstead (Holly Bush Hill). 149, 225.

Rosenauer, M i c h a e l (In practice 1970). Architect of the Time and Life Building and Westbury Hotel (Bond Street/Bruton Street junction)

1952; Carlton Tower Hotel (Belgravia), opened 1961.

Rossetti, Dante Gabriel (1828–82). Pre-Raphaelite painter and poet. Well represented in the Tate Gallery, V. & A., N.P.G. etc. Lived at 16 Cheyne Walk, Chelsea Walk, Chelsea, and earlier at 17 Red Lion Square, W.C.1. 175, *175*, 225.

Rossi, John Charles Felix (1762–1839). Sculptor to George IV and William IV. *Apollo and Diana* (pediment, Buckingham Palace); statue of *Tragedy* and a relief (Covent Garden Theatre façade). Among his monuments, five of which are in St Paul's Cathedral, the most elaborate is that to *Admiral Lord Romney* and a bust by him is in the N.P.G. (*James Wyatt*).

Roubiliac, Louis François (1702 or 5 –62). French sculptor. Worked in London from c. 1755 till his death; one of the most brilliant of 18th-century European sculptors. Statue of *Shakespeare* (British Museum); several important monuments in Westminster Abbey (Poets Corner) —*Handel, Mrs Nightingale* and *John, Duke of Argyll*, of which a model is in the V. & A. Portrait medallion of *Elizabeth Smith* (St Botolph Aldersgate) and several busts in the N.P.G. (*Colley Cibber* etc); National Maritime Museum; the V. & A.; Royal Academy; Royal Collection, and elsewhere. 150, 190, 217, 220, 222, 232.

Roumieu, R. L. Architect, responsible for buildings in Hammersmith, Islington, Wandsworth etc. often in association with other architects; best known for the very emphatic Gothic of Nos 33-5 Eastcheap, 1877 *162, 164.*

Rovezzano, Benedetto da (Active in England, c. 1524–35). Italian sculptor. Sarcophagus in black marble, Nelson's tomb (St Paul's Cathedral) 1524-9, intended for the tomb of Cardinal Wolsey. 112.

Rowlandson, Thomas (1756–1827). Prolific satiric draughtsman and illustrator of London life; well represented in the V. & A., British Museum, London Museum. A comprehensive collection of his prints is in the British Museum. Lived on the site of 16 John Adam Street, W.C.2. (marked with a plaque).

Rubens, Sir Peter Paul (1577–1640). Flemish painter; knighted by King Charles I when visiting England, 1629–30. Nine allegorical ceiling paintings, including *Apotheosis of James I* in the central oval (Banqueting House, Whitehall). There are examples of his work at Wellington

Museum, Apsley, House; the Courtauld Institute Galleries; Dulwich, and the Royal Collection. A group of works at the Wallace Collection include *The Rainbow Landscape* but the most representative collection is in the National Gallery. 69, *74,* 192, 198, 223, 228.

Ruskin, John (1819–1900). Artist, critic and social reformer. His architectural gospel had great effect on Victorian exploitation of the Venetian Gothic idiom in London streets: patron and apologist of J.M.W. Turner. Examples of his drawings and watercolours are in the British Museum and V. & A. 152, 164.

Rysbrack, John Michael (1693/4–1770). Sculptor; came to England *c.* 1720. Statues of *Sir Hans Sloane* (Physic Garden, Chelsea Embankment); *Inigo Jones* and *Palladio* (by the steps, main front, Chiswick House); relief overmantel *Roman Marriage* (State Apartments, Kensington Palace). A group of monuments in Westminster Abbey include his masterpiece, *Isaac Newton,* also *Ben Jonson, Sir Godfrey Kneller* and *John Milton*; busts in the British Museum; N.P.G.; National Maritime Museum; and the V. & A. where some of his designs and sketches are also housed. 190, 217, 232.

Saarinen, Eero (1911–61). American architect of the United States Embassy (Grosvenor Square) 1960. 120.

Salviati, Antonio (1816–90). Italian mosaicist; glass mosaic, *The Last Supper* (Westminster Abbey Sanctuary); mosaics also in St Paul's Cathedral and the Houses of Parliament, the latter designed by Sir Edward Poynter.

Savage, James (1779–1852). Architect of St Luke (Sydney Street, Chelsea) 1820–4, the earliest stone-vaulted church of the Gothic revival; St James (Spa Road, Bermondsey) 1827–29, with G. Allen. 164, *164.*

Scheemakers, Peter (1691–1781). Sculptor, from Antwerp, working in London from the 1720s to 1771. Best known for his statue of *Shakespeare* 1740, (Westminster Abbey), a copy of which is in Leicester Square gardens; *Thomas Guy* (forecourt, Guy's Hospital, Southwark). Monuments in Westminster Abbey include those to naval commanders, *Admiral Balchen, Lord Howe* and *Sir Charles Wager.* 232.

Scott, Sir George Gilbert (1811–78). Architect. Responsible for restoration work at Westminster Abbey, 1849 onwards, St Michael's (Corn-hill), St Margaret's (Westminster) and elsewhere. Designed the Albert Memorial, the group of Government offices in Whitehall—Commonwealth Office, Foreign Office, Home Office; and St Pancras Station and hotel 1867–74. 154, 161, *162,* 203, 206.

Scott, Sir Giles Gilbert (1880–1960). Architect. Responsible for restoration or rebuilding following damage sustained during the Second World War—e.g. House of Commons 1948–50. Designed Waterloo Bridge, completed 1939, and Bankside Power Station, 1953. 172.

Scott, Samuel (c. 1702–72). Marine and view painter. Represented in the National Maritime Museum; London Museum (*View of Covent Garden*); Soane Museum; Tate Gallery.

Sedding, John (1838–91). Architect of Holy Trinity (Sloane Square) 1890.

Seifert, Robin (Richard) and Partners (In practice 1970). Architects responsible for the Royal Garden Hotel (Kensington High Street) 1965; Centre Point (Tottenham Court Road/Oxford Street junction), etc.

Semper, Gottfried (1803–79). German architect, in London 1851–55. Designed the Duke of Wellington's funeral carriage (St Paul's Cathedral) 1852: adviser on the beginning of the South Kensington complex of museums and art schools. 112.

Shaw, John (1776–1832). Architect of St Dunstan-in-the-West (Fleet Street) 1831–33.

Shaw, Richard Norman (1831–1912). Architect. The Swan House, Chelsea, 1876 and Albert Hall Mansions (Kensington Gore) 1879—the first block of flats to be built in London. The Piccadilly Hotel (Piccadilly and Regent Street frontage) 1908 and New Scotland Yard—the building formerly occupied by the Metropolitan Police (Victoria Embankment) 1891; many domestic and other buildings, in the so-called 'Queen-Anne' style. 168, 175, 206.

Shepherd, Edward (?–1747). Architect of No, 4 St James's Square; layout of Shepherd Market, Mayfair. *86.*

Sickert, Walter Richard (1860–1942). Painter: leader of the Camden Town Group. Represented in the Tate Gallery; portraits at the N.P.G. His studio was 19 Fitzroy Square (1911–13). 220.

Slater, Crabtree and Moberley with **C.H. Reilly.** Architects; built Messrs Peter Jones (Sloane Square) 1936.

Smirke, Sir Robert (1781–1867). Architect; son of Robert Smirke the painter. Responsible for altering, completing or remodelling many public buildings and houses in London e.g. Royal Mint (Tower Hill) 1807–9, begun by James Johnson. Designed Union Club now Canada House (Trafalgar Square); St Mary's Church (Bryanston Square) 1835 but best known for The British Museum (Bloomsbury) 1823–47. 131, 142, 147-8, 199, 201, *203*.

Smirke, Sidney (1798–1877). Architect, younger brother of Sir Robert Smirke (q.v.). Designed the domed Reading Room, British Museum, 1854–57; rebuilt Carlton Club (Pall Mall) 1847–54, designed by his brother Sir Robert Smirke with whom he also designed the Oxford and Cambridge Club (71 Pall Mall). Designed 74 St James's Street 1843, with George Basevi; Exhibition Galleries, Royal Academy 1869. 226.

Smith, S. R. J. (1858–1913). Architect designer of several houses in the west end (32 Green Street, Park Lane, etc); libraries; etc; also the Tate Gallery (Millbank) 1897. 224.

Smithson, Alison and Peter (In practice 1970). Architects; leaders of the Brutalist school. Designed the Economist Building (St James's Street) 1966.

Soane, Sir John (1753–1837). Architect. Nos 12-14 Lincoln's Inn Fields which include the Soane Museum (*see* list of Museums) where he lived from 1812 until his death. He designed Dulwich Picture Gallery (see list of Museums); the Mausoleum for his wife in St Giles' Burial Ground (St Pancras); Pitshanger Manor, Ealing. Among surviving monuments is that to J.P. de Louterhbourg (Chiswick Churchyard) and churches designed by him include Holy Trinity (Marylebone Road). He was Surveyor to the Bank of England but only part of his extensive work there—the girding wall—survives. 151, *155*, 192, 201, 202.

Steell, Sir John Robert (1804–91). Sculptor. Statues of *Robert Burns* (Embankment Gardens) and *Lord de Saumarez* (National Maritime Museum) with busts of *Wellington* (Wellington Museum, Apsley House) and *Florence Nightingale* (N.P.G.).

Stevens, Alfred (1817–75). Painter and sculptor. Monument to the *Duke of Wellington* (St Paul's Cathedral); an important collection of his work is at the Tate Gallery. 112, 232.

Stone, Nicholas (1587-1647). Sculptor; worked with de Keyser in Holland before 1613. Tomb of *Thomas Sutton* (Charterhouse Chapel); monuments in Westminster Abbey include the very Michelangelesque *Francis* and *Sir George Holles* also important tombs for *Sir George Villiers* and *Viscount Dorchester;* his statue of *Elizabeth I* made for the first Royal Exchange is in the Guildhall. 25, 27, 29.

Stowell, Robert (Working 1452–1505). Master mason of Westminster Abbey. Rebuilt St Margaret (Westminster).

Street, George Edmund (1824–81). Architect. Law Courts (Strand) begun in 1874—completed by his son A. E. Street and Sir Arthur Blomfield; St James (Paddington), etc. 161, *162*, 165.

Strong, Edward the elder (c. 1652–1724). Mason and carver; was responsible for the masonry of several city churches but, in particular, for much carved stonework for Sir Christopher Wren at St Paul's Cathedral.

Stuart, James 'Athenian' (1713–88). Architect and antiquary. Responsible for No. 15 St James's Square, 1763.

Stubbs, George (1724–1806). Painter. Three works (Royal College of Surgeons); represented in the National Gallery, Tate Gallery, and N.P.G., Royal Collection (Windsor); important drawings belong to the Royal Academy. 191, 202, 225.

Taylor, Sir Robert (1714–88). Architect and sculptor. Designed the Stone Buildings (Lincoln's Inn) 1774–80; houses in Dover Street and Grafton Street are attributed to him—apart from No 37 Dover Street, Ely House, which he built *c.* 1772. His best known sculpture is the composition in the pediment of the Mansion House.

Telford, Thomas (1757–1834). Architect and engineer. Designed the St Katharine's Docks buildings, warehouses etc, 1827–28. 170, 173, *181*.

Theed, William, the Elder (1764–1817). Sculptor. *Hercules Taming the Thracian Horses* (pediment, Riding House, Buckingham Palace), earliest (1817) example of the impact of the Elgin Marbles, acquired for the nation the previous year.

Theed, William, the Younger (1804–91). Sculptor. *Africa* (Albert Memorial); statues of *Bacon, Locke* and *Adam Smith* the philosophers (Burlington House façade, Burlington Gardens).

Thornhill, Sir James (1675/6–1734). Painter; the finest English decorator in the Baroque tradition. Sergeant Painter to the Crown, 1720. Best known for his scenes from the life of St Paul (St Paul's Cathedral) and the Painted Hall etc, at Greenwich Hospital (*Glorification of William and Mary* etc); also Queen Anne's Bedroom ceiling (Hampton Court). Represented in the N.P.G.; Tate Gallery; an important sketch book in the British Museum; drawings and sketches also at the National Maritime Museum; V. & A. 110, *111,* 116, *125.*

Thornycroft, Thomas (1815–85). Sculptor. Group of *Commerce* (Albert Memorial); statue of *Boudicca,* the native queen who revolted against the Romans, AD 60/61 (Westminster Bridge approach, Westminster side of the Thames). 11.

Thornycroft, Sir W. Hamo (1850–1925). Sculptor; son of Thomas T. Monuments include *G l a d s t o n e* (Strand/Aldwych junction); *General Gordon* (Victoria Embankment); *Cromwell* (outside Westminster Hall); *Dean Colet* (St Paul's School, Barnes); work also represented in National Portrait Gallery (*Thomas Hardy*).

Thorpe, John (*c.* 1565–1651). Architect; reputed to have had a hand in the design of Holland House (Kensington) 1605 onwards, little of which now remains. An important book of drawings of Elizabethan and Jacobean houses is in the Soane Museum. 201.

Tijou, Jean (Active in England from *c.* 1670). French metalwork craftsman. Worked for Wren. Examples of his work can best be studied at Hampton Court and at St Paul's Cathedral; chancel aisle gates and screens and staircase railings; balcony ironwork executed for Lincoln's Inn Fields, is now in the V. & A. 112, 115.

Tite, Sir William (1798–1873). Architect of the third Royal Exchange finished 1844; involved in the building of the Thames embankments.

Torel, William (*fl.* 1291–1303). Sculptor/Goldsmith. Effigies in bronze of *Eleanor,* Queen of King Edward I and *King Henry II* on their tombs (Westminster Abbey). 39.

Torrigiani, Pietro (1472–1528). Italian sculptor, worked in England 1511–20, and made the tombs of *Henry VII* and *Lady Margaret Beaufort* (both Westminster Abbey, and also a bronze relief medallion of

Sir Thomas Lovell). Other works ascribed to him are the effigy of *Dr Yonge* (Rolls Chapel, Public Record Office) and a polychrome bust of *Henry VII* (V. & A.). 32, *36, 43,* 46, 63, 187, 226, 232.

Townsend, C. Harrison (1852–1928). Architect. Designed the Whitechapel Art Gallery (Whitechapel High Street) 1899; Horniman Museum, 1900-1902.

Trehearne and Norman Preston and Partners (In practice 1970). Architects. Designed Gateway House (Cannon Street) 1956 and State House (High Holborn) 1960.

Turner, Joseph Mallord William (1775–1851). Greatest of English landscape-painters; the great body of his work (bequeathed to the Nation by himself) is in the Tate Gallery and (watercolours) in the British Museum; some select masterpieces are in the National Gallery; also Soane Museum; Iveagh Bequest, Kenwood; V. & A. A statue of him is in St Paul's Cathedral. 155, 191, 199, 201, 224, 225, *232.*

Tweed, John (1869–1933). Sculptor. Equestrian statue of *Sir George White* (Portland Place); *Earl Kitchener* (Horse Guards parade) and *Lord Clive* (Parliament Street, Whitehall).

Vanbrugh, Sir John (1664–1726). Architect and playwright. Comptroller of Her Majesty's Works to Queen Anne and succeeded Sir Christopher Wren as Surveyor to Greenwich Hospital. His work at Greenwich included the completion of the Great Hall and the design of the King William Block, from 1703 onwards; the Orangery (Kensington Palace) is attributed to him and Hawksmoor, as are the Old Kitchen (St James's Palace) and The Royal Foundry (Woolwich Arsenal). Vanbrugh Castle (Maze Hill, Greenwich) was built for himself in 1717–26 (now a school).

Van De Velde, William, the Elder (1610–93). Marine painter.

Van De Velde, William, the Younger (1633–1707). Marine painter, son of William Van de Velde, the Elder. The Van de Veldes, Dutch-born, switched sides in the Anglo-Dutch wars. Both are represented in the National Gallery, but especially in the National Maritime Museum (including a great series of drawings). 227.

Van Dyck, Sir Anthony (1599–1641). Flemish painter; working in England for Charles I and the Court from 1631. Represented in National

Gallery, and especially the Royal Collection (Windsor Castle—portraits of *Charles I* and family etc.); also in the Wallace Collection; Iveagh Bequest, Kenwood; Syon House; Dulwich Picture Gallery; Lambeth Palace; copies after him in the N.P.G.; Chelsea Hospital, and elsewhere. Buried in Old St Paul's. 57, 60, 73, 188, 190, 192, 198, 220, 223, 224, 229, 230.

Vardy, John (?–1765). Architect; Clerk of the Works at the Royal Palaces and Chelsea Hospital. Horse Guards (Whitehall)—with William Kent and erected with William Robinson after Kent's death; Spencer House (St James's Place, overlooking Green Park) 1756–1765. 122.

Verrio, Antonio (1639–1707). Painter, worked in England from *c.* 1672 until his death. Wall and ceiling decoration, allegorical subjects, in the State Apartments—Banqueting House, King's Staircase, Queen's Drawing Room (Hampton Court Palace) and ceilings at Ham House. 115.

Vertue, William (*d.* 1527). Mason architect. Probably responsible, with his brother Robert (*d.* 1506) for much of St George's Chapel, Windsor, and Henry VII's Chapel, Westminster. 41, *41,* 52, *59.*

Vulliamy, Lewis (1791–1871). Architect. Responsible for the alteration or design of a large number of churches, houses and other buildings in London and the suburbs. Designed the Law Society (Chancery Lane) 1832 and Christchurch (Woburn Square) 1833.

Ward, Edward Matthew (1816–79). Victorian genre painter. Eight frescoes on slate depicting episodes during the Commonwealth and Restoration periods of English history (Houses of Parliament—corridor of the Commons) 1853; a group of works at the Tate Gallery and V. & A.

Ward, Ronald and Partners (In practice 1970). Architects. Designed Agriculture House (Knightsbridge) 1956, the Institute of Marine Engineers building (Fenchurch Street) 1957, Holborn Viaduct Station 1962 and the Millbank Tower 1963.

Ware, Samuel (1781–1860). Architect. Designed the Burlington Arcade (Piccadilly) 1819. *145.*

Waterhouse, Alfred (1830–95). Architect. Designed the Natural History Museum (Cromwell Road, South Kensington) 1873 onwards; the Prudential Assurance Company building (Holborn) 1879 and University College Hospital 1897 onwards. 168, 218.

Watts, George Frederick (1817–1904). Portrait and mythological painter, sculptor. Copiously represented in the N.P.G.; Tate Gallery (*Hope,* etc). Statue, *Physical Energy,* in Kensington Gardens. Murals at Lincoln's Inn. His old house, at Compton, near Guildford, is a museum of his work. 220.

Webb, Sir Aston (1849–1930). Architect. Designed several buildings in the South Kensington area, notably the Victoria and Albert Museum, completed in 1909; he was responsible for the design of Admiralty Arch, 1910; the Queen Victoria Monument, 1911, and the reconstruction of the façade of Buckingham Palace, 1913. An earlier work is the French Protestant Church, built in terracotta in 1893. 146, 169, 208.

Webb, John (1611–72). Architect: Inigo Jones's son-in-law. Ashburnham House (Little Dean's Yard, Westminster) is attributed to him; he added the bridges at each end of the road dividing the Queen's House (Greenwich) and was responsible for the Charles II block of buildings at Greenwich Hospital. 115, 116.

Webb, Philip (1831–1915). Architect; friend and colleague of William Morris, for whom he built the famous Red House, Bexleyheath, 1859; No. 1 Palace Green (Kensington Palace Gardens) for the Earl of Carlisle, 1863; Green Dining Room (V. & A.) with Burne-Jones and Morris.

West, Benjamin (1738–1820). American-born painter. President of the Royal Academy. Tondo and ceiling paintings—*Air, Earth, Fire* and *Water* (Royal Academy entrance hall); *The Martyrdom of St Stephen* (St Stephen Walbrook—north wall); altarpiece, *St Paul shaking off the viper* (Greenwich Hospital Chapel); a group of works is in the Royal Collection (Kensington Palace and Windsor) and at the Tate Gallery. He also designed the Nelson pediment at Greenwich Hospital.

Westmacott, Sir Richard (1775–1856). Sculptor. Succeeded John Flaxman (q.v.) as Professor of Sculpture at the Royal Academy. Statue of *Achilles* (south east corner Hyde Park); *Frederick, Duke of York* (surmounting the column at head of Duke of York steps, Carlton House Terrace / The Mall); *Francis, 5th Duke of Bedford* (Russell Square); *Charles James Fox* (Bloomsbury Square); and *Canning* (Parliament Square). Several monuments in St

Paul's Cathedral and Westminster Abbey—*Mrs Warren, Pitt the Younger, C.J. Fox.* Sculpture in pediment of British Museum. *203, 235, 237.*

Westmacott, Richard, the Younger (1799–1872). Son of Sir Richard Westmacott. Sculpture in pediment of Royal Exchange.

Wheeler, Sir Charles (*b.* 1892). Sculptor. President of the Royal Academy. Bronze fountain group (Trafalgar Square) designed by Sir Edwin Lutyens; *Earth and Water* (flanking new entrance, Ministry of Defence, Embankment); *Winged Springbok* (South Africa House, Trafalgar Square); sculptures on the Merchant Seamen's Monument 1939–45 (Tower Hill), etc.

Whistler, James Abbott McNeill (1834–1903). American painter, working in England from 1859, and responsible for a great series of Thames views. Represented in the Tate Gallery; the famous etchings richly represented in the British Museum and the V. & A. *175, 175.*

Whistler, Rex (Reginald John) (1905–44). English painter and illustrator. A large mural decoration by him (the *Pursuit of Rare Meats*) is in the Tate Gallery Restaurant. *226.*

Wilkins, William (1778–1839). Architect. University College (Gower Street) 1827–28; St George's Hospital (Hyde Park Corner) 1828–29; National Gallery (Trafalgar Square) 1834–38. *179, 188, 199.*

Wilson, Richard (1714–82). Portrait and landscape painter. *Admiral Thomas Smith* (National Maritime Museum); roundels with views of London Hospitals (Thomas Coram Foundation); Tate Gallery—*Hadrian's Villa; On Hounslow Heath;* National Gallery. *225.*

Wilton, Joseph (1722–1803). Sculptor. *Great urn* (Churchyard, All Saints, Chelsea) designed for Sir Hans Sloane whose monument, by Wilton, is in the churchyard of Chelsea Old Church. Several monuments in Westminster Abbey— *General Wolfe* (Ambulatory chapel); *Laocoön* (V.&A.) and the bust of *Lord Chesterfield* (British Museum); *Wolfe* (N.P.G.); Royal College of Physicians, etc.

Winterhalter, Franz Xavier (1806–73), German court painter. Portraits of *Queen Victoria* and *Prince Albert* (Royal Gallery, Houses of Parliament); Royal Collection (Windsor Castle, etc); National Portrait Gallery.

Wolfe-Barry, Sir John (1836–1918). Architect and engineer; son of Sir Charles Barry. Tower Bridge 1886– 94—with Sir Horace Jones; extensions to Docks and Underground Railway. *173, 174, 181.*

Wood, F. Derwent (1871–1926). Sculptor. *Machine Gun Corps Memorial* (Hyde Park Corner) 1925; *Atalanta* (Albert Bridge approach, Chelsea).

Woolner, Thomas (1825–92). Sculptor; member of the Pre-Raphaelite Brotherhood. Statue of *Lord Palmerston* (Parliament Square); busts of *John Hunter* (Leicester Square), *Charles Kingsley* (Westminster Abbey) and, among several, *W. E. Gladstone* (N.P.G.); monument to *Sir Edwin Landseer* (St Paul's Cathedral).

Wren, Sir Christopher (1632–1723). Architect. Responsible for the rebuilding of 52 city churches following the Great Fire. One of King Charles II's Commissioners for the rebuilding, he became Surveyor General of the King's Works in March 1668/9. Held appointments as Surveyor at Greenwich, Westminster Abbey as well as St Paul's. Surviving churches (in whole or in part): 1) City: St Paul's Cathedral; Christ Church, Newgate Street; St Alban, Wood Street; St Andrew, Holborn; St Andrew-by-the-Wardrobe, Queen Victoria Street; St Anne and St Agnes, Gresham Street; St Augustine, Watling Street; St Benet Guild Welsh Church, Queen Victoria Street; St Bride, Fleet Street; St Clement, Eastcheap; St Dunstan-in-the-East; St Edmund the King, Lombard Street; St James Garlickhythe, Garlick Hill; St Lawrence Jewry, Gresham Street; St Magnus the Martyr, Lower Thames Street; St Margaret Lothbury; St Margaret Pattens, Rood Lane, Eastcheap; St Martin Ludgate, Ludgate Hill; St Mary Abchurch, Abchurch Yard; St Mary Aldermary, Watling Street; St Mary-at-Hill, Lovat Lane; St Mary-le-Bow, Cheapside; St Mary Somerset, Lower Thames Street; St Michael Paternoster Royal, College Hill; St Michael-upon-Cornhill; St Nicholas Cole Abbey, Queen Victoria Street; St Olave, Old Jewry; St Peter-upon-Cornhill; St Stephen Walbrook; St Vedast, Foster Lane. 2) Outside the City: St Clement Danes, (Strand); St James Piccadilly. St Mary Aldermanbury is now at Fulton, Missouri. Work at the Royal Palaces: Kensington (reconstruction for William and Mary) 1689–1702; Hampton Court (rebuilding of south and east wings) 1689–94; Greenwich (general layout, Painted Hall and twin domes). Chelsea Hospital. Houses in King's Bench Walk, Temple, are ascribed to him, and the

Deanery, St Paul's. *48, 55, 57, 58,* *81, 82, 83, 86,* 92, *93,* 94, *96, 99, 102, 104, 105, 108, 111, 112, 114,* 116, 117, *117,* 118, 119, *122, 125,* 168, 174, 201.

Wyatt, Benjamin Dean (1775–*c.* 1850). Architect. Drury Lane Theatre 1809–12; The Duke of York's Column 1831–34 (Carlton House Terace); Lancaster House 1825–26 begun by Sir Robert Smirke; Devonshire Club (formerly Crockfords) 1827 (St James's Street); also alterations to Apsley House. *138, 139, 142,* 174.

Wyatt, James (1746–1813). Architect. Younger brother of Samuel Wyatt (q.v.). Little of his work now visible in London; a fine stucco-fronted house by him—No. 9 Conduit Street 1779. The Strawberry Room from Lee Priory, Kent, a neo-Gothic design by him is preserved at the V. & A. 139.

Wyatt, Matthew Cotes (1777–1862). Sculptor, son of James Wyatt, the architect. Equestrian statue of *George III* (angle of Cockspur Street and Pall Mall East). Monument to *Princess Charlotte* (St George's Chapel, Windsor). 234.

Wyatt, Samuel (1737–1807). Architect; succeeded Robert Adam as Clerk of the Works at Chelsea Hospital. Elder brother of James Wyatt (q.v.). Trinity House (Tower Hill) rebuilt by him 1793–5.

Wyatville, Sir Jeffrey (1766–1840). Architect. Messrs Scott's Bank (Cavendish Square); remodelled parts of Windsor Castle for King George IV; designed the Pantheon Temple (Kew Palace) for King William IV. 54, 57.

Yevele, Henry (*d.* 1400). Architect. Master mason to Edward III. Completed the nave of Westminster Abbey *c.* 1376–1388; rebuilt Westminster Hall 1394–9; probably built the Jewel Tower (1366)—the last surviving domestic part of the Palace of Westminster. *31, 32,* 38.

Yorke, Rosenberg and Mardall (In practice 1970). Architects. Jesus College (Montagu Square) 1957 designed by them; since 1963 they have been responsible for the new St Thomas's Hospital (Lambeth).

Young, William. Architect. Designed the War Office building (Whitehall) 1906.

Zuccaro, Federico (*c.* 1543–1609). Italian painter, in England 1574–75. Countless Elizabethan portraits are attributed to him, but the only certain English works are two drawings (*Elizabeth I, Earl of Leicester*), British Museum.

Zucchi, Antonio (1726–95). Venetian decorative painter; worked in England with the Adam brothers. Married Angelica Kauffmann in 1781. Small examples of his work as part of the Adam scheme in No. 20, Portman Square (Home House-Courtauld Institute of Art). An Adam ceiling with paintings by Zucchi is preserved at the V. & A. Panels painted by him in the Library, Iveagh Bequest, Kenwood. 140.

ACKNOWLEDGMENTS

Illustrations pp. 17, 18 by courtesy of the Ministry of Buildings and Public Works; pp. 22, 23, HMSO (Crown copyright); p. 34, National Gallery; p. 98, Goodwood House; p. 32, Pitkin Pictorials. Ltd; pp. 28, 29, 202, British Museum; p. 169, Victoria and Albert Museum; p. 191, National Gallery; p. 221, National Portrait Gallery; pp. 227, 229, 230, Tate Gallery.
End-paper: Weinrebb and Douwma, Ltd.